Neil Boyd is the pseudonym of Peter de Rosa, a former Roman Catholic priest who became a BBC producer and is now a full-time writer. Besides his best-selling books, A FATHER BEFORE CHRISTMAS and BLESS ME, FATHER, he has also written the scripts for the highly-successful London Weekend Television series, BLESS ME, FATHER, starring Arthur Lowe and Daniel Abineri.

Also by Neil Boyd

BLESS ME FATHER
A FATHER BEFORE CHRISTMAS

and published by Corgi Books

FATHER IN A FIX

Neil Boyd

CORGI BOOKS
A DIVISION OF TRANSWORLD PUBLISHERS LTD

FATHER IN A FIX
A CORGI BOOK 0 552 11271 2

Originally published in Great Britain by Michael Joseph Ltd.

PRINTING HISTORY
Michael Joseph Edition published 1979
Corgi Edition published 1980

Corgi Books are published by Transworld Publishers Ltd., Century House, 61-63 Uxbridge Road, Ealing, London, W.5. Made and printed in the United States of America by Arcata Graphics Buffalo, New York

Contents

*FOR THE ONE
IN WHOSE HONOUR
I THREW SNOWBALLS
AT THE MOON*

One

NEW YEAR'S RESOLUTIONS

New Year's eve. The lights were already out in the presbytery of St. Jude's.

Stretched out on my bed, my hands behind my head, I was reflecting on how momentous a year 1950 had been.

Six years of seminary life had been crowned by a summer ordination; and then St. Jude's in West London. I thought back to the pangs of my first confession, first sermon, first baptism, first reception of a convert. Six months had passed and, though I had aged ten years, I could scarcely kid myself I was an old pro yet.

On the floor above was our housekeeper, dear, kind, belligerent, white-haired Mrs. Pring. In the last hour before midnight I hoped she was sipping her crème de menthe or pink gin. She deserved it.

Strange and somehow reassuring that the pious Catholic was out of step with the world around. Next door, for instance, the noise of the New Year's party came to me in waves of music and laughter. But Mrs. Pring, wanting to receive Holy Communion on January 1st, would lower her glass at the very moment the revellers in Billy Buzzle's house raised theirs to toast the new year in.

'He's as lean as Lent,' I had heard Mrs. Pring say of me, 'and he pads around this house quiet as a giraffe.' I admired the terseness and accuracy of her

7

description as I looked down the long promontory of my blanketed body. Six feet from eye to toe and it looked all of six miles.

A window clunked open and a roar with a brogue to it: 'Will you God-forsaken heathens quit that infernal racket and let a Christian sleep.' That was the third time in less than twenty minutes. I doubt if next door they heard or cared about my revered parish priest.

Mrs. Pring had sketched Fr. Duddleswell, too, with a few strokes of the pen. 'The inside of his head,' she said, 'must be shaped like a french horn.' And another time: 'That man could sit on a pot-scourer and slide up the banister rail.'

But Mrs. Pring had acquired her virtuosity with words only through twenty years of apprenticeship under the master of conscientious abuse. 'That woman,' he said to me once, scratching his sparsely covered dome, his blue eyes blazing behind his round spectacles, 'that *woman* could put a tank out of action with a knife and fork.'

'You've got the measure of her, Father,' I had replied to boost his unflagging self-confidence.

' 'Tis true what you say, Father Neil, but 'tis very discouraging, all the same. Arguing with herself is like fighting a doughnut. I always end up in a terrible mess even when I win.'

How could anyone give off so many sparks and seem so harmless, even innocent? I never ceased to wonder at it. As Mrs. Pring observed in a more pacific mood, 'In spite of his gall-stone face, he is that generous he would burn his harp to warm your toes.'

Another clunk. 'Will you God-forsaken heathens . . .'

Tonight Fr. Duddleswell was as jumpy as a grasshopper. He had been like it since Christmas. He had even gone for me. When, in one slight particular, I had dared to question his infallibility he had rounded on me with, 'If I died and rose again, you

8

foreign buck, would you believe a word I say? You would not.'

Another time he called me 'Nathanael, an Israelite in whom there is no guile'—and meant it as an insult.

As for the doggess of the house, she was taken to task for the incompetence of her cleaning and cooking as well as for the noise from her propeller (her tongue). 'That blarney-tongued woman,' he said, 'could blast a tree just by talking to it.'

Mrs. Pring received it well as if it were part of a post-Christmas pattern she was used to. Whenever Fr. Duddleswell appeared, she slipped away murmuring, 'Here comes the Great Depression'. And once, taking me aside, she said, 'Wear your crash helmet for the last few days of the year, Father Neil.'

A barn owl cried eerily from the garden as if it too found the noise of merrymaking distasteful. Rain lashed against the window-pane. A white Christmas had turned to slush in the south, although the north of the country was still snowbound.

I momentarily took my hand out of the rag-bag of memories to pray about my New Year's resolution. My advice to myself was brief: 'Wise up.' It was imperative that I shake off some of my naivety and become more a man of the world. That's why I had decided to fork out threepence a day on *The Times*, read Cardinal Newman and Dostoievsky, and make a study of Impressionist paintings.

I looked at my watch. A few minutes to midnight. A distant bell rang out prematurely, a few fireworks went off. I switched on my radio at a low level to hear the chimes of Big Ben heralding the New Year. There was a commentary on the scene in Trafalgar Square. The Christmas tree, Norway's annual gift to London, was illuminated as were the fountains. The war was still fresh enough in our minds for us to appreciate the lights.

Fr. Duddleswell had one more Wagnerian outburst before the midnight chimes, after which he was silent. The voices of the revellers in Trafalgar Square mingled discordantly in my ears with those in Billy Buzzle's house as they boozily sang *Auld Lang Syne.*

In the Square, heavy rail fell and everybody scattered for shelter. Funny people, the English, I reflected. If a bomb falls, they stroll leisurely together to find out what's wrong. A shower of rain and they race off panic-stricken in all directions.

I sat up in bed and raised an imaginary glass full of imaginary wine. 'To 1951,' I said. 'God bless us all.' And I drained it to the imaginary dregs.

January 1st, the Feast of our Lord's Circumcision, was a holy-day of obligation. I celebrated the first two Masses at seven and seven-thirty. At each of them, I preached a two-minute sermon on honesty in money matters.

The sermon was inspired by a local grocer, Tony Marlowe, who told me that shop-lifting had reached epidemic proportions. 'I'm losing so much stock,' he said, 'I'm thinking of employing a lad just to keep an eye on the customers.'

My preaching had an unexpected result. After the seven-thirty Mass, Mrs. Murray, an elderly widow with the popping eyes of a thyroid sufferer, came into the sacristy. Red-faced, she admitted that she had stolen some stockings and would like, in the spirit of the new year, to give them back.

'Would you help me, Father?'

'Of course, Mrs. Murray,' I said, doing my best to conceal my surprise.

Mrs. Murray was an excellent Catholic and very rich as well, a case of money marrying money. Why should she need to steal stockings? With the slight light-headedness that comes from wine on an empty stomach, I thought, What a rum old world this is.

Mrs. Murray wasn't asking me to hear her confession so I asked what she wanted me to do.

10

'Father, I wouldn't have to admit publicly that I stole them, would I?'

'Not at all, Mrs. Murray. No one is obliged to incriminate himself. Tell you what I'll do. I'll drop in on you first chance I get and take them off your hands.'

'Would you do that for me, Father?' Her big brown eyes were glistening with appreciation.

I nodded. 'Are there a lot, Mrs. Murray?'

'A couple of pairs, Father.'

I smiled reassuringly. 'No bother.'

She took a five pound note from her purse. 'Would you say a Mass for me, Father?'

'Of course.'

'Pray, Father, that God will forgive me and that 1951 will see a new Margaret Murray.'

Almost half a year's subscription to *The Times,* I calculated, as the lady left.

Later, I listened to Fr. Duddleswell preaching. His New Year's theme was keeping control of the tongue.

'You cannot unsay words,' he mourned. 'Words once spoken will not obligingly pop back down your throat. 'Tis like the toothpaste. Once out of the tube you cannot squeeze any of the stuff back in again.

'The Apostle James tells us the tongue is a wild beast no man can tame. 'Tis a fire, a tiny spark from which will set a forest ablaze. That is the way of it, talk begets talk.

'So, me dear people, let every one be swift to hear but slow to speak, and slow to anger. For the Apostle James promises, "If any man offend not in word, the same is a perfect man." The same is true of women, naturally. So let them stop telling tales taller than policemen and whispering snakes in one another's ears!'

Fr. Duddleswell spoke so passionately, he was clearly addressing himself first of all. It wasn't hard to guess *his* New Year's resolution. His wild outbursts since Christmas were all accounted for. A last fling before he relapsed into a holy silence.

Even as he descended the pulpit he was put to the test. Francis Martin, a three-and-a-half-year-old who lived across the road, having eluded his parents, wandered over to the crib. He picked up the baby Jesus to cuddle him and, splash, there was a mess of multicoloured plaster on the floor.

'Daddy,' Francis cried, as Don his father advanced menacingly towards him, 'Jesus died early this year.'

Fr. Duddleswell went back to the pulpit to say that the child had unwittingly delivered a symbolic sermon of his own. 'What,' he challenged, 'would Christmas be like without Christ?'

The father was spared embarrassment, though not costs, and the child escaped a smack.

For a few days, until a replacement could be found, we had to make do with the Infant Jesus of Prague, who, in rich vestments and with a bejewelled crown perched on his head, didn't seem altogether at home in the hay.

The same forgiving spirit characterized Fr. Duddleswell's second Mass that morning. We had discovered earlier that a window at the back of the church had been broken by a flying beer bottle.

'One of the Billy Buzzle's guests last night,' I suggested.

'Father Neil,' he had remonstrated, 'Judge not and you will not be judged, you wicked young feller.'

Now through that same broken window one of Billy's pigeons flew in. It perched on the baldachino above Fr. Duddleswell's head as he celebrated Mass and made a clatter as if it had wings of wood.

Fr. Duddleswell proceeded unperturbed. In the pulpit he turned the visitation to advantage by telling the tale of Mohammed stuffing his ear with grain. A white dove perched on his shoulder and pecked at the grain so that his followers were convinced the Holy Ghost was speaking personally in the Prophet's ear.

'What is the Holy Ghost whispering in our ears this New Year's day, me dear people? That we should get a grip on our tongues and judge even the heathen more generously than heretofore.'

I felt properly put in my place.

Dr. Daley, Fr. Duddleswell's lovable, bibulous friend, was not slow in taking advantage of the truce.

'A thousand blessings on you, Donal,' Fr. Duddleswell said after Mass, 'come and join us in me study for a cup of tay.'

'Dear, dear, dear, Charles,' the Doctor groaned. 'You preach about kindness in speech and no sooner are you down from the altar than you are insulting me like I was a Protestant. I have come for a New Year's alms, don't you know?'

'No liquor from me today, Donal, or any day. You are pretty well softened by the drink already, as far as I can see, with your head over your shoulder like a plaice.'

'You refuse me blankly?'

'I do.'

'What a dry, disobliging man you are for one so full of sweet charity, you would even buy the flame-licked devil an ice cream.'

' 'Tis for your own good I am mean, Donal.'

'Dear, dear, *dear*. You are an old Molly and no mistake. You speak in church like the white dove of peace and here you are dropping on me like a greedy gannet.'

Fr. Duddleswell took his hand. 'I do apologize for the form me kindness has to take, me dear old friend.'

'Accepted, but do not throw the evil eye at me while you're saying it.'

'God bless you, then, Donal.'

'Here is myself,' Dr. Daley said sadly, 'solemnly

13

purposed this year to fight against man's oldest enemy . . .'

'The devil?' I said.

'Thirst, Father Neil.'

'But, Donal, could you not keep away from the mischief at least until the evenings?'

The Doctor frowned amusedly. 'You know the old saying, Charles, a man without his dinner makes two for supper.'

Fr. Duddleswell nodded in acquiescence. 'Very well, I will pour you a little slip of a drink since 'tis the new year. But you are incorrigible, all the same.'

'Clever of you, Charles, without any medical qualifications, to confirm my own expert diagnosis.'

As Fr. Duddleswell poured, the Doctor was muttering happily, 'God, doesn't the stuff make your teeth water.' He raised his glass to me. 'You over there, here's to you, Father Neil. May you live long enough to comb your silver locks.'

'Thanks, Doctor. In this house, that'll be in about two weeks time.'

The Doctor drained his glass. 'Now I come to look at the pair of you soberly,' he said, 'I can see you are not looking as grand as you did last year.'

'There was a heathen hooley and a half till the early hours next door,' Fr. Duddleswell sighed. 'I'm at the end of me whistle.'

'If you die now, Charles, our loss is Heaven's gain to be sure. I can just see it, the Almighty on His golden throne pointing a finger at you and saying, "Come, Charles Clement Duddleswell, come home to Myself. Pick up that harp there and brighten the place up for us."

'*Donal.*'

'And all the choirs of angels and archangels tapping their wings in rhythm with your playing.' He saw Fr. Duddleswell was not pleased, though his New Year's resolution prevented him saying so. 'You do want to be with God, Charles?'

'I am in no tearing hurry.'

14

'You are right, Charles. God knows you have important things here to do.' And he held out his glass for a refill. 'Why die, say I, when there's sage upon the hill?' He raised his glass to toast the donor. 'May you see nothing worse in life, Charles, than your holy self.' His glass emptied, he made for the door.

'A happy New Year to you, Donal.'

'And to both you Fathers.' The Doctor paused, his hand on the door knob. 'If you see your next door neighbour, Charles, will you give him a message from me?'

'I will.'

'Tell him a big thank you for entertaining me so royally last night.'

Soon after the midday Angelus, I was in my study when I saw Fr. Duddleswell in the garden. His face was like that of one recently bereaved.

Languidly he cast his bread upon the waters of the rain-drenched lawn until he was surrounded by pecking sparrows, starlings, thrushes, blackbirds and, of course, Billy Buzzle's pigeons. He was doing his best to be at one with all living things.

He called across the fence to his arch-foe:

'A very happy New Year even to you, Mr. Buzzle.'

A roseate Billy emerged unsteady on his pins from his kitchen and stretched out a hairy hand. 'And to you, Father O'Duddleswell.' Billy's black labrador, Pontius, also put up a muddy paw and my parish priest took that, too. 'How's tricks, Father?'

'I am merry as a rope's end, Mr. Buzzle.'

'Hope our little get-together didn't disturb your slumbers last night.'

Fr. Duddleswell caressed the hamster-like pouch under his left eye. 'I was tucked up in bed so warm and well, so does it matter, Mr. Buzzle? Besides, a celebration like that, God be praised, happens but once a year.'

'It's nice to know,' Billy said, 'that the second half of the twentieth century has just begun.'

15

I had read my *Times* that morning. I could see the drift of Billy's argument and knew he was out to rile his adversary.

'I beg your pardon,' Fr. Duddleswell said politely.

'Today, January 1st 1951, sees the beginning of the second half of the twentieth century, don't it?'

'It does? And it did not begin a year ago today?' His motto was, Quick to hear and slow to speak.

Billy adjusted his stiff white cuffs. He looked a bit upset that the Third World War wasn't already breaking out over the fence.

'It's a common mistake of the ignorant,' he said, stirring things up. 'They forget there is no year nought. So 100 A.D. belongs to the first century.'

'And 1900 belongs to the nineteenth century,' Fr. Duddleswell took up.

'*Right*,' Billy Buzzle said gloatingly.

'Then the twentieth century did not begin on January 1st 1900 but on January 1st 1901?'

'And, Father O'Duddleswell, as I was just at pains to point out—'

'We have only just begun the second half of the twentieth century.'

'Correct,' Billy said, but by now the light of battle was dim in his eye.

'Mr. Buzzle, may I shake your hand again.' Billy allowed it. 'I am most grateful to you for taking the trouble to explain such a conspicuously simple matter to one as dull-witted as meself.'

He left Billy standing there wondering how he had been drubbed as he wandered back to the house shaking his head sadly at the unexpected depths of his own ignorance.

'Now, Father Neil, a pinch of advice for you. Curates are always coming and going like the Holy Ghost at the Last Supper, whereas housekeepers are . . . almost as immovable as parish priests.'

I showed no sign of doubting it.

'So I would like you to take care not to bruise or

16

belabour the good lady of the house in any way at
all. Try and be as tidy in your habits as a blind man,'
he said, tapping his paunch in a self-satisfied way.
'Make sure, for instance, that you put your tooth-
brush back in the bathroom cabinet and do not leave
a scum-mark on the wash bowl.'

We were in Fr. Duddleswell's study prior to lunch.
Already his special brand of kind censoriousness
was getting me down. Even 'bloody' had been ex-
punged from his vocabulary and replaced by
'blessed'—albeit accompanied by an unconscious little karate chop.

'Twenty years she has been with me, Father Neil,'
he said wearily, his top teeth scraping his tongue,
'and none but meself knows the worth of her. She is
clever enough to make a cat with two tails. And
clean! Why she would whitewash a piece of chalk,
did I but let her.'

At the meal, Mrs. Pring, knowing that Fr. Duddleswell would complain of the pillows in Paradise,
apologized in advance for the stringy joint.

He lifted his podgy hand, refusing to hear more of
it. 'Mrs. Pring, I realize surely that the meat ration
was reduced only yesterday. You have performed a
miracle with the poor material the Minister of Food
has provided you with.'

And he would not change his mind even when,
with the sharpest knife in the house, he couldn't cut
it.

His uncanny politeness was in danger of poisoning the atmosphere. Something happened or was
said and I watched him get the range, take aim and
then stop short of firing.

After he had praised the unmatchable flavour of
her cabbage—of all things—Mrs. Pring grunted, 'So
I'm not the last teaspoon left in the washing-up
bowl, after all.'

He opened his mouth and, remembering his resolution, shut it like a piano.

I had troubles abroad as well as at home. About

17

tea-time I cycled to Mrs. Murray's. With each revolution of the pedals I repeated my New Year's resolution, 'Wise up.' Since being posted to St. Jude's, I had seen enough of rich, harmless old ladies to recognize the danger signs. Strapped to the rack of my bike was a carrier bag, in case she had stolen more than stockings and was keeping it from me.

'Father,' Mrs. Murray whispered, her eyelids fluttering as she passed me a cup of tea in the parlour, 'I am so grateful to you for relieving me of my shame.'

What a heel I felt for suspecting that a nice, respectable lady like Mrs. Murray might be guilty of anything but a temporary lapse.

Still, I had made a resolution, I had better keep it. 'There isn't something besides stockings, is there, Mrs. Murray?'

'Oh, Father!' She went red. '*No.*'

'I'm terribly sorry,' I said, 'I only wanted to help in every possible way.'

To rid us both of embarrassment, I turned my attention to Tinker, her old English sheep dog. I frisked his ears.

'A superb animal, Mrs. Murray.'

Tinker was certainly that. A big black and white woolly plaything with white forelegs and a face white with hairs that hid all his features except the black sensitive nose.

When tea was over, I said, 'Now, those stockings, Mrs. Murray.'

She blushed. 'Would you care to come with me, Father.'

She led me upstairs.

Careful, Neil, I told myself. Wise up. Don't let yourself be compromised so early in the year.

It was too late. There, in a bedroom with its pink wall-paper and with only a white alabaster clock for ornament, were thousands of pairs of stockings. They were neatly stacked in piles about three feet high.

'All these, Mrs. Murray.' My lips formed the words but no sound came.

'Yes, Father.'

'But,' I managed to get out, 'you said a couple of pairs.'

'At a time, Father. Only two pairs at a time.' She turned quickly and went from the room.

I rushed after her, anxious that in her shame she should not think I had rejected her. I saw her disappear into the adjoining bedroom.

My New Year's resolution was practically stillborn. Instead of running away while there was still time, I knocked on the door of what looked suspiciously like her boudoir.

A quavery woman's voice said, 'Come in', and I entered to see another roomful of stockings.

Having taken in the appalling scene, I asked warily, 'Is this all, Mrs. Murray?'

'My entire collection,' she said. 'Apart from a few pairs in my wardrobe. But honestly, Father, I paid for those.'

I noticed the stockings she wore were of the knitted kind.

'Would you leave us alone for a few minutes, Mrs. Murray.'

'*Us*, Father?'

'Me and the stockings.' They presented such a threat to my well-being they had almost taken on a personal reality.

When she went downstairs, I examined the piles of stockings. The old girl must have taken years pilfering that lot. Many of them, I guessed, were too old-fashioned to wear. They came in all shapes and sizes. They were of cotton, silk, nylon and rayon. Between thirty and forty thousand pairs?

My original intention had been to return two pairs of stockings through the post, anonymously. What was a curate to do with forty thousand pairs?

Mrs. Murray was sitting on a sofa in the parlour wringing her hands and twitching nervously. It was difficult to tell whether she was ashamed of herself or more than a little proud.

'Why, Mrs. Murray?' I asked weakly.

She gave a wan smile. 'I'm very fond of stockings, Father.'

'*How*, Mrs. Murray?' It occurred to me that Mrs. Murray must be something of a genius to take stockings out of stores year after year and never be detected.

'I think it's Tinker, Father. Whenever I go in a shop, all eyes turn to Tinker and it makes . . . taking things . . . so much easier.'

Tinker was a fascinating dog. Even so, the lady must have possessed a talent it was not easy to guess at.

'Give me a day or two, Mrs. Murray, and I'll come up with something.'

As she and Tinker showed me to the door, she called after me, 'Happy New Year, Father.'

Cycling home in the rain, I prayed to God as to the calm centre of a hurricane, 'Tell me, Lord, why do I have to suffer because of other people's New Year's resolutions?'

I wanted to ask Fr. Duddleswell about Mrs. Murray, but she had spoken to me in confidence. If her shop-lifting had shocked me, what would it do to him who always spoke of her in such glowing terms?

'Wise up,' I said to myself. 'Father Duddleswell *must* know about Mrs. Murray's idiosyncracy.'

On second thoughts, how could he? If he knew, he would have stopped it. That was his duty as parish priest. Had she been confessing to him week after week that she had stolen stockings he would have been obliged to refuse her absolution until she had amended her life and given back the stolen goods. This had not happened. No, this was clearly Mrs. Murray's secret vice; and I was not going to speak out of turn and ruin her reputation.

At the evening meal, Fr. Duddleswell was still in

his polite, impossible mood. Marvellous, I thought. Here's a golden opportunity to pull his leg without reprisals.

He started to tell me a funny story. On the side, Mrs. Pring had repeated to me quite a number of his stories. When, subsequently, Fr. Duddleswell brought them up in conversation I usually had to pretend they were completely new to me.

'Did y'ever hear about the Irish doctor looking after a patient, Father Neil, for a couple of months? No? Well, now, the patient passed away at the end of it, God rest him, and the doctor sent the widow a bill.' He stopped to laugh. 'Know what the bill said on it?'

'Yes.'

It was a nasty shock to him. 'Y'never did.'

'Ten shillings. For curing your husband till he died.' Since he didn't comment, I added, 'I don't suppose for a minute I'm right.'

'Um. Wait, now, till I come to the punch-line. The widow would not pay it, of course, Father Neil. So the doctor took her to court and know what she said to the magistrate?'

He was cheating by putting two stories together. Well, he had made his New Year's resolution, let's see if he could keep it. I said in some sort of a brogue:

'Sir, if that doctor had not cut up and *postmortemed* my husband after he passed away, himself might be still alive today.'

Not a word or a smile from Fr. Duddleswell. He was absorbed in trying to slice his meat into manageable proportions.

When he had got a grip of himself, he said:

'There was this old feller, Con O'Neil, who used to walk through the churchyard at five every morning.'

He glanced nervously in my direction to find out if I had heard it before. I gave no sign.

'All his pals said to him, "Con," they said, "one of

21

these fine mornings, like, you will see a ghost there among the gravestones surely." Con took no notice, of course.'

Another furtive glance to see if I was reacting. Nothing.

'Anyway, one of his pals, Danny Delancey, thought inside himself, I'm goin' to give old Con the fright of his life. So Danny gets up early of a foggy morning and hides himself in the cemetery back of a stone, like. And just as old Con passes by on his way to the fields, Danny with a sheet over him screams and scrabbles in the sod and shouts, "Let me get back, let me get back." '

Fr. Duddleswell paused to laugh in a laboured way and to search my face for one last clue before finishing.

'But old Con raises his blackthorn stick and brings it down, thud, on Danny's skull. Know what Con said?'

I continued munching.

'I asked you a civil question, Father Neil. D'you know what—'

'Yes.'

'What?'

'But, Father,' I protested, 'this is your story.' He heaved a sigh and turned his head away disgustedly.

'I don't want to ruin your story.'

'You have *already* blessèd well . . . Tell me, damn you. I mean, bless you.'

'I may have got it wrong, Father.'

'Father *Neil!*'

'What was the point you had reached, Father?'

There was a glint in his eye as if he hoped I might not know the ending after all. ' 'Twas where Danny Delancey says, "Let me get back," and Con cracks his skull for him and cries—'

' "Take that you silly old beggar. You should not have got out in the first place." '

Fr. Duddleswell took out his handkerchief and blew his nose unnecessarily. After the trumpet blast, we chewed in silence for a while before I took the initiative.

'Did you ever hear the story, Father, of a lady telling a bishop about her aunt's narrow escape from death?'

He looked up at the ceiling. 'I cannot say that I do.'

'Well, the lady says, "My Lord, my aunt was booked to travel on an aeroplane. She missed the flight because she got stuck in a traffic jam." '

'That is very good, Father Neil,' he said charitably. 'I never heard that one before and that is the truth.'

'I haven't finished yet, Father.'

'Not . . . I *am* sorry.' He seemed sincere about it. ' "Stuck in a traffic jam",' he repeated as if *that* coming from me, was hilarious.

'As I was saying, Father, before I was interrupted, the aunt missed the flight. The plane took off without her.'

'And it crashed, Father Neil.'

I nodded.

'I was only guessing, mind. But I think that is a delightful story.'

I looked at him sternly.

'You are still not finished?'

'All seventy-three people aboard,' I continued, 'were killed,' He made the sign of the cross. ' "Now," the lady in question said to the bishop, "Don't you think that was providential, my Lord?" And the bishop said to the lady . . .'

I gave Fr. Duddleswell ample time to consider the bishop's reply. He eventually shook his head in defeat.

'The bishop said, "Madam, I'm afraid I can't tell you if it was providential or not. You see, I've never met your aunt." '

Quick as a flash, he said, 'That is a good un—'

Quicker still, I got in, 'As the divil said when he got a parson.'

23

'No, I mean it, Father Neil,' he said, giving me a withering look for pinching another of his favourite lines. 'That is good, very good.' He did his New Year's best to laugh. 'I must remember your talent for telling funny stories when we hold our next St. Patrick's Day concert.'

Two

MY FIRST FIX OF THE YEAR

How was I to dispose of forty thousand pairs of women's stockings? In my six years in the seminary, no solution had been provided to a moral dilemma of this magnitude. In fact, considering the thoroughness of the studies, including discussions about how many angels could sit on the end of a pin, it is surprising that it was never even mentioned.

At a loss for an answer. I decided to call on professional help. It was rough on me, though Dostoievsky would have understood, that the only person I could rely on in the parish was a reformed con-man, Archie Lee.

'Pleased to see you, Father,' Archie said, as he led me upstairs to the room he shared with his associate, a former accountant called Peregrine Worsley. 'Perry's at the races.'

I was glad. I only trusted Archie. He even looked dependable, a head like Table Mountain and a body built like a low, thick wall.

'Archie,' I said frankly, 'I'm in a frightful fix.'

When I had explained it, Archie said:

'These stockings wouldn't be nicked by any chance?' Before I had a chance to reply, he added, ' 'Course not, Father. I knows you wouldn't be in the stealing lark. You're as straight as me.'

'Thank you, Archie.' I appreciated the sentiment and the fact that I didn't have to explain the origins of the merchandise. 'All proceeds are ear-marked for charity. For Catholic orphans, to be precise.'

Archie made plans. Everything had to be above board to satisfy Archie. He'd apply to the Council for a trading licence, hire a market stall for a few Saturdays as well as a wheelbarrow for Peregrine to transport the stockings from the lady's house.

I took Archie with me to Mrs. Murray's to see the merchandise for himself. He whistled with incredulity. 'If I didn't know,' he said, 'I'd've sworn that little lot was knocked off.'

His advice was that we ought to remove all the stores' labels and put the same price on every pair for the sake of a quick turnover.

'How much shall we charge, Archie?'

'A bob a pair, Father. Ten bob the dozen. Even the old 'uns should be snapped up in days like these.'

For three evenings I joined Archie at Mrs. Murray's, removing labels, grouping the stockings and tying them into bundles.

Meanwhile, I looked up 'kleptomania' in the medical section of the Municipal Library. I learned that it's a complaint of which remarkably little is known. So various are the causes, no general remedy can be proposed. Usually, it's psychological in origin; it affects people who are otherwise normal but for whom the stolen objects satisfy some often unidentifiable need.

In a footnote, I discovered that under British law kleptomaniacs are held to be sane and, therefore, punishable for their actions. Another strong motive for not disclosing Mrs. Murray's secret whim.

Having resolved to wise up in the ways of the world, I decided to compensate Mrs. Murray for the

25

loss of her stocking collection. I went to the Convent to see Sister Augusta who was an expert on pottery. She agreed to decorate a mammoth cup and saucer for me, inscribed with the words: 'Margaret Murray, Once Holder of the Finest Collection Of Stockings In Private Hands.'

What I liked about nuns was their lack of inquisitiveness.

In three days, I was able to collect Sister Augusta's handiwork. A fine matching set in yellow glaze with gold lettering.

Mrs. Murray was visibly moved by the gift. 'How did you *know*, Father?' she said hoarsely.

'I thought you might feel . . . a bit lonely . . . when the stockings go.'

She placed the cup and saucer on the table in the centre of the parlour. 'Beautiful. And the inscription. I am so honoured, so *honoured*, Father.'

As Saturday approached, I became more nervous. By helping Mrs. Murray, I was in danger of compromising Archie who was innocent and trusted me. If he was picked up by the police, both he and Mrs. Murray would go to gaol and I would be arrested myself as an accessory.

There was a steady drizzle on Saturday morning. I celebrated the early Masses for the Feast of the Epiphany and was in the market before ten o'clock. Peregrine in full regalia—bowler hat, black jacket, pin-striped suit—had recently arrived with a wheelbarrow full of stockings. Barely were they unloaded before they were sold out.

As I stood there for a while, I recognized some of the customers. Mrs. Conroy, the butcher's wife. Mrs. Rollings, my first convert, with her twin boys. Miss Bottomly, the Matron of the Kenworthy General, and, later, two of the nurses. Mr. Bottesford, the undertaker, no doubt buying for his many girlfriends. I guessed from their furtive looks that they all thought the goods had fallen off the back of a lorry.

During a lull, Archie caught my eye. I went across to him and he asked, 'Got some sort of bag to keep the lolly in, Father?'

I promised to get him something. At the presbytery, Mrs. Pring was busy taking down the Christmas decorations. The only thing I could find in a hurry was the small black suitcase I used when visiting the sick. I tossed out the contents and took it to Archie.

'Just the job,' he said gratefully.

That was when I saw a policeman in the line. He was a cool one. He looked as if he was waiting his turn to buy stockings. I felt the urge to run but I couldn't bring myself to desert Archie.

All innocent, Archie said, 'Yes, Copper. How many would you like?'

'You couldn't spare a couple of dozen pairs, I suppose?'

'Anything to oblige,' Archie said cheerfully. 'One quid. Thanks. Next, please.'

That's his exhibit in court, I told myself. But, no, the policeman walked away, greedily clutching his bundle. God, I groaned, is Archie the only honest bloke in town!

In the next quiet period, Archie came across to me, carrying the black case for safety. 'At this rate, Father, we're a-going to get rid of the 'olc bloomin' lot in one day.'

I said I wouldn't be sorry. With luck, I'd be taking home two thousand pounds.

Archie held up a brightly coloured scarf. 'Found this tucked in among the stockings, Father.'

I looked at it. 'Nice,' I said, wondering where Mrs. Murray had pinched that.

'Can I have it?'

'Of course, you can, Archie.' I took a half a crown out of my pocket. 'Put that in the till to pay for it.' I looked up at the clouds bulging with rain. 'You've earned it.'

27

Archie tied the scarf round his neck like a choker. 'Ah,' he said, 'Perry's 'ere again. Back to work.'

I returned at five. The day's trading was nearing its end. Peregrine's wheelbarrow was abandoned, empty. Archie, with a sack round his shoulders and a beret on to keep the chilling rain off his gingerbread, as he put it, was selling off the last of his wares by the light of a hurricane lamp.

I was about to go up and congratulate him on his sterling efforts when a smartly-dressed gentleman approached the stall with two policemen.

'That's the thief, officers,' the stranger said, indicating Archie.

Archie, all smiles, said, 'There's some mistake, Mister, I ain't pinched nothin'.'

'I think you'd better come along with us,' the senior policeman said.

Archie caught sight of me, shrugged his shoulders, winked in the direction of the money and walked off under escort.

I took charge of the case and waited five minutes until Peregrine returned from a café. On hearing what had happened, he said:

'Poor old Archie, you know he had no idea those stockings were stolen. So innocent.'

I returned home thoroughly miserable. From force of habit, I set my black bag containing the notes by the umbrella stand in the hall and carried the canvas bag with the change up to my room.

What was I to do? I could hardly inform on Mrs. Murray, equally I couldn't let Archie suffer for a crime in which he had no part.

My problem resolved itself. During supper, there was a call from the police station. Mrs. Pring announced:

'Father Neil, there's a Sergeant O'Hara wants you on the phone immediately.'

The Sergeant requested my presence at the station because a suspect said I could provide them with important information.

As I was about to leave, Fr. Duddleswell touched my arm. 'Can I be of help?'

'It's nothing, Father,' I lied. 'I'll be back in no time.'

At the station, Sergeant O'Hara of the enormous nose greeted me respectfully. 'Sorry to involve you in this jamboree, Father, but there's a chap here who's mentioned your name in connection with some cock-and-bull story.'

I swallowed hard. 'Is that so, Sergeant?'

'Porbably somebody who's touched you for a few bob in the past. Archie Lee's his name.'

'I have met him,' I admitted.

'He's not been charged yet. Only helping us with our enquiries at this stage, Father.'

'What've you picked him up for?' I said, as if I didn't know.

'Theft.'

'Of ladies' stockings?' I bit my tongue for stupidly revealing my knowledge of the crime.

Sergeant O'Hara gave me an odd look. 'No, Father. What made you think of ladies' stockings?'

'The first thing that came into my head, Sergeant.'

'Oh,' he said.

I was relieved that Mrs. Murray's reputation was still untarnished and, to be honest, that I was off the hook. I was only sorry that Archie, the sinner who I thought had repented, had returned to a life of crime. What if he had even pocketed part of the day's takings?

'Did he have a lot of money in his possession, Sergeant, when you picked him up?'

'Five bob,' he replied, and I felt ashamed for having misjudged Archie, my faithful friend. 'Follow me, Father.'

In an interrogation room, Archie and the plush-looking gentleman in a Crombie overcoat faced each other silently across a table. A constable stood with folded arms, keeping watch.

I smiled at Archie and he jumped up to shake my hand. 'I knew you wouldn't let old Archie down, Father, oh no.'

When we were all seated, I asked, 'What is Mr. Lee supposed to have done?'

'This gentleman,' the Sergeant said, indicating the stranger, 'is Mr. Travers. He's sales manager at Brittains.'

I nodded to Mr. Travers. Brittains is the biggest store in the borough, one of the biggest in town. Their sales-line runs, 'If you can't buy it in Brittains, you can't buy it in Britain.'

'To put it in a nutshell, Father,' Sergeant O'Hara said, 'Mr. Travers is accusing Mr. Lee of stealing a very expensive silk scarf.'

I let out a gasp.

'Brittains made a special purchase of six Persian silk scarves. Two were sold and yet only three are left. One has been stolen and Mr. Travers is convinced that the suspect is wearing it now.'

'Tell him, Father,' Archie pleaded.

'Be quiet, Lee,' Sergeant O'Hara said kindly but firmly. 'I am not wanting you to put words into the Father's mouth.' He turned to me. 'Now, Father, have you any idea how the suspect came to possess a silk scarf valued at £30?'

'Yes,' I gulped. 'I gave it to him.'

Archie's face lit up while Mr. Travers' correspondingly darkened.

'I can assure you, Sergeant,' I said, choosing my words carefully, 'I did not steal it from Brittains store.'

Mr. Travers said, 'Believe me, sir, it would never have occurred to me . . .' and trailed off.

'I paid for it,' I said, availing myself of a mental reservation of which Fr. Duddleswell would have approved. After all, I was under an obligation to defend Mrs. Murray and Archie Lee. Not to mention myself.

Archie seemed more hurt than angry when he

30

said, 'They know I've got a record, Father. But once a crook . . .'

'Look,' Mr. Travers put in with old world courtesy, 'I cannot tell you how deeply embarrassed I am at this whole affair.' He looked repentantly at Archie. 'Mr. Lee, I have shamed you and I have smirched the good name of the venerable firm I work for. If you would do me the honour of coming to my office first thing on Monday morning, I promise you, you may choose anything in the store you wish. Compliments of Brittains.'

Archie and I went to a café for a quiet cup of tea. He stretched across the table and gripped my arm. 'I knew there was one man 'oo believed in me, Father,' he said gratefully, 'but what a ripe, shabby business, eh?'

'Archie,' I said, 'I'm up to my ears tomorrow with Sunday Masses and evening Benediction but I'll call round on Monday evening to settle up with you and Peregrine.'

As I cyled off, he saluted me like a saviour.

'Father Neil, d'you want to tell me about it?'

Fr. Duddleswell put the question before I could even remove my cycle clips.

'No trouble, Father. Sergeant O'Hara just wanted me to vouch for the honesty of a suspect.'

'I was referring, Father Neil,' he said, 'to the money.'

I got on my high horse. 'Have you been opening my case while I was out?' I said. 'You've no right to. . . .'

'Father Neil,' he interrupted me, ' 'tis the first Saturday of the month when I anoint Mrs. Hately. I grabbed your case by mistake and instead of giving her extreme unction I nearly buried her in pound notes.'

There was nothing for it. I followed him into his study to begin my long explanation. 'That money came from the sale of stockings.'

'It never did!' So he didn't know. 'Not Meg Murray's collection?' Damn it, so he did know.

'Yes,' I sighed.

'But why did you make her give them up, Father Neil, her house is big enough?'

I couldn't understand his lax attitude. 'Theft is theft, Father. You say you know about it and you didn't discourage it.'

'Look, Father Neil. Every shopkeeper in the district knows about it.'

'How?'

'I told them.'

I wiped my brow, astonished. 'They know she's a thief and they let her steal as and when she likes?'

'Not exactly, Father Neil. When I first discovered Meg's little peculiarity I went round to every store that sells stockings and told them that whenever she buys so much as a reel of cotton they are to add to the bill the price of two pairs of stockings.'

'Does she know she's being charged for them?'

'Probably.' He looked at me grimly. 'Over the years, I have asked three consultant physicians about her. They all agree that stealing stockings is her hobby and, if she can afford it, she should be allowed to continue.'

'But she's as rich as Croesus,' I said, 'why does she have to steal?'

'According to the experts, 'tis her way of combining the pleasure of the thieving poor with the stability of the stinking rich.'

'Oh yes,' I said.

'She is compensating, poor soul, for the lack of insecurity in her life.'

'Lack of insecurity!' I gasped. 'And I suppose I've just rid her of life's only little pleasure.'

'No matter, I will award you an apple, lad, for your good intentions. But tell me, now, why are you so blessèd secretive?'

'You mean if I had asked, you would have told me about her?'

'Certainly not, Father Neil. A priest's ear can never let his tongue in on a confidence. But by your asking, you would have put me in the picture and I could have set things to rights.'

Many things became suddenly clear. How, for example, the inept Mrs. Murray had managed to be such a successful thief and why Fr. Duddleswell had been able to give her absolution week after week without demanding of her a purpose of amendment. Another thing: the whole clandestine operation of selling the stockings had been legal after all.

'Has she been at it long?' I asked.

'Twenty years, Father Neil. It began in me last parish when her husband died. Riddled with cancer was he, with cancer of the spine as a secondary. A big, upstanding man was he in his prime, but by this time you could have emptied out a can of beans and put him in it, instead. I anointed him and they were saying the rosary quietly together. On the third joyful mystery, his head dropped like a bird with a broken neck. The doctor told me after that his spinal column just snapped.'

'I'm sorry,' I murmured.

'What with her husband's death and her undergoing the change of life, she took to pilfering stockings. I warned the shopkeepers at me last parish. When I was transferred to St. Jude's she followed me and I warned the shopkeepers hereabouts.'

I told him the thefts had definitely stopped. I had arranged the stockings at her house in such a way that, had she added to the piles in the last few days, I would have known it.

'But what concerns me, Father Neil, is that if she has stopped stealing, she is probably terribly miserable now.'

I said she seemed not to be and told him about the cup and saucer as a memorial of her collection. He congratulated me on my inventiveness.

'It might just work, Father Neil.' He squeezed my

33

hand. 'Anyway, grateful to you for your efforts, even though you did mess everything up.'

My hackles rose at that. 'I'll take her money back to her tomorrow, Father,' I said.

For the first time he looked agitated. 'You will do no such thing, Father Neil, d'you hear me? 'Twould break the dear soul's heart to realize we knew she was not stealing all those years.'

I conceded the point. 'I'll take charge of the money, then.'

'After twenty years of slaving and worry,' he barked at me, 'I think I am entitled to dispose of the proceeds meself.'

The visit to the police station must have frayed my nerves because I rushed out of the room crying, 'No, you can't have that money. I'm looking after it.'

I picked up my case from the hall and was half-way up the stairs when it hit me that the case was empty.

As I turned to descend, he explained, 'A thief might have stolen it, you follow?'

'A thief *has*.' I yelled.

'Father Neil, you need not pique yourself on that,' he yelled back. 'The dough is in the sacristy safe.'

'I want it to go to charity.'

'Father Neil, what a great half-the-house lad y'are, to be sure. May I remind you who is the bloody parish priest of this place? I intend giving it to the Crusade of Rescue for Catholic orphans, and that is me final bloody word.'

I lifted the case to hurl at him. At which point we burst out laughing together. Both of us knew that at least I had got him to break his intolerable New Year's resolution.

The only sobering thought was, If *his* resolution cracked so easily, what about Mrs. Murray's?

'Come up and see it, Father,' Archie said, his face glowing. 'Perry's gone to Cheltenham for the day's racing.'

34

I was at Archie's place as promised, to pay him and Peregrine five pounds apiece for their work.

The two beds had been swept against the wall and in the centre of the room was a baby grand piano. Archie had rested his plate of kippers on the shiny black surface. Worse, next to the kippers was Mrs. Murray's alabaster clock.

'Ain't it lovely?' Archie said, admiring the gleaming black instrument that monopolized the room.

'Certainly is, Archie. Do you, um, play at all?'

'A bit, Father. Well, chopsticks with two fingers and *this*'—he played *God Save The King* with one. 'But I'll get better, Father.'

'From Mr. Travers?'

Archie clicked his lips in admiration. 'Ain't it funny, Father. All those years when I was crooked, I never 'ad a thing. Now I've gone straight, I've got me a grand piano and, y'know, I didn't even 'ave to tell a lie.'

I broke it to Archie that Perry had perhaps unwittingly taken Mrs. Murray's clock. He shook his head despairingly.

'Perry said that nice old girl gave it 'im. 'E's real classical, ain't 'e, Father?'

Without another word, Archie placed the clock in my hand.

'By the way, Archie, would you mind telling Peregrine that, whatever he thought, those stockings were not stolen.'

'Did 'e think they was?' Archie exhaled deeply. 'Funny 'ow 'is mind works, ain't it?'

I wrapped up the clock and took it to Mrs. Murray's. When she answered the door, she did not immediately invite me in. In fact, she seemed very upset at seeing me at all. Was that guilt on her face or was my New Year's resolution, 'Wise up', making me far too suspicious?

I showed her the clock. 'Someone took it by mistake on Saturday, Mrs. Murray.'

She brightened up. 'No, I gave that clock to the

nice gentleman who wheeled my stockings to the market. What I have lost is a lovely silk scarf I paid thirty pounds for in Brittains.'

In the hall, Mrs. Murray said, 'If that man doesn't want the clock, would you mind taking it upstairs, Father?'

'Of course.'

It seemed strange that instead of accompanying me she beat a hasty retreat into the parlour. As I ascended, I was wondering what surprise was awaiting me in the bedroom this time. Another heap of stockings perhaps?

The bedroom was empty. I put Peregrine's clock on the shelf and, in my new spirit of inquisitiveness, I walked on tiptoe and peeped into the second bedroom. Empty. The lady's conversion was complete and she wanted me to know it.

As I walked downstairs, I could hear sounds of scuffling in the parlour. Probably only Tinker bounding about. Just because Mrs. Murray had stolen stockings before it didn't mean she would go on doing it for ever. There was such a thing as the grace of God. I remembered Archie's plaintive words, 'Once a crook.'

On the table in the centre of the parlour was the prize cup and saucer resting on a hand crocheted doily. I smiled. 'It looks splendid, Mrs. Murray.'

'Care for a cup of tea, Father?'

My suspicions had made me dry. 'Thank you very much, I would.'

When she withdrew, I couldn't stop myself. I went across to the sideboard and opened it. *Deo gratias* No stockings there. I looked behind the books on the shelf, even in the polished brass coal scuttle. Again, nothing.

I sat down on the sofa with relief and stroked Tinker's coat. Until it occurred to me to turn round, kneel on the sofa and look behind it.

And there they were. Stacked in neat piles were eighty or ninety cups and saucers.

Three

THE BIRDS AND THE BEES

'See here, Lucifer—' Fr. Duddleswell had made a complete recovery from his New Year's resolution.

'Father Duddleswell,' I said, responding with a thin-lipped formality that seemed to me to suit the situation, 'I will *not* do it.'

That was the fifth time I had made it plain I wouldn't do it and it wasn't the last. But he was very persuasive. As Mrs. Pring said, 'He could sell mothballs to moths, that one, and two pairs of hiking boots to an archangel.'

Miss Bumple, Headmistress of the Junior School, had informed Fr. Duddleswell of a request from the Ministry of Education that in selected schools pioneer experiments be carried out in sex-education.

'The idea, Father Neil,' Fr. Duddleswell had relayed to me, 'is that you start teaching the kiddies about sex at the age of nine or ten.'

'Very interesting,' I mused, not yet appreciating the war clouds on the horizon.

'Y'think so? Anyway, the point is, I believe, you teach them all about the birds and the bees before they have the slightest notion what you are talking about.'

'Like the catechism, Father?' I suggested with a grin.

'Something like. Miss Bumple advised we bring in a local nurse or midwife.'

I said I saw the wisdom of that but he disagreed.

' 'Tis not just a question of describing the ins and outs and roundabouts of the anatomy, you follow? You must inculcate sound Catholic *attitudes* to sex.'

'*You* must?' I was suddenly suspicious of the second person singular.

He never used the thin end of a wedge. 'No, Father Neil, *you.*'

That was when I rebelled and did my Lucifer-like 'I-will-not-serve' piece. To no avail, as I have hinted already.

'You admitted the project was very interesting to you, Father Neil. You really should have the courage of your convictions. I will accompany you to the pet shop before you give your first lesson to the tribe of darlin' little savages.'

He pleged himself not to put me in for a job without providing the necessary tools.

He went to his bookcase and, having blown the dust off, handed over a couple of Catholic Truth Society pamphlets: *Sex And The Catholic* and *The Pope's Teaching on Marriage And Procreation.*

'The latest?' I enquired, noticing they were dog-eared and jaundiced.

'Some things do not change, thank the dear Lord,' he replied sternly.

He also promised me two animals from the pet-shop as a kind of classroom visual aid to interpersonal relationships.

In my study, I leafed eagerly through the pamphlets. I knew as much about the human anatomy as about mediaeval weaponry. Afterwards, the equation was about the same. The pamphlets, full of pious phrases, lacked pictures or any precise information.

The Penny Catechism let me down, too. Under 'Virtues and Vices' it listed lust and the sin of Sodom but it didn't elaborate. The commandment against adultery forbade 'whatever is contrary to holy purity in looks, words or actions'. Immodest plays and dances came into this category 'and it is sinful to look at them'. Likewise 'immodest songs, books and pictures because they are most dangerous to the soul and lead to mortal sin.' Not much help there with the nines and tens.

Since *The Catholic Dictionary* jumped in cowardly fashion from 'The Seven Gifts of The Holy Ghost' to 'Sexagesima' I went to the library to borrow *A Manual Of Practical Medicine*. The gum-chewing girl at the desk laconically told me it was a reference book and couldn't be taken out except by thieves.

I carried the tome back to a corner and secretly copied diagrams and mugged up terms like *'vas deferens'*—which at least sounded polite—and 'Fallopian tubes'. I learned things that quite shook me, so I could scarcely imagine how I was going to put them over to God's darlin' little ones.

'Of course,' I consoled myself, 'sex and cycles and puberty are all very well. My job is to concentrate on sound Catholic—what was Fr. Duddleswell's word? —*pl—attitudes.*'

'Is that a hamster, Father Neil?'

I glanced sickly at the fur, the claws, the large cheek-pouches of the creature in the cage. 'I think so Father.'

'I will buy him for you, Father Neil. And the other in the next cage.'

The second rodent was lying under straw. Only its nose and whiskers were visible.

'Father,' I whispered, so the assistant couldn't overhear, 'how do you know which is male and female?'

'I do not,' he whispered back, 'but I am certainly not asking an assistant about the sex of hamsters. He will think us cranky or worse. Besides, I am not buying them to *perform* for you.'

He put on his determined look, pointed at the two

rodents and said, 'I'll take a pair of 'em. Put the big one in with the little critter hiding in the straw.'

'Sure you want them both in the same cage?' the assistant asked.

'I do,' Fr. Duddleswell answered. 'I am no prude.'

'Amen, Reverend,' and the assistant did as he was told.

Fr. Duddleswell escorted me to the school that Monday morning carrying the cage.

'Thank you, Father,' I said pointedly at the gates.

'Thank *you*, Father Neil.' Instead of turning to go home like a gentleman, he marched ahead of me to Mrs. Hughes' class.

This was caddishness of a high order. First he insisted I give sex-instructions to the children and now he intended sitting in and witnessing my humiliation. Having Mrs. Hughes, a pretty young married woman present was already torture enough.

With Fr. Duddleswell and Mrs. Hughes seated on the side, I took my place behind the desk. 'Catechism question number 228, "Are we bound to obey the Church?"' It was best to establish from the start who was in charge.

Thirty feverish arms were raised in the air.

'Yes, Philip.'

Philip in the front row stood up and chanted, 'We are bound to obey the Church, because Christ has said to the pastors of the Church, "He that heareth you, heareth Me; and he that"'—a hesitation—'"disgorges you, disgorges Me."'

'Not *disgorges*, Philip,' I said. 'Anyone else?'

Fat Frank proposed, 'Disguises, Father. He that disguises you, disguises Me.'

Jimmy Baxter set the rest right. 'He that despises you, despises Me.'

We continued working through the commandments of the Church as slowly as I could reasonably allow. At the end, I judged that two children had tied for first place in the speed with which they parroted the answers: Jimmy Baxter and Patricia, a girl with big glasses perched on a thorn of a nose.

I called them out to the front—anything to delay matters for a few moments more—and tossed a silver threepenny piece high in the air to decide the winner: heads for Jimmy, tails for Patricia.

I heard Fr. Duddleswell's chair creak and glanced across to see him clasping the cage and tensing himself in expectation of delights to come.

It was fatal taking my eye off the coin. As I lifted my head, the threepenny piece dropped into my open mouth. It barely touched the tip of my tonsils en route down my gullet. Instinctively, I swallowed like an ostrich and knew the coin was not recoverable for a day or two.

There was a few seconds' silence and then pandemonium in class. 'Where's it gone?' 'Fr. Boyd's a magician.' 'Was it heads or tails?' Patricia's mournful cry, 'He's eaten my threepenny piece.' Wittiest was Dean's, 'Cripes, he's put his mouth where his money is.'

Fr. Duddleswell came across, handed me the cage and three pennies. 'So you do not choke altogether, Father Neil.'

Jimmy won the next toss and returned to his place. Patricia broke down saying she was sure the coin had come down tails. Mrs. Hughes embraced and soothed her, and I turned with relief to Adam and Eve.

In the beginning of time, I told the children, God made the first man. But because Adam was lonely, God put him to sleep, took one of his ribs and made a woman out of it. Afterwards, Adam wasn't lonely any more. He had someone like himself to talk to: Eve, his wife.

I realized with the first question, that the threepenny piece was the nicest thing I was likely to swallow all week.

'This Eve, Father, was she Adam's daughter?' There was a look of spite on Patricia's face as if she was determined to make me pay for consuming her reward.

'No, Patricia.'

'Brother and sister, then?'

'No, Patricia.'

'They must've been. They had the same father, didn't they?'

'God, you mean?' I said. 'Yes. But they didn't have the same mother.'

'That's naughty, isn't it, Father,' Patricia persisted, 'having the same father and not the same mother?'

I explained that Adam and Eve didn't have *any* mother but Patricia looked really pleased with herself for opening the flood-gates.

Fat Frank asked, 'Was Adam and Eve a Catholic, Father?' and Robert said, 'Was they married, Father?'

I hedged. 'In a manner of speaking.'

'What manner's that?' Patricia asked.

'In church, Father?' Robert wanted to know.

'No, Robert.'

Dean, a lad always in trouble with the police and destined to cause me troubles of my own that week, put in, 'The bride wore white fig leaves, didn't she, Father?'

'Dean!' I snapped and looked angrily at him as he stood there with his socks down to his ankles, his shorts down to his shins and his greasy hair shooting off in all directions.

Dean, undeterred, said, 'My mum says when she got hitched, she put a gold ring on my dad's nose.'

'Dean!'

'My old man tells a story about Adam putting his arm round Eve and she slaps his face and he says, "Why you do that, Evie? I was only tickling my rib.'

Mrs. Hughes now had Dean by the arm and was marching him to the corner where he was left to stand facing the wall for the remainder of the lesson. From time to time, he looked over his shoulder and muttered, 'Boring. Ain't it boring?'

Patricia, meanly referring back to a catechism question we had been through together not long before, said, 'The Church says it's a mortal sin to marry within degrees of kindred and not in front of a priest.'

'Patricia, there weren't any priests in those days,' I said as kindly as I could. I wish I had given her threepence as a consolation prize. 'Adam and Eve weren't related. It would only be a sin for them to marry if they were brother and sister.'

Patricia smiled crookedly. 'Ah, so it was their children who committed mortal sins by marrying each other, then.'

I looked up at the ceiling but no answer to the conundrum was written there. It had never occurred to me before that if Adam and Eve were the first and only parents of the human race, there must have been quite a bit of incest early on.

'See these hamsters,' I said.

'Do you like being alone, Father?' Barbara, an Indian girl with big brown almond eyes was genuinely concerned about me. 'Even Tarzan had a mate.'

'I'm not alone,' I said, really thrown by this time. 'I live with . . .'

I stopped when I saw that Fr. Duddleswell, his head in his hands, was rocking to and fro.

'See these hamsters, children.' I was feeling desperate. 'Male and female. They are company for one another. It's not good for hamsters to be alone. They love one another and from their love proceed little baby hamsters. God said to all living things, "Multiply and fill the earth".'

No sound in the class. Even Patricia relented, sensing that things were not going well for me.

'So, children,' I concluded. 'Thank you for your very intelligent questions.'

I went over to Dean and touched his shoulder, convinced he must be subdued by now. 'Back to your place, Dean.'

'Did you ever hear the one about Adam, Father—?''

'No *thank* you, Dean.'

'When he finds Evie squatting under a tree?'

'No, Dean.' I was really quite interested but I didn't dare show it. 'Children,' I said, 'keep an eye on the hamsters for me. Feed and water them. And I'll see you tomorrow, God willing.'

We recited a Hail Mary together and I left in company with Fr. Duddleswell.

'Well, Father,' I sighed on the way home, 'what do you think of that?'

'I now know why our blessed Lord said, *Suffer* little children to come unto me.' A bit farther on: 'Father Neil, you owe me threepence.'

I acknowledged the debt.

'Not the coin you mislaid, mind. I do not want any of your filthy lucre.'

'Where is the other hamster, Mrs. Hughes?'

Fr. Duddleswell, in his mercy, had decided to let me go it alone. I was feeling in a more confident mood as I gestured to the solitary rodent nibbling away in his cage.

Mrs. Hughes took my arm and whispered, 'It wasn't a hamster, Father. The one under the straw must have been a mouse.'

'Must have been?'

'The hamster ate it, Father.'

So much for the noble themes of yesterday: 'The end of loneliness', and 'Multiply and fill the earth.'

After completing the catechism session quickly, I addressed the class:

'Now, children, you are not going to be little boys and girls all your life. You will grow up—'

Johnny, a Jamaican lad, interrupted me. 'When I grow up, Father, I wanna be a bully.'

'I want to be a snake or a policeman,' an unrepentant Dean called out.

'Tell me why, Dean,' I said wearily. 'Tell me why.'

'So I can frighten the pants off my dad.'

Jimmy Baxter, Dean's best friend, said, 'Don't take any notice of him, Father, he has to show off because he's no good at anything else.'

Mary Fitzgerald, a thin angular girl, rose to her feet like a snake that has swallowed a plate of bones. 'When I grow up, Father, my mummy wants me to be very, very holy.'

'A saint, Mary.'

She shook her head. 'Much, much holier than that.'

'What could be holier than a saint?' I said.

'When I grow up, my mummy wants me to be the virgin Mary.'

I grabbed the reins again. 'When you grow up, children, you will be men and women. You won't want to be alone all your life. You will get married. You will become mummies and daddies yourselves.'

'I like cuddling my mum,' Dean volunteered, 'cos she wears cushions in front.'

'You will become mummies and daddies,' I repeated.

Lucy Mary told me, 'My mummy's gone to the dentist to have a baby out.'

I started to explain that women don't have babies at the dentist's when Dean again intervened with, 'Babies should tell us where they come from 'cos they'd been there, ain't they?'

Burt said, 'My mum carried me around for years in her pouch and then a sergeant in the hospital put a zipper in it and let me out.'

Debbie stood up. 'My dad told me that I started life as tiny seed, Father, so I'm quite lucky I didn't grow into a tree or something.'

Now Sean was on his feet. 'D'you know what, Father? When our baby cries, mum sticks him quick inside her shirt.'

Rebecca capped that. 'Our mum feeds baby with milk from her elbows.'

'Oh, yes,' I sighed.

'Course, dad has to use a bottle,' Rebecca admitted.

'As soon as our Dicky was born,' Dean, in a devilish mood, called out, 'we 'ad to take 'im to church.'

'Good,' I muttered, but thought it a dubious blessing that another of Dean's family might plague me in years to come.

'It wasn't good, Father,' Dean insisted. 'Old Father Duddleswell tried to drown 'im.'

There were cries of 'idiot' and 'wicked' before a rich, slightly accented voice put in, 'I see a babe born.'

The speaker was a gypsy. He was called 'Ross' but nobody knew if this was his first or second name.

Ross was small with skin the colour of a raisin. He had entered the school after Christmas and this was the first time he had opened his mouth in my presence.

'Pardon, Ross,' I said, as an interested silence settled on the class.

'I see a babe born. Once I do.'

He had the edge on me. 'You did?' I gulped.

'One summer it happens. Under a tree.'

'Under a *tree*.' It came from thirty throats like the sighing of the wind.

All eyes turned to Ross in his corner seat:

'What was it like?' 'All babies look the same, silly.' 'No, I mean, what was it *like*?'

Another silence.

'It hurts,' Ross said.

'Ah,' came from the class.

'And after, the babe don't breathe.'

The children held their breath.

'The babe is white all over. 'Cept for a little black face.'

'Ah,' sighed the class.

'His whole head is black an' clenched like a man's

46

fist. They slap hard an' hardest. And the babe don't breathe.'

'Ah,' the class contributed again in deepest sympathy.

'When it don't breathe for like an hour, someone says, It won't breathe never, no, never. So the dad lays his mite in a box. Like a match.'

'Like a *match*.'

'They don't tell the ma. They say, "He's a nice un, your little un. A boy an' all".'

'A *boy*.'

'But he's not a boy or gal. He's a dead.'

'Didn't they tell the baby's mum?' Patricia asked him.

'Afterward, they do. They says, God comes and takes your little un. But,' Ross shook his curly head, 'I am watching an' He don't come.'

'What did the baby's mummy say,' Lucy Mary asked, 'when she heard?'

'God bless God for His kindness, she says.'

'And you, Ross,' I put it to him, 'what did *you* think?'

For some inexplicable reason, Ross stood up at this point. Perhaps to convey the significance of what he had to say. Certainly, it gave him tremendous dignity. The little fellow looked to me then like a tall pine tree topping a hill.

'I tells God, I hopes one day, *You* is white all over with a black face.'

'Sit down, Ross,' I said gently. 'And thank you.'

It was nearly time for the break. I prayed with the children and joined Mrs. Hughes in the staff room for a cup of tea.

Mrs. Hughes, pretty with short black boyish hair and dark eyes, wasn't a Catholic but we seemed to hit it off together.

'Tell me about him,' I said.

According to Mrs. Hughes, Ross was a genuine Romany. A local education officer had called at the caravan site where some gypsies were camping during the winter months. He told Ross's mother the boy had to go to school.

'He seems too old for your class,' I suggested.

'As soon as he began speaking today, I realized that. His mother—she's a widow, by the way—doesn't know exactly how old he is. The education people went by his size. That's why he ended up in my class.'

'What age would you say he is?'

'About twelve or thirteen. One thing I'm sure of. He hates school. What he said wasn't nice—'

'It was beautiful.'

'You know what I mean. A young lad shouldn't have to witness such things. But I was about to say, you are the first person who has got him to speak in class.'

'Perhaps,' I laughed, 'my sex-education lessons are bearing fruit after all.'

The next day's surprises began with breakfast. There wasn't any.

'Mrs. Pring has not stirred this morning, Father Neil. Not even as little as usual.' Fr. Duddleswell faced me across the bare board. 'I will evict her like an Irish peasant, so I will.'

'Perhaps she's ill.'

The thought had struck him already. I could tell by his worried look.

'Would you care to risk trespassing on her parish, lad?'

I went up to the top floor, calling, 'Mrs. P., Mrs. P.' There was no reply but I thought I heard a movement in her sitting room. I knocked and, receiving no reply, entered.

Mrs. Pring was sitting in her dressing gown in front of a makeshift altar illumined by candles. There was no other light in the room but it enabled me to see the sheet of paper in her hand. On the altar was a crucifix, a tiny statue of the Sacred

Heart and a faded photograph of a soldier in a silver frame.

"Mrs. P.' I spoke guiltily as if I was intruding on her only zone of privacy.

'Yes.'

She turned towards me and I could make out her puffy eyes.

'Are you ill? Shall I call a doctor?'

She shook her head. 'I'll be all right, Father Neil. In an hour or two. No,' she anticipated my question, 'there's nothing I want.'

Very worried, I left her and reported back to Fr. Duddleswell. I think he had guessed in a general way what was wrong.

'I'll ring her daughter,' he said.

Within the hour, Helen had arrived in her Morris Minor. She was with her mother for ninety minutes and afterwards went into Fr. Duddleswell's study. Before he closed the door, I heard Helen say enigmatically and in a cracked voice, 'My dad just spoke to her.'

What did that mean? Mr. Pring had been dead over thirty years. He had been killed in the First World War.

I couldn't stay to unravel the mystery because it was time for my next sex-lesson at school.

Things were in turmoil there, too. First of all, I was told that the hamster had now disappeared. Someone—Dean was the prime suspect—had unlocked the cage and Harry the Hamster had vamoosed. Not that I was particularly sorry to see the back of that cannibal.

If Dean was the culprit he was devoid of any guilt feelings. 'We lost our dog last week, Father.'

I waited for the punch-line that was bound to come.

'Yah, a truck run over 'im and now 'e don't work.'

Fat Frank said, 'We can't have a dog in our house, Father, because they're allergic to my dad.'

49

'I like dogs,' tender-hearted, pig-tailed Lucy Mary whispered, ' 'cos they're the only people who're kind to fleas.'

'Our dog's eight years old,' Patricia contributed, perhaps to prove she had forgiven me, 'and he still only crawls. But ever so fast.'

'We've got one in our garden, Father,' Dean said in his best conundrum voice, 'that barks so quiet you can 'ardly 'ear it.'

I'm a sucker for punishment. 'What have you got in your garden, Dean, that barks so quietly you can hardly hear it?'

'A tree, Father.'

Dean, encouraged by my straight-man act, broke into verse:

> Mary had a gold wrist watch
> She swallowed it one day,
> And now she's taking laxative
> To pass the time away.

The Headmistress interrupted the children's groans by bouncing into the room. The boys and girls jumped to their feet as if God had just arrived.

'Children,' Miss Bumple, in aggressive tweeds, proclaimed as she breathed out the last of the smoke from her discarded cheroot, 'something has happened, is happening but will not happen any more, which is excessively egregious.'

Even Dean knew Miss Bumple meant that something intolerable had been brought to her attention.

Neighbours whose houses backed on to the school playground and playing fields were making angry noises. Miss Bumple demonstrated with shivering effect.

Someone—it might be one of her children, though she was not pointing a nicotined finger—had taken it into his or her tiny little head to enter the neighbours' gardens.

'And what has he or she done?' Miss Bumple demanded to know. 'Damage. Not to property but to defenceless animals. In short, some joker has let dogs off their leads, rabbits out of their hutches and chickens out of their coops.'

She was absolutely certain this excessively egregious lark would stop but if it didn't she would summon the police.

With that, the Head stamped out benignly to trumpet her message, unnecessarily it seemed to me, to the class next door.

I looked at the cage recently vacated by Harry and did point the finger—if only mentally—at Dean, the pest of the class.

As soon as I returned to St. Jude's, I hurried to Fr. Duddleswell's study.

'How's Mrs. P.?'

He shrugged and lifted his hands to heaven. There were creases about his eyes and his face was the colour of a burned out fire. Mrs. Pring was wrong, then: his skin wasn't thicker than roast pork.

'Can I pop up and see her?'

'She has gone, Father Neil.'

'*No.*'

'Only for a couple of days, to Helen's, you follow?'

I didn't. I said:

'I'm sorry, but I overheard Helen say something about her father communicating with her mother.'

He explained.

Mrs. Pring had only known her husband briefly. A penny wedding they had had during the First War. Yesterday had been the anniversary of his birthday. Mrs. Pring's custom was on that day each year to take out her husband's letters and read them through in the evening.

One letter she always placed on the altar: her own last letter to her husband. It had been sent back to her unopened at his death. This was the letter in which she had written him that a child, Helen, was on the way.

I said I did know that. Mrs. Pring had told me herself.

'Well, y'see, Father Neil, last evening as she put the letter on the altar she noticed it had come open. The gum had given out at last on the envelope, she thought. Then, wisely or foolishly, who can tell? she decided to read the letter.'

Fr. Duddleswell had difficulty continuing.

'To her surprise, she found that her husband *had* read the letter and it had got re-sealed, I suppose. Before he went into battle.'

'How could she possibly know that?'

'Because,' he said with an effort, 'in the margin, next to where she told him of the awaited one, he had written something in pencil. Faded 'twas. Barely legible.'

'Yes?'

' "Wonder—full." ' He lowered his eyes. 'Just that. "Wonder—full." '

'Ah,' I said, and left him there.

We lunched at the Clinton Hotel. Fr. Duddleswell offered to cook for us next evening.

He proudly drew up a menu: breast of lamb, peas and potatoes with sherry trifle as dessert. But while he was preparing it, there was a bang and afterwards a strong smell of burning came from the kitchen. I was not surprised when he served us poached eggs on toast, followed by tinned pears.

' 'Tis exceeding quiet with the screech owl of the house abroad,' he said at table, breaking the silence.

'Yes.'

'I miss her like a lost leg, Father Neil, and that is the truth. She still pains me even when she is not here.'

It was the nearest he had ever come in my hearing to expressing devotion to Mrs. Pring.

'Her husband did know, then,' I said tentatively, worried lest I touch a raw wound.

'And herself had thirty lonely years thinking he

did not.' He had a far-away look. 'When he fell face down in the mud, Father Neil, at least he was a happy man. I am pleased for herself. After the initial shock, 'twill be heart's ease to her.' He sniffed and came back to earth. 'And what is wrong with me cooking, you ingrate, that you are not eating it?'

'Best breast of lamb I ever tasted,' I said, filling my mouth with cold egg and water-logged toast.

He asked how my day had gone at school.

First, I told him I'd bought a couple of turtle doves out of my own pocket to illustrate the theme of 'Mummies and Daddies' and the differences between them.

'And how did the kiddies react to that?'

'Debbie said, "My dad's bald but he wears a wig under each arm," and Sean said, "I have to love mum more than dad 'cos she's fatter." '

Fr. Duddleswell smiled and tapped his tummy.

'Johnny stood up,' I went on. ' "Father, would you come round our place and put my mum straight. She will say cabbage is good for me even if it does make me always sick." '

'You are a first-rate mimic, Father Neil, you know that?'

'And you're a pretty good liar yourself, Father. Anyway, Rebecca told us, "An angel looks like my mum when she's ready for bed." '

'Pity her poor father, then. And our friend Dean Smiley?'

I turned grim. 'Miss Bumple came in again today to say the neighbours are still complaining about losing their animals.'

'Nuisance, Father Neil. What did Dean say to that?'

'First he informed me that his dad always works as an unemployed builder and then that his sister has to get herself fixed up married before she has an illiterate baby.'

Fr. Duddleswell laughed with an effort. 'Dean

53

may surprise you in the end. Remember, with children, there is many a wave 'twixt ship and land.'

'Tomorrow,' I continued breezily, 'is my last day. Miss Bumple has agreed to let me take the whole class to the Aviary.'

'And to the Apiary, when?'

'The birds are enough,' I chuckled, 'I'll give the bees a miss.'

'Anyway, Father Neil, I am happy for you that your experiment has turned out so intensely well.'

Was this irony? 'How so, Father?'

'It has proved beyond doubt, Father Neil, that this whole business of sex-instruction is utterly senseless.'

I didn't argue the point.

Much against his will, I insisted on washing up. I found the kitchen ceiling spattered with potatoes and peas.

'Dean's been here as well?' I asked.

'You remember that pressure cooker I gave Mrs. Pring for Christmas . . .' he said.

When I reached the Fairwater Aviary at eleven, the children were already there.

Mrs. Hughes took me aside. 'Keep your eyes open, Father. This morning at school, someone opened the cage and the doves have flown.'

I promised to do my best but how can you keep tabs on thirty boisterous kids? I decided to tail the prime suspect.

I spoke to Patricia. 'Where's Dean?'

'Don't know, Father.'

Trouble straight away. I left the main party to their own devices. I scoured room after room, outhouse after outhouse, and raced round every pond looking for Dean Smiley. I passed parrots and cockatoos, jays and blue rock thrushes, ducks, storks, egrets, an eagle, herons and hundreds of other billed species. But no Dean Smiley.

I was comforting myself with the thought that

Dean must have played truant when I was accosted by an irate keeper.

'Are those kids in your charge, Reverend?'

I said they were.

He took off his black peaked cap and scratched his head. 'Sabotage. That's what it is. Sabotage.'

Already he had found three valuable birds fluttering around outside their cages and God alone knew what further mischief was waiting to be uncovered.

I excused myself, ran to Mrs. Hughes and told her to gather the children together quickly—Dean, I noticed, was not with them—and return to school at once. I promised to explain later.

I accompanied the keeper on his rounds to find out the extent of the damage.

Dean was a fast worker. Sixteen birds had been let loose and although seven were recovered, the rest, valued at over two hundred pounds, were given up for lost.

The Director of the Aviary, Mr. Brandon, had been notified. He and I agreed that the police would have to be informed and if it were proven that one of ours was responsible the school would have to pay.

'Just look at this,' the keeper said. 'Ruddy hooligan.'

He showed me a golden oriole, still warm, with its neck broken by some predator.

I asked if I could hold on to it to show my parish priest. The keeper put it in a small cardboard box for me.

Before returning to the presbytery I went to Dean's house in a fury. I prayed he had gone straight home so I could tear strips off him.

His unemployed-builder father with a taste for saucy stories opened the door. He was wearing a once-white, now mustard-coloured vest, shapeless grey flannels supported by a boy-scout belt and his feet were bare. He was by no means the brutish sour-faced fellow I had been expecting.

'Mr. Smiley,' I snapped.

He didn't invite me in but neither did he appear to resent my visit. 'Yes, Guvnor.' He wasn't a Catholic, I remembered.

'I've come about Dean.'

Mr. Smiley ran his fingers through a mop of greasy hair. 'Bad news don't half travel fast, don't it?'

'It does,' I said. 'Well, can I see him?'

'No, Guvnor.'

I gritted my teeth. 'Why not?'

'Don't want you to get it, do we?'

'Get what?'

'The 'flu, of course.'

Mr. Smiley explained that Dean had come home from school the day before with a temperature of 102. 'I carted 'im off to the doctor and he ordered Dean to bed for a couple of days.'

'So that's what it was,' I said lamely.

'Nice of you to notice 'e was under the weather.' As he closed the door on me, he said, ' 'E's got no idea you're so fond of 'im.'

He didn't fool me. Even if my New Year resolution, 'Wise up,' had worn a bit thin, I knew a cover-up job when I saw it.

I phoned Dr. Daley. Though he admitted to being a little fuzzy in the head, he was quite sure he had not treated anybody by the name of Dean Smiley.

I went to the school where Mrs. Hughes insisted that Mr. Smiley's story was true.

'Someone's made a mug of you, Mrs. Hughes.'

'My husband, Father.'

'What about your husband?'

'My husband's the doctor who ordered Dean to bed for a couple of days.'

'Oh, is he?' I said, taken aback. 'I don't suppose your husband could get him to stay there for six months.'

Outside the building, on the wet grass, I saw something that made me shudder but I picked it up with my handkerchief and placed it in the cardboard box alongside the dead bird.

Fr. Duddleswell was not too upset about the incident at the Aviary. It was the least of his worries. As for me, I now had no doubts about who the culprit was.

That evening I phoned Mrs. Hughes at home, questioned her about Ross and asked her for his address.

Next afternoon, Saturday, I cycled to the small field reserved by the Council for gypsy encampments. It was raining hard but I was dressed for it in galoshes—a Christmas present from Mrs. Pring—cape and oilskin hat. There were a few early snowdrops and the tips of the first daffodils spiked the grass under dripping trees.

Ross lived with his mother in a caravan on the edge of the encampment. It was of the old-fashioned sort, shaped like a huge barrel on its side with the horse-shafts protruding from the front. It had been bright green once but the paint was peeling everywhere. Under it, an old black Alsatian, blind in one eye, was lying on clean straw. He looked at me suspiciously but fortunately did not bark.

Nearby were the smouldering remains of a wood fire; a bare washing line hung from two poles. Two horses, a mare and a colt, were nibbling the lank grass and shivering in spite of the sacking thrown over them as a protection against the icy rain.

I knocked on the rear end of the barrel. Nailed to the door was a big black feather, a crow's perhaps. The door swung open outwards and a striking-looking woman stood framed in the doorway. She wore a brightly coloured shawl almost to her knees. Her hair was jet black, parted in the middle, she wore ruby earrings and her eyes blazed above a long straight nose.

'You've come for him, then.' It was an affirmation not a question.

'Yes.'

She looked alarmed. 'You're not going to take him away from me.' The same tone of voice. 'He's the breath of my breath.'

'No,' I said. 'I'm not a policeman. I'm a priest.'

She relaxed. 'Come in, Father.' She took my hand and kissed it. 'A wild colt makes a good horse, Father.'

'Father Boyd,' I said, introducing myself, as I brushed my shoes on the wire mat and shook my cape and hat.

'My Ross speak of you.'

The dim interior, with only a small box window, was lit by a kerosene lamp. I made out a bundle of dried leaves of which I only recognized burdock and serpent's tongue. There were bunches of herbs, piles of seeds and two wicker baskets full of white wooden pegs. Ross was seated at a table holding a cup to his mouth.

'It *is* me,' Ross said, 'I do it.'

As I sat down beside a bunk, I thanked him for owning up. 'I guessed it was you, Ross.'

'I knows you would.'

Ross's mother came up and whispered in my ear. 'He likes you, Father.' She retired to a corner and said no more.

I sensed that Ross had been confronted many times before for his misdemeanors by people he liked a good deal less.

'It can't go on, can it, Ross?'

'What?'

'Opening cages. Letting out animals and birds.'

Gorgio!' Ross spat out. 'Nothing should be locked up. 'Taint natural.' He softened towards me. 'You're a nice man, Father, our dog not bark at you, so why you let these things?'

I shrugged. I had expected to be the one asking the questions.

'Animals, birds, they should be free. *Always*. Like sparrows. Roam free they should, like a horse. Our

58

horse eats grass when she's hungry, drinks in the stream when she's dry. There's some as would lock air in cages if they could.'

'I thought you felt like that, Ross.'

'I do. Yes, I do.'

'I didn't expect a Romany would like to see anything locked up.' I smiled. 'Not even a schoolboy.'

He smiled, too. His face was not used to it.

'Mrs. Hughes told me, Ross, that when all the animals were released in the gardens, there wasn't a sound. No bark from a dog, no cluck from a hen.'

'That's right. They knows I love 'em, see.'

'Yes, I do see.'

'If you put a bird in a cage, you might as well chop his wings off,' Ross said. 'There's people'd learn rabbits their sums if they could.'

Sure I had Ross's confidence, I told him I thought he was only partly right. Usually people lock up animals and put birds in cages for their protection.

'Your dog under this caravan, Ross. What would happen to him if you didn't look after him? And your horses, you put sacks on their backs to keep them dry and warm.'

'We don't lock nothing up,' he said stubbornly. 'Not even our dog is allowed in here. He don't have *no* prison, him.'

I took the cardboard box from inside my jacket. It was wet and crumpled. I handed it to the boy.

Ross took the lid off. He stared first at the hamster and golden oriole lying side by side on the straw and then at me. 'That's life, isn't it?' A nerve twitched in his temple.

'Try telling that to them, Ross.'

'You try telling dead things in cages they're alive.' I said nothing. 'Death's not important, everything dies. But to be free—' He broke off as if he could never make a Gorgio understand.

I rose to go. Ross walked with me to my bike. The rain had stopped. The sun was trying to pierce the clouds.

'I don't like what you say about being lonely,' Ross said, as I stood my bike up.

'You don't believe it?'

'I do, which is why I don't like it. My mum is lonely.' He pointed to the caravan, and, though perhaps I imagined this, to the black feather nailed to the door. 'And so are you lonely.'

'And you, Ross?'

He looked really puzzled. 'I don't never think of it.'

I lightly punched his arm. 'See you, Ross. Bless you.'

Mrs. Pring was back. I could tell as soon as I opened the back door. I even knew before seeing her that her hair had been permed.

I placed my bike against the wall, ran into the kitchen and took her into my arms. 'I'm so sorry,' I began.

'Whatever for, Father Neil? I'm the happiest woman in the world, don't you know?' and she cried to prove it.

We sat at the kitchen table opposite each other and I told her about Ross and the animals and his widowed mother.

'Poor little chap,' Mrs. Pring said, 'and the poor mother, too.'

She promised to speak to Fr. Duddleswell about it. She was sure he would sort things out. 'If he don't, I'll flatten him like a hedgehog on a main road.'

Half an hour later, she came to my room. She had persuaded him to phone the Aviary Director. Fr. Duddleswell had promised Mr. Brandon to pay the cost of replacing the birds if the police were kept out of it.

'That man,' she said admiringly, 'could make the sun go from North to South if he liked.'

Fr. Duddleswell was so pleased to have his sparring partner back he would have done anything for her. Not that he gave any overt sign of it. At supper, he whispered to me, 'She is not back above one hour and she comes rushing at me like a lobster.'

The neighbours whose houses backed onto the school stopped complaining. My sex education lessons were over. Peace of a sort descended on St. Jude's.

The following Friday, Mrs. Hughes told me that Ross was leaving Fairwater. The incessant rain—three times the January average—had turned their camp-site into a quagmire. The gypsies were leaving on Sunday for another site on higher ground.

Early Saturday afternoon, I cycled to the encampment for the last time. Ironically, the sky was blue and an enormous sun almost warm.

Ross was lying along the bank of a stream to the north of the field, tickling a trout. Dr. Daley had told me he used to do it when he was a boy in Connemara but I had never seen it with my own eyes.

Slowly, Ross dipped his arm in the water and stroked the trout. The murmur of his voice came to me across the still waters and the wet grass. '*Ek, dui, trin,*' he counted and then, flip, the fish was on the bank, jumping and somersaulting.

Seeing me standing there, the boy flipped the fish back into the stream. 'Too small to eat, Father.' I smiled. He stood up. 'I am expecting you.'

'I just come to say goodbye.'

His hands hung down clumsily by his side. 'Goodbye, Father.'

That seemed to be the end of it. I had really come on an errand. I wanted to say to him:

'Ross, you know you spoke hastily to God once. Well, you're wrong, Ross. Not one tiny sparrow falls to the ground without God knowing it.

'You remember, Ross, you said the dead baby in the box looked like a match? Well, one day, Ross, at the Resurrection, God will come and light that match with His Holy Spirit and that little baby's face will glow like the face of Christ Himself.'

I had prepared it all. But when the time came, I

couldn't say it. This soul of mine, I thought, is so dull and prosaic while Ross's is like sunlight and birdsong, pure poetry.

'Can I walk to your bike with you, Father?'

I smiled. 'Thanks, Ross.'

He came with me, carrying a kind of bell-shaped object covered with a cloth which he brought from the caravan. I stopped to put on my cycle clips and when I rose he held out his hand. 'A present for you, Romany.'

I lifted the cloth. There was a cage and, on its perch, a golden oriole.

'But, Ross,' I protested almost angrily, 'how could you do . . . ?'

Ross was smiling broadly. The golden oriole was the one I had given him, now stuffed.

He opened the cage door. 'See, Father, he don't mind a cage, his sort.'

I placed my free arm round the boy's shoulders. He smelled of wild garlic and damp green grass. A warmth went from me to him, from him to me.

'Ross,' I said, 'I've been meaning to ask you something.'

'Yes, Father?'

'You know the time you saw a baby born dead.'

'Yes.'

'And you said something . . . rough . . . to God.'

'I remember. Want to know what He says to me?'

'Well . . . If you like, yes.'

'God says, "You don't need to worry none about Me, Ross boy. I always *is* white all over with a black face."'

Four

PORGY AND BESS

'I will not allow the peace and quiet of me nose to be disturbed by Billy Buzzle's pigs.'

It was surprising that it took Fr. Duddleswell three days to discover that Porgy and Bess were there. But I had received no visit from the Angel Gabriel. Why should I consider myself chosen by Providence for the unenviable task of breaking the news to him?

A big sty was built at the bottom of Billy's garden in early January and a few days later the two pigs arrived, grunting and squealing, to take possession.

'There is a startling odour hereabouts,' Fr. Duddleswell remarked in my study, grossly understating the case.

From that moment on, I knew there was no sense in which peace and quiet would be a feature of our domestic scene.

His nose twitched like a rabbit's as he attempted to sniff down the source of the smell. His quest led him to the window in spite of it being tightly closed.

Then he saw them. Bess's silky, whitish back and the broad ringed snout and muddy forelegs of Porgy as he looked laughingly over the stye.

'Did you have previous cognizance of this Father Neil?' he snapped.

'Um.'

'Father Neil, I have told you a power of times be-

63

fore that your face is a postcard for everyone to read.' And he stamped out.

A minute later, I heard Billy's cheerful voice coming from the garden. 'Morning, Father O'Duddleswell.'

I caught sight of my parish priest banging the fence with his fist. 'The Third World War, Mr. Buzzle. Right here 'twill commence. Over this blessèd fence.'

Billy flattened the kiss-curl above his right eye and slowly adjusted the cuffs protruding like white cylinders from his jacket sleeves. 'What's eating you, then?'

'I will not tolerate oinks, slurps and stinks in the vicinity of me abode. They will have to go.'

'Father,' Billy said patiently. 'Father O'Duddleswell. Pigs are beautiful, friendly animals.' He pointed to the shining face peering over the sty. 'Ain't he lovely, now? Tell me if he ain't.'

Fr. Duddleswell took a quick look at the pointed ears, the broad wrinkled snout, the dribbling chin and, for reply, turned his head towards his left shoulder. 'Phew. The stench of it.'

'Stench?' Billy was really indignant. He breathed in air generously as if he were paddling up to his knees at the sea-side. 'That's not even a smell. That's an aroma, that is, an agricultural perfume. It's not fair to judge pigs by their reputation.'

Fr. Duddleswell pegged his nose with thumb and forefinger. 'Why must you do this to me, Mr. Buzzle?' he enquired nasally.

Billy shrugged and held out the fat, ringed fingers of both hands as if he was completely bewildered by such an accusation.

'Why do you take divilish delight, Mr. Buzzle, in always being right-left to my left-right?'

'Ooink, oink.' Porgy seemed to side with his owner in the dispute before dropping into the mud and effluent of the sty with an almighty splash.

'Look, St. Francis,' Billy said, 'I love all God's creatures.'

'Excepting me, Mr. Buzzle,' Fr. Duddleswell roared.

'Yeah, well, I've never been quite sure where *you* came from.'

'Right, 'tis war. War bloody and horrible. I am taking you and your blessèd cloven-footed demons to court, God is me witness.'

Billy shouted after Fr. Duddleswell's retreating figure, 'If only people realized when they buy a house that the bloody neighbours go with it.'

Our garden door slammed to and I heard Fr. Duddleswell muttering, 'Friendly creatures, he says. Harmless creatures, he says. The smell of 'em alone would register 6 on the Richter scale.'

There was silence as he retired to his study to recite the divine office.

I went on gazing through the window. Billy, joined by Pontius, his big black labrador, was leaning over the brick wall of the dunging yard uttering endearments.

'Lovely girl, Bess. C'mon Porgy, old chap.'

He dangled potato peelings in front of their snouts, hoping they would beg for them like dogs. It was like watching the beginnings of an improbable romance.

Fr. Duddleswell's attitude was quite different. 'Mrs. Pring,' he commanded at table, 'for tomorrow's lunch I am wanting roast pig.'

'You'll have to chop your own leg off, then,' Mrs. Pring retorted, 'we've got no meat coupons to spare.'

Dramatically, Fr. Duddleswell took two pound notes out of his wallet. 'Get it, if need be, without coupons.'

He turned to me, shaking his head and tapping on the table with his fork in tune with the words: ' 'Tis sore hard on a peaceable man like meself. I was born, y'see with this quiet, loving disposition.' On the last three words, his fork almost spiked the table.

When Mrs. Pring returned to her kitchen, I asked him if he really intended taking Billy to court.

Instead of answering, he fell to musing on why Billy needed the company of animals—a dog, pigeons and now pigs—to survive.

'He has no wife or children, you follow? and no religion. He is thirsting for love and affection, poor misguided feller that he is. More to be pitied, really. Let's pray the pigs teach him some manners.'

His New Year's resolution still had some life in it.

At that moment, Mrs. Pring screamed hysterically in the distance and dropped a trayload of cutlery. I was with her only a few seconds later to find this grinning, porcine face pressed against the window pane.

I put my arm round Mrs. Pring's trembling shoulders. 'It's only a pig, Mrs. P.,' I said soothingly.

Fr. Duddleswell, in the meanwhile, had grabbed the carving knife and was scampering off in search of retribution. 'Billy Buzzle. That Abomination of Desolation. Now his odious bloody pig is trespassing on me land.'

I left Mrs. Pring, caught up with Fr. Duddleswell and held his arm back to prevent him throwing the knife pig-wards.

In any case, Porgy, smelling danger, had trotted off to the safety of his own garden *via* a fresh hole in the fence.

'There,' Fr. Duddleswell cried, 'did I not say the next War will start over that bloody fence?'

He went to the official border and called to Billy in his house as if he were Goliath summoning the Israelites to do battle with him.

'Come out, Mr. Buzzle, before me axe flies off its handle and finds a home in your head.'

Billy immediately took up the challenge and showed himself. 'What's up?'

'What is *down*, you mean, Mr. Buzzle. 'Tis me fence that is down, that's what.'

'You know what they say, Father O'Duddleswell,

good fences make good neighbours. You should keep your fence in better repair, shouldn't you?'

'Dear God in heaven or wherever! I did not erect me fence to be proof against invasions by pigs.'

For the first time, Billy noticed the instrument in Fr. Duddleswell's hand. 'What're you doing with that? You weren't intending to stab my poor Porgy?'

'There is a hog traipsing about me garden at his own free will,' Fr. Duddleswell retorted, 'nearly frightening me beloved housekeeper to death, and he has the nerve to ask me about me intentions.'

'Father O'Duddleswell,' Billy sighed, 'why can't we be friends?'

'Mr. Buzzle, 'tis surely bad enough having you for an enemy.'

'Can't you be kind for once in your life?'

'I will be kind as a brick wall to your head. You are a most complete rogue and no mistake, a most abandoned villain.'

'Go away, you pompous little rotter,' Billy yelled, realizing a peace treaty wasn't on. 'No air-raid warning from me. You'll just get a bomb on your bloody house, you will.' He reached forward to pick up the fallen piece of fence. 'Don't want you coming through here upsetting my pigs.'

Porgy, with a supreme effort, scrambled over the brick wall into the sty and squealed with what sounded suspiciously like mockery.

'Out of me garden,' Billy threatened, 'before I give me foot a free hand.'

Fr. Duddleswell, a good match at mixing metaphors, growled, 'You are as pig-headed as a mule.'

That was the first of Porgy's many forays into our garden and he gave our fence quite a battering. His muscular snout, bull-ringed though it was, dug up our lawn, vegetable patch and flower beds. For his part, Billy accepted it with characteristic forebearance.

One day when Fr. Duddleswell was out visiting

the parish, I asked Billy how he came by the pigs in the first place.

He was standing next to a huge tin bath he had sited in the middle of his garden. He dropped into it every species of food: carrots, parsnips, peas in their pods, acorns, horse-chestnuts, as well as barley meal, balancer meal and ground wheat. He was just about to drop in a bundle of nettles.

'They need it for the iron, Father,' he explained. 'How did I get 'em? Sheer luck, if you ask me.'

A punter, unable to pay his gambling debts, offered Billy two pedigree pigs instead. Billy had hired a van to transport them and, for some reason, they had gone as berserk as Fr. O'Duddleswell and nearly kicked the sides in. But they were converted and calm after that. Unlike somebody he knew.

'I never thought I'd grow so fond of 'em as this,' Billy said, eyeing the pigs dreamily.

'They look easy to feed, Mr. Buzzle.'

'Yeah, well, they've got a digestion like you and me.' He started stirring the mess up with a garden fork. 'Can swallow anything but insults, pigs can. You tell your boss-man, if he wants to help this country, which he don't, grow pigs.'

When Billy drew out a bucket of pig-swill from the bath and put it on a brick kiln to be warmed up, I excused myself saying I had very important things to do.

Up in my room, I took out my air-freshener and sprayed for five minutes.

'Dear saints in heaven,' Fr. Duddleswell exploded on his return, 'the odour of pig is loud as a brass band. I do not know that I can put up with this much longer. Not when the west wind is whistling up me nose.'

He lit a bonfire in the garden. On it he dumped two whole packets of expensive incense-coals which we put in the thurible at High Mass and Benediction. Even that failed to sweeten the atmosphere.

Once, I saw him stamping up and down in the garden reciting his breviary with a gas mask on.

'Not a fair nor a wake will I enjoy,' he groaned, lifting his gas mask for a moment, 'till I have driven those pigs to the knacker's yard.'

By Sunday the smell of pig was stupendous. The congregation at the first two Masses, which I celebrated, seemed in purdah. Only their eyes were visible above their handkerchieves.

At the eleven o'clock Mass, Fr. Duddleswell ignored the prescribed Gospel reading for the day and chose in place of it a passage from Mark 5. It was the story of Jesus casting devils out of a man named 'Legion' and sending them into a herd of pigs which promptly rushed down the hill into the sea.

'All of them drowned,' he concluded, rubbing his hands. 'Drowned.'

In his sermon, he developed the theme, not at any length because of the lack of air, of Jesus' righteous hatred of pigs.

'I want you to remember, me dear people, at this peculiar Mass which is High in every sense, how our Blessed Lord clearly indicated the best way to deal with this depraved, gluttonous and disgusting beast.'

After Mass, the congregation dispersed so rapidly we barely had a chance to bid goodbye to half a dozen of them. When we returned to the sacristy, the place was in turmoil. The altar servers were screeching, laughing and holding their noses and one of them was sick.

Fr. Duddleswell's demand for silence went unheeded. The source of the trouble was obvious. Two of the boys were locked in battle in the big brown cupboard that held the servers' cassocks and cottas.

He opened the door and called imperiously, 'Come out, d'you hear me speak to you?' And out came Porgy, his head sticking out of a cotta, smiling lewdly.

Having no other instrument handy, Fr. Duddleswell tried to lassoo him with the vestment girdle but Porgy eluded him with ease and, making a mess on the cotta, strolled nonchalantly out of the sacristy. He scrambled through a new hole in the fence and homewards to his pen.

'Sunday or not,' Fr. Duddleswell rasped, 'holy-day or not, enough is more than enough. That pig and his pong will drive me to the crazy-house.'

I followed him in case he did something he might regret. He did not like my attentions. 'Father Neil,' he snapped, 'must you be always following me around like me own backside?'

He crawled through the hole in the fence into Billy's garden and planted himself underneath the bedroom window.

'If you want to make yourself useful, Father Neil, give me some beggar's bullets.'

I gave him a handful of pebbles over the fence and he threw two or three at the window pane. The window opened and Billy's head and pyjama-ed shoulders appeared.

'What the . . . Father O'Duddleswell? I was abed.'

'I will put you to bed, you heathen, you. With a shovel.'

'And if you don't shift your plates of meat off my daff' bulbs, I'll come down there and tear out your shrivelled little trinkets.'

With frosted breath that turned them into two dragons in argument, Billy called Fr. Duddleswell the son of a bachelor and Fr. Duddleswell retaliated with something meant to be far worse:

'You, Mr. Buzzle, are the son of a policeman.'

Billy tried the oil-technique. 'All right, Father O'Duddleswell, all right, calm down and tell me what my Porgy's done.'

'Your pig is a swine.'

'What has he *done*?'

'I did not invite your blessed pig to become one of me choristers. Nor me gardener, come to that. I am claiming five pounds in damages.'

'Okay, St. Francis, if you won't talk sense.' Billy withdrew his head and lowered the window.

Fr. Duddleswell demanded more ammunition and I gave it. He threw the second pebble with more vigour than he intended and a big crack appeared in the glass.

'Father Neil,' he said accusingly, 'I asked you for bullets not six pound shells.'

Inside the room upstairs, there was a rumpus and Billy's voice could be distinctly heard. 'C'mon, Pontius old boy, follow me quick. I'm gonna give you clergyman's backside for breakfast.'

We scrambled.

After the last Mass that morning, Fr. Duddleswell pleaded with parishioners to stay on to sign a petition for the removal of the pigs. I was detailed to put it through Billy's letter box. Before lunch was over, it had been re-mailed to us in confetti form.

Fr. Duddleswell threatened Billy with various things, from planting a lump on his head to making a centre aisle between his teeth. But for a few days the pressure was lifted from us. Porgy took to leaping over Billy's garden gate and terrorizing the neighbourhood. There followed a chapter of accidents with many verses.

First, Porgy was found entangled in the washing of Mrs. Martin who lived opposite us. Next, he held up traffic in the High Street for several minutes, frightened old ladies, causing one of them to faint, and ended up in the Gents' lavatory next to the Fire Station. Fortunately for Billy, the firemen treated it as a big joke and reunited pig and owner without informing the police.

Fate dealt less kindly with Fr. Duddleswell. Next day, when he chanced to park his old Chrysler car in the street, Porgy came bouncing down from the gate and, failing to stop in time, left a distinct impression of himself on the near-side wing. I was the only witness of the accident.

'Definitely a court case now and I am off to the

lawyers,' was Fr. Duddleswell's instinctive response when I told him. But he didn't go. I suspect it was because he considered lawyers even more greedy and unwholesome creatures than pigs. He contented himself with sending Billy another demand, fruitless as before, for damages.

Billy wisely doubled the height of his gate so that Porgy's only recreation left was digging up our garden afresh. Billy did at least put up special wiring on his side of the fence.

'What is the use of this?' Fr. Duddleswell complained to me as we examined it together.

He put out his hand to test the strength of the wire and received a terrific shock. He rebounded into me and his glasses fell off.

'That . . . that cursed bloody Bookie has electrocuted me,' he cried. 'Why did he not tell—?'

Porgy chose that moment to investigate the incident and one of his trotters smashed the left lens of the glasses.

Fr. Duddleswell groped his way at manic speed to Mrs. Pring's kitchen. 'The carving knife, quick,' he demanded, shaking all over.

I took his arm and led him like a blind man with malaria to his study where he kept his spare pair of spectacles. His vision and temper restored, he said despairingly:

'After a while of this it gets you down. B.O. is bad enough but P.O. Ugh.'

'What I don't understand, Father, is how Billy can stand it himself.'

'When the breeze is westerly he takes up residence in "The Blue Star", that is how.'

'What can we do?'

His reply sounded ominous. 'Look, boy, if the wind blows your hat off, me advice to you is, Don't wait for the wind to change. Run after your bloody hat.'

'Oh, yes,' I said, making for the door.

' 'Tis up to you, Father Neil.' The tone of his voice

72

stopped me in my tracks. '*You* are going to get rid of it.'

What did he mean? Was he expecting me to murder the pig? I had a startling childhood memory of my father killing our three cockerels one Christmas. Instead of wringing their necks, he chopped their heads off and for several minutes decapitated cockerels were racing all over the yard, knocking things over. A murdered pig, I thought, can still kill.

'Don't expect me to kill Porgy,' I said. 'I'm too attached to him.' It sounded a lame excuse.

Fr. Duddleswell made a slurping noise through his closed teeth.

'Who said anything about killing him?'

'Sorry,' I said, much relieved.

'No, I just want you to help me kidnap him.' I gulped. 'Take him on a journey, like.'

I protested strongly. 'Do you expect me to ride my bike with a pig?'

'Of course not.'

'And I'm not taking him on a bus, cither.'

'Father Neil, will you at least allow me a speech from the dock?'

Mrs. Pring was given leave that evening to attend the whist drive. At seven-thirty, the lights in Billy's place went out indicating he had left for "The Blue Star". Fr. Duddleswell called Billy's number to make sure. No reply.

We crept out into the garden. ' 'Twill be as easy,' he whispered, switching on his torch, 'as the road from your hand to your mouth. But watch that pig narrowly, mind.'

The plan was this: corner Porgy, put a rope round his neck and a bag over his head, truss up his trotters, put him on his back in a wheelbarrow, wheel him to Fr. Duddleswell's car, cover him with a blanket so as not to terrify passers-by and transport him to a friendly farm on the edge of town for safe-keeping until Billy paid the damages owing.

With such a spine-chilling scenario, we were extremely lucky not to get through the opening scene.

Sleet was falling, and cornering Porgy was like trying to track down a clever ghost. Taking advantage of the fact that we only had Fr. Duddleswell's 'search-light' to guide us, he led us a dance all over Billy's garden, then all over ours. When, finally, I over-balanced into Billy's swill-tub, Fr. Duddleswell called the chase off.

I retired in my wrath to get out of my clothes and rid myself of some of the stench in the bath.

When I emerged, powdered to the eyebrows, he confronted me.

'There's a scum mark all round the bath,' I said defiantly. 'I left it there specially for you.'

'Father Neil before you start spitting at me like fat in hell's frying pan, let us—'

He was about to say, 'Let us shake hands on it,' but being downwind of me he thought better of it.

'Let us forget about the whole thing,' he said, turning sharply to go.

'So, I'm a leper now, am I?' I called after him.

'No,' he called back, 'you are the Prodigal Son returned. And I am just off to inform your father.'

For a while, even the all-suffering Mrs. Pring raised her nose in my presence. I consoled myself with the thought that kidnapping a pig was no longer on the parish agenda.

My suspicions were aroused anew when Fr. Duddleswell adopted an entirely different attitude to the pig.

Several times I caught him feeding Porgy over the fence. He offered him potatoes, beetroots, dandelions, even chocolate. I was afraid in case he had treated the food with rat poison. I need not have worried. Afterwards, Porgy romped all over our garden with his usual abandon.

'Father,' I suggested once, holding my sniffer, 'don't you think it's about time you made peace with Billy?'

'One Munich is enough in my time,' he rasped back.

A few malodorous days passed and on Mrs. Pring's day off, Fr. Duddleswell said:

'I am watching an opportunity for days to kidnap the enemy and now it has arrived. If the mountain will not come to Mohammed . . .'

The revised plan was to strew Porgy's path with the food he loved best: apples. By trial and error, Fr. Duddleswell had discovered that pigs find them irresistible. He intended enticing Porgy not into the car which he could probably demolish in two minutes but into an open truck. Fr. Duddleswell had consulted a farmer who told him that pigs are good travellers provided they can see where they're going.

I objected heatedly. 'Look, Father, this is stealing and—'

He stopped me and explained that he was only taking Porgy into custody until Billy paid all expenses owing. 'Justice demands it, Father Neil.'

This time the plan worked very well. Porgy chewed his way to the van and we drove under the stars to the sound of him munching contentedly a dozen more apples. The rumblings of his belly were sensational.

'Jed Summers will look after him fine,' Fr. Duddleswell assured me.

The Summers' farm was three miles away. Jed, Essex born and bred, lived with his son, Tom, who now ran the place.

Jed was an old man. He wore a cloth cap, his eyebrows were long and yellow like stacks of straw and his eyes, deep-set though they were, shone with gentleness and humanity. His dialect, coming through thick grey moustaches and beard, was a strange, wonderful music. And difficult, but only at first.

'There,' Jed said, his face creasing into a smile of approval at seeing Porgy. 'I'll look after him like one of me own. Won't be a case of self first, then m'wife, then me agin.'

75

'I hope he will not be too much trouble for you, Jed,' Fr. Duddleswell said.

'I creak a good bit, true. And I can't work hard like what I used to could. No diggin' for me, I ain't neither gristle nor grit fer it.'

One of his teenage grandchildren, Bob, put in, 'Gramps ain't s'green as he's cabbage-looking but still he works a lot harder'n most.'

'Ay,' Jed said, 'I put my coffins on my feet, time to time, and muddle about and do a bit of gardenin' an' that. But I'm four score year, you knows, come next April.'

Fr. Duddleswell said, 'I am sure, Jed, I could not commend this pig into better hands.'

Jed stroked Porgy's back affectionately. 'When he's adry I'll let him guzzle so he don't suffer none from salt poisoning and I'll see to it he has plenty to bite on.' He examined the sack we had brought with us. 'I sees you have a tidy lot o'apples for him. I won't feed him no mucherooms an' that sort o'rubbage. No, I'll treat him jes' like one of my.'

He led us to the sturdy, high-walled pen where Porgy was to be kept.

'Sixty degree in there. No draught come in at the winders here where he sleep and,' indicating the dunging yard, 'he'll happy himself enough paddling away in his slaps o'wet there.'

Jed explained he'd have to call the vet in to give Porgy crystal violet vaccine as a precaution against swine fever.

Fr. Duddleswell willingly coughed up for the vet, the food and the daily care.

As we left, we shook Jed's hand. 'Hap I'll see ye agin soon,' he said.

The magnitude of the harm we had done only hit me when I next saw Billy Buzzle anxiously looking around his garden.

'Porgy,' he called. 'Are you there, Porgy?'

He examined our fence. No break there. We had

mended it on our return the night before. When, in the dark, I had hit Fr. Duddleswell's thumb with the hammer, my apology had in it less than the fullness of my heart.

Billy got his car out and went, I presumed, on a tour of the town looking for his lost pig. He returned two hours later and started again his plaintive, 'Porgy. Are you there, Porgy?'

He asked Mrs. Pring if she had seen his pig and she, quite truthfully, said no. Billy took her word as Gospel and didn't bother to ask Fr. Duddleswell or me.

'It stands to reason,' he told Mrs. Pring, 'he's got to come home some day. Like a pigeon or a dog.'

But he didn't.

For three successive afternoons, Fr. Duddleswell visited the Summers' farm and came back with glowing reports of Porgy's progress. I really believe that he, like Billy, had taken a fancy to that mischievous pig. It explains why he became so aware of Billy's melancholy.

'I wanted to be upsides with Billy Buzzle,' he confessed to me, 'and now I feel guilty as a 'flu bug.'

He had made up his mind to relent and give Porgy back when Tom Summers rang to say that Porgy was dead.

'Rest in peace,' Fr. Duddleswell said instinctively.

Porgy might, I thought. We certainly won't.

We raced to the farm and there sitting alongside Porgy's prone form in the freezing dunging yard was old Jed.

He looked up at us, still stroking Porgy's flank.

'He ate plenty turnups. He were in the pink and nobbly in every way, he were. He don't want for nothing, don't Porgy.'

We were too stunned at first to ask how it had happened. There didn't seem to be a mark on the pig. He hadn't been run over.

'Me children's childern comes and plays with Porgy,' Jed said wiping his forehead with his sleeve.

'He were good company and pretty-behaved. The bestest pig I ever do see. Could've come with mine any day and rest him by the coals.'

Jed shook his capped head and sniffed. 'He ain't owd is Porgy an' a rare'un, ever so rare. If ever anyone loves that pig, I'm him.'

' 'Twasn't your fault,' Fr. Duddleswell said, 'that's for sure.'

Jed found difficulty in breathing. 'You happen unlucky, I reckon, Fr. Duddleswell. The wicked Old Un must of put the kibosh on him. It's shameful sad, though.'

'How did it happen Mr. Summers?'

He looked up at me momentarily and blinked.

'Two hour ago, it were. I go t'light the lamp. It were jes' gone eight. I came to give him a apple. I give him a many afore that. This time there's a sickish smell to 'im an' he acts wunnerful strange, wanky on his feet, he were.'

Jed shook his head in unbelief. 'He lays down do Porgy an' slips his wind. Jes' like that. Dead as last year. Then my two gran'children come. "What's up, Gramps?" they says. "He's gone," I says, "an' that's all about it." '

Jed took his cap off, scratched his head and finished his story.

'Our vet do live hard near. I sent off the fastest of the two chilern. It were a rough mornin' but Bob ain't no watery-head. "I've gone a'ready," says Bob. But he warn't there, the vet warn't.'

'The kids' eyes is that sore, my childern's childern. And I come over cold as what Porgy is now.' He breathed in and released the air slowly. 'An' white as a hound's tooth.'

Tom walked up and told his dad to get up from the mire. 'You do look like you're reg'lar haggled, Da.'

Jed didn't budge. 'The twinkle went out in Porgy's two little eyes. Like stars turned to planets.'

'Get you up, Da. Don't want you followin' that there pig.'

Jed stood up. 'I did all possibles for that pig. Every one of these things I tell you, Fr. Duddleswell, are true, God so help me.'

Fr. Duddleswell took hold of his hand and arm. 'I believe you, Jed. Every word.'

'We shall have to bury him,' Jed said, 'shan't us?'

'What did Billy say, Father?'

'Nothing much, Father Neil. One word, in fact. Repeated and repeated. 'Twas as if I had sung *God Save The King* in a Dublin bar.' He became sympathetic. 'But 'tis a miserable expression of countenance he has and no mistake.'

In a more tranquil moment, he described the whole episode. He had knocked on Billy's door and invited himself in.

' "I am sure I beg your pardon, Billy, but Porgy has gone." "Escaped again?" "By gone I mean gone." "Dead?" "Dead as roast p . . . Dead as one of Mrs. Pring's doughnuts." '

That was when Billy resorted to his single-word attack.

Now long afterwards, I was in the garden. A disconsolate Billy was trying to get some Parish's food, a red liquid concoction given to babies, down Bess's throat.

'I'm very sorry, Billy,' I said.

'I ain't blaming any human being for it, Father. Only your boss-man.' To console himself, he turned to stroke Pontius's sleek black coat.

I told Billy that Fr. Duddleswell had gone to tremendous trouble on Porgy's account. Jed Summers, the keeper, really loved the pig and gave him the best of treatment.

'Porgy died laughing, I suppose,' Billy said bitterly.

'Even Jed doesn't know what he died of. It wasn't swine fever or pneumonia or pleurisy. One moment he was well and the next he just keeled over.'

'Died of a broken heart did Porgy. That's the worst way to go, that is.'

'I just thought you'd like to know, Billy, that Fr. Duddleswell is cut up, too.'

'Not in small enough pieces for my liking,' Billy growled.

Half an hour after that conversation, I said to Fr. Duddleswell:

'Father, with due respect, you made a mess of things.'

'Do I not know it, Father Neil. I have already made me confession over it and begun me penance.' He beat his breast. '*Mea maxima culpa.* I never should have lifted that pg.'

'Maybe, Father, but what I meant was, you should have taken Billy to court in the first place.'

'Father *Neil*.' He was hardly able to believe his ears. 'Me dear old neighbour Billy Buzzle has lost the pig dearest his heart and I am entirely to blame. And while he is still in mourning you are suggesting I should have taken his sweet self to court.' He was astounded at the hardness of my heart. 'Why do you say that, Father Neil? *Why?*'

'Because, Father,' I said, not without satisfaction, 'he wouldn't now be taking *you* to court.'

Five

A PIG IN COURT

'Taking *me* to court,' Fr. Duddleswell exclaimed when I told him what Billy had said. 'What scoundrelism. I should be the one to take that pig to court. Why, the beastly animal . . . I mean Porgy . . . did more destruction to me garden than twenty legions of atheist moles.'

I took no sides.

'Oh, Father Neil, 'twas no offence to me though Billy Buzzle were hanged, smoked and quartered. He takes his best enemy to court after I have said six miles of prayers on my knees for him and for his darlin' pig but recently deceased.'

He paused, doubtless to pray another mile of silent prayer for Porgy alone. Then:

' 'Tis strange how I grew exceeding fond of that pig and would give every particle I possess to have him back.'

The Law was not long in taking over. A summons arrived instructing Charles Duddleswell to appear at the County Court in four weeks time. The case was to be heard before His Honour Judge Turnbull on the plaintiff's claim of £15 for the wrongful conversion of a pedigree pig by the defendant Duddleswell to his own use.

I went with Fr. Duddleswell to the St. Jude's solicitor, Josiah Tippett, the elder statesman of Tippett, Tippett and Wainwright.

Josiah Tippett invited us into his neat little pan-
elled den adorned with Law Reports and musty
tomes. He was a small crumpled man dressed in
black and grey, with a white face as if he had died
last week. Of the two wings of his shirt collar one
went up and one went down as if to symbolize his
talent for moving in whatever direction his client's
case required.

'There isn't any need to go to court, you know, Fr.
Duddleswell,' he said, straightening his tie.

'No, Josiah?'

Mr. Tippett sniffed and shook his head as if even
he had a loathing for the labyrinthine workings of
the law. 'You could let the Court Registrar arbitrate.'

Fr. Duddleswell turned down the suggestion flat.
' 'Twould look like an admission of guilt on my part.'

Another sniff from Josiah as if he was satisfied
he had done his best to warn a prospective client of
the terrors to come. 'So be it. You can either let me
handle the case in court for you or I could instruct
counsel.'

'Why cannot I argue me own case?' Fr. Duddleswell wanted to know. ' 'Tis unassailable.'

Mr. Tippett permitted himself a smile. I felt sure
he was mentally making a charge for it.

'Father Duddleswell,' he said, 'we have a dictum
in the profession, He who is his own lawyer, has a
fool for a client.'

Fr. Duddleswell, about to comment, thought better
of it.

'Now, Father, is the plaintiff instructing counsel?'

I said yes because Billy had told me so.

'Then,' Josiah said, 'I suggest we talk to Nathan
Flitch, K.C. He's a tin-lid.'

'Pardon, Josiah.'

'A pot o' glue. One of the chosen,' he said, touching the side of his nose. 'But sharp, really sharp.'

'That will cost me a few potatoes,' Fr. Duddleswell said gloomily.

Josiah sniffed dismissively as if the little matter of legal fees did not enter into the calculation of legal men. 'First of all, what did you do with the distrained pig?'

'Porgy? Buried him,' Fr. Duddleswell said. 'With honours.'

'Pity, Father. Great pity.'

'We could not eat him. 'Tis probably against the law, even.'

Josiah waved a minute white hand to intimate he was well aware that more things than not were against the law. 'I mean, Father, you should have called in the vet.'

'The blessed pig was completely dead, Josiah.'

'A vet would have ascertained the cause of death. By interring the pig in a hurry you may appear to the court to have wanted to destroy any evidence of neglect on your part.'

'I am *innocent*, Josiah.'

Mr. Tippett made a tired gesture as if to say that innocence or guilt had nothing to do with the matter in hand.

'Josiah, it did not occur to me to hold a *Postmortem* on a pig.'

'So many things do not occur to laymen, Father Duddleswell.' Another sniff. 'What are we lawyers for, after all?'

At the end of an hour's consultation, it seemed to me that Fr. Duddleswell ought to reconsider the offer of the Registrar's arbitration.

In the street, I said:

'I reckon Mr. Tippett thinks he could have got Jesus off before Pilate.'

A curious thought struck him. 'If so, how would the world have been redeemed, Father Neil?'

'What are the signs that it *has* been redeemed?'

'Apart from me own heroic sanctity, not many, I

83

grant.' He laughed grimly. 'Did I ever sing you the Judge's song from *Trial By Jury*?'

'Hundreds of times.'

'Good. Then I will sing it you again.' And he did, with special hostility on the verse:

> All thieves who could my fees afford
>> Relied on my orations,
> And many a burglar I've restored
>> To his friends and his relations.

'There's one advantage in having a Jew for an advocate,' I said to cheer him up.

'Oh, yes?'

'He'll dislike pigs as much as Jesus.'

Fr. Duddleswell stayed glum. 'But I did not dislike Porgy,' he said.

Mrs. Pring was delighted to hear that Fr. Duddleswell was to stand trial at last.

'But what about *that* one in the dock telling the truth, the whole truth, and nothing but the truth,' she laughed. 'If I were you, Father D, I'd restrict myself to telling them the time of day.'

He stamped out, growling, 'Are you me barber that I have to stay and listen to this?'

The hearing was arranged for four o'clock on a Wednesday afternoon. In the corridor beforehand we nodded to Billy and met our counsel, Mr. Flitch, for the first time. Billy's counsel, Timothy Banks, was also in attendance.

His Honour Judge Turnbull appeared, bewigged and in a blue robe with a purple sash, on the dot of four. And battle commenced.

Banks's opening was admirably concise:

'May it please Your Honour, the case is being brought by William Rufus Buzzle, owner of the distrained animal which went sick and died of neglect after being purloined by the defendant, Charles Clement Duddleswell.'

Billy was called. From my vantage point immediately behind Josiah Tippett, he looked a convincing and poignant witness.

In between sobs, Billy gave his counsel an account of the pig's disappearance. He related how Fr. Duddleswell had told him what had happened only after the pig was dead and buried.

There was no need for other witnesses as to the basic facts; about them there was no dispute between the parties.

The defendant's case was argued quietly by Nathan Flitch. He put it to Billy that he had shown no concern for private property or public safety in allowing his animal to wander away from his pen at will.

'I submit, Your Honour, that the defendant had the right of any damaged person to "distress damage feasant". This included the right to keep the animal under detention "in pound" until the plaintiff paid the damages demanded by my client. This the plaintiff steadfastly refused to do.'

When Flitch had finished with Billy, I thought he was worth every penny of the many pounds we would have to pay him.

Fr. Duddleswell's turn to take the stand. He went forward clutching his Douai Bible in case he should be asked to swear an oath on a Protestant version full of heretical translations.

Mr. Flitch elicited from him that he had no personal animosity towards pigs as such nor towards the particular estranged pig, Porgy by name.

'Indeed not, sir.'

'Address the court, please,' Mr. Flitch demanded.

'Indeed, not, Your Honour. It was to me a matter of genuine regret and lamentation that Porgy, a beautiful creature, passed away. Especially, Your Honour, in view of the current shortage of meat in the country.'

Flitch further established that Porgy was an unusually savage example of a swine. In spite of this

85

the plaintiff made but pitiable efforts to restrain him.

'The plaintiff also failed,' Flitch continued, 'to provide his beast with the secure, spacious and happy home of which he stood so obviously in need. Indeed, Your Honour, I suggest there are *prima facie* grounds for believing the plaintiff contravened the "Cruelty to Animals Act of 1847".'

The Judge gave no sign of being impressed either way by this submission. If the truth were told, he looked more than three quarters asleep.

'As to damage,' counsel said, '*res ipsa loquitur*. The said pig dented the defendant's vintage car, repeatedly battered down his fence and dug trenches deep enough for soldiers in his garden.

'More, the pig, of substantial weight and volume, collided with numerous unsuspecting members of the public, entered a Gentlemen's lavatory wherein he interfered with natural functions and caused patrons of the said lavatory to leave without adjusting their dress. The distress of women shopping in the vicinity is best left to the court's imagination.'

Fr. Duddleswell was coaxed to describe his sterling efforts to enlist public support for improvement in the pig's behaviour. However, the plaintiff, who lives next door, tore up the petition.

'When,' Mr. Flitch concluded, 'the plaintiff twice refused *to pay or even discuss* compensation for the pig's misdemeanours, the defendant impounded the pig—in the pig's own interests as well as everyone else's—and transported him to a place of maximum porcine pleasure and safety.' He coughed. 'Where he died.'

As counsel sat down, I judged that Fr. Duddleswell deserved a medal for public service. Until the long, lean Timothy Banks, distinguished by his apparent lack of eyebrows, got at him. I rapidly came to the conclusion that we had hired the wrong counsel.

'Charles Duddleswell,' Banks began, as if he had

not noticed him until that moment, 'I am touched by your deep affection for the deceased pig.'

'I liked him a lot.'

'A generous sentiment seeing he was such a savage beast.'

'He was not exactly savage, sir. I mean, Your Honour.'

'I am so sorry,' Banks said with exaggerated politeness. 'I received the distinct impression from counsel it was of the essence of the case for the defence that the said pig was a *savage* beast. Did he not dent cars, demolish fences and dig canals in your garden?"

'That he did,' Fr. Duddleswell said, uncomfortably committed for the first time in his life to total truth. 'But he was more playful than savage.'

Banks turned away from Fr. Duddleswell to ask:

'Did you ever attempt to knife this pig?'

'I beg your pardon, sir, Your Honour.'

'Knife.' Banks rounded on him suddenly before spelling out the word for him, slowly. 'Did you ever try to stick a knife in this lovable, playful animal?'

'I did.'

'Interesting. Once?'

'Or twice. *Twice.*'

'Why on earth, or should I say in heaven, did the defendant attempt to lodge a carving knife in a live pig?'

Fr. Duddleswell gulped. It was a little difficult to explain.

'I suppose I was wanting to do him some harm.'

'You *suppose.*'

'I *did* want to harm him.'

'I would draw the court's attention to the explicit avowal by the defendant that he desired to do harm to a pig which eventually died in suspicious circumstances while in his custody.'

'There was nothing suspicious about Porgy's death.'

'Nothing.'

'No, Your Honour.'

'Except the pig was perfectly well when you ab-ducted him and dead three days later.'

'Objection,' Flitch said languidly.

'Sustained,' the Judge said.

'There was nothing suspicious about a perfectly healthy pig dying,' Banks went on, 'but you decided, for some reason known only to yourself, to bury him before informing the owner.'

'I did not think Mr. Buzzle would want to attend his funeral.'

A polite titter from the dozen or so people in court greeted this transparently honest observation.

'It was an act of Christian charity?' Mr. Banks asked.

'That it was, sir. And I never meant *real* harm to that pig.'

'Ah,' Banks exclaimed. 'if you had wanted to do the pig *real* harm, what instrument more lethal than a carving knife would you have considered employ-ing?'

'I mean, Your Honour, that I know for sure I could never harm anything by throwing a knife at it.'

'You are not an expert with a knife.'

Fr. Duddleswell allowed himself a solitary flash of his usual humour. 'Only when 'tis paired with a fork, Your Honour.'

Only Billy laughed and said to his solicitor, 'A good one, that.'

Banks ignored the witticism. 'But you did like the pig a great deal?'

'Not at first.'

'When you abducted him, did you like him then?'

Josiah Tippett indicated to Flitch he should inter-vene on the grounds of counsel leading the witness. Flitch whispered in reply:

'Window-dressing, Tippett. Banks hasn't a chance in hell and he knows it.'

What a ridiculously optimistic and irresponsible attitude, I thought.

Fr. Duddleswell said, 'I did not like the pig at all when I took him away.'

'I see. This was still the period, then, when you were trying to stick a knife in him, once or twice. Yes? Yes. Love came later, I recall. But I can only assume it was not affection that motivated you to abduct the pig.'

As Tippett nudged Flitch again, Fr. Duddleswell cried, 'No, 'twas justice.'

For a fleeting moment the witness box was transformed into a pulpit.

'Justice,' Banks repeated. 'I *see*. You formed an explicit intention of taking the law into your own hands.'

Fr. Duddleswell's mind had to work at a furious pace to keep up.

'I was wanting to defend both me property and members of the public.'

Banks nodded. 'How much compensation did you ask of the plaintiff?'

'Five pounds, Your Honour.'

'And the pig was worth how much?'

'Fifteen, so I am told.'

'Ah,' Banks said, 'this lovable, playful pig did such slight damage to your property you demanded only five pounds in compensation, yet you took away a property valued at fifteen until it was paid. Is that *justice*, would you say?'

'I am no longer sure,' an admirably honest Fr. Duddleswell admitted. 'But I do know I generously underestimated the damage the pig did.'

'And why did you do that?'

'Out of friendship for Mr. Buzzle, the plaintiff.'

'I presume it was the same friendship that led you to deprive him of the company of his pig.'

'In a certain sense, Your Honour, 'twas that. Y'see, the plaintiff and I do play such pranks on each other.'

Banks was not used to such limpid replies. 'You mentioned members of the public. Counsel for the defence has given the court to understand that the pig terrorized the entire neighbourhood and did considerable damage.'

Fr. Duddleswell avoided rhetoric. 'He did some.'

'Do you happen to know how many of that public for whom you showed such tender solicitude were in fact hospitalized as a result of the sallies of this savage, lovable pig?'

'None that I am aware of, Your Honour.'

'None that *anyone* is aware of, Your Honour.' Banks shook his head as if he genuinely grieved that the defence had such a pitiable case. 'I have examined the records of the Fairwater Constabulary for the entire period of the pig's domicile in this district. Does the defendant happen to know how many complaints were registered in matters pertaining to the said pig?'

'None that I am aware of, Your Honour.'

'In this instance your awareness does not entirely match the facts. There was *one* complaint recorded.'

Fr. Duddleswell looked relieved.

'Yes, by the plaintiff against the defendant.'

Fr. Duddleswell was amazed. 'I cannot think for why.'

'I will tell the defendant for why. It was because the defendant was alleged by the plaintiff to have trespassed on his land and broken the plaintiff's bedroom window by hurling a stone at it.'

Once more Josiah asked Flitch to intervene on the grounds of irrelevance. Flitch declined with a smile.

' 'Twas an accident,' Fr. Duddleswell whispered.

Banks turned his back on him in mock surprise. 'An accident. The defendant seems not to realize that accidents cannot be ruled out when bricks and knives are tactlessly flung in all directions.'

Fr. Duddleswell penitently bowed his head.

'You did of course offer to pay compensation.'

Fr. Duddleswell bit his lip. 'He never asked me, Your Honour.'

Ominously, the Judge scribbled again in his note-book.

Banks said, 'It did not occur to you that in the plaintiff's mind the damage you are alleged to have done and the damage his pig is alleged to have done cancelled each other out?'

'I never thought for—'

'How much would it cost to replace a window pane these days?'

'I have no idea.'

'Five pounds?'

'I suppose it could.'

'I heard Flitch mutter, 'Banks is magnificent. I wasn't expecting anything like this.'

'The plaintiff,' Banks went on, 'magnanimously, as is his nature, decided not to proceed with an action for damages to property. It was only *when his heart was broken* by the abduction and subsequent death by neglect of his lovable pet pig that he was forced to resort to the due processes of law.'

Banks paused to run his long fingers over his non-existent eyebrows. 'My client did not think at any time to take the law into his own hands by breaking three of your windows to compensate for the one of his that *you* broke.'

The Judge intervened to do Flitch's work for him.

'Would counsel be so good as to move away from the window.'

Banks bowed low in acquiescence. He passed to certain technical considerations of Billy's pen. He established it was of a height and standard approved by the Ministry of Agriculture.

I was no longer listening. I was too incensed at the injustice of the court's proceedings. Even I, a legal innocent, knew Banks should never have been allowed to get away with saying that Porgy died through Fr. Duddleswell's neglect. The Judge himself should have intervened when Flitch remained on his backside.

What was our counsel expecting to be paid for? After a promising start, he had let the case drift away from Fr. Duddleswell. Flitch seemed to acknowledge as much by almost applauding every new point Banks made at Fr. Duddleswell's expense.

When Banks had finished and my parish priest, in a terrible sweat, was allowed to leave the stand, Flitch had the audacity to whisper to Josiah Tippet, 'Superb handling by Banks. It's all sewn up, I'm afraid.'

That 'I'm afraid' was said without the least note of regret. I was disgusted.

My fury abated only when old Jed Summers was called.

Banks tried to make Jed, as Fr. Duddleswell's agent, own up to neglect. Perhaps the children of the farm had tormented the pig.

'That ain't partly right,' Jed said.

'You mean,' Mr. Banks asked, 'I am not right at all?'

'That's every partly right,' Jed said. 'I don't keer none what you open about owd Jed but the childern ain't to blame. The little owd uns stroke Porgy with their little paddies, tha's all. I'd have given 'em a tongue-pie if they'd misbehaved theirselves.'

'You would have scolded them?'

'Tha's right, Your Honour. No, Porgy didn't have marks of the measles or the jaundice. I treacled up the pen—'

'Treacled?' the Judge enquired, interested for the first time.

'Polished it up. He were a bit peaky that mornin' and he went rusty like leaves seared by frost. But no blame of me, Your Honour. I ain't no never-sweat. Nor am I that clumsy I'd hurt a kindful thing like Porgy were.'

Banks, to his credit, let him get down from the

stand. Even he was unwilling to insinuate that Porgy had died from neglect at the hands of one as kindful as old Jed Summers.

The time came for the Judge to sum up. It was plain to everyone, I thought, that Billy had won. Fr. Duddleswell's only hope was that the Judge really had been asleep most of the time and missed the vital evidence.

'There are many unusual features in this case,' the Judge began, when all the lights went out.

The usher, in the pitch dark, said, 'It must be a power-cut, Your Honour.'

'Get a lamp,' the Judge commanded.

There was a lot of commotion, matches and lighters were lit, and there was the sound of knees knocking into benches before the usher's voice proclaimed, 'No lamps to be found, Your Honour, nor candles, either.'

'We endure five years of war,' the Judge said caustically, 'and there is not a solitary candle in His Majesty's County Court! Am I expected to read my notes by the light of the stars?'

He brought his fist down on his desk. 'Case adjourned until tomorrow morning at ten thirty.'

'Silence,' the usher cried. 'Be upstanding.'

Then there was a fearful crash as the Judge missed his step and fell off the dais.

'Billy's counsel has been dipped in the Shannon and no mistake.'

We were at supper and Fr. Duddleswell took the same dim view of his prospects as I did. Before we left the court house, even the usually non-committal Josiah Tippett had approached Fr. Duddleswell and clasped his hands sympathetically. 'I am very, very sorry about that, Father,' he'd sighed.

Holding the case over had added to our expenses because the useless Nathan Flitch, K.C. would have to attend the morning session, too.

'Father,' I said, trying to lighten his load, 'I thought your absolute honesty in the box was a credit to the priesthood.'

'Y'think so,' he said, munching miserably away. 'Telling the truth, the whole truth and nothing but the truth is the most unnatural experience of me life to date.' He paused. 'I feel soiled all over.'

There was a scream from the kitchen and the sound of Mrs. Pring's feet pounding the corridor.

'Things are desperate enough already, Father Neil, without that woman causing an epidemic of earache in the neighbourhood.'

Mrs. Pring burst in. 'Another face at the window,' she spluttered.

'Where are You, God?' Fr. Duddleswell roared. 'First Porgy and now Good Clean Bess.'

As I raced to the kitchen to investigate, he called after me, 'No knives, now, Father Neil.'

I found it wasn't a pig at all. It was Billy Buzzle. He was alternately hammering on the window and pressing his face grotesquely against the pane.

'He is astray of his wits,' Fr. Duddleswell groaned. 'He has come to break me windows, after all. What have I done to me dear old enemy by pinching his precious pig?'

I let Billy in. He was shivering and saying, 'It's Bess. She's ill. Been with her for an hour. There's something awful the matter with her. Must be the same disease as Porgy.'

'Dial 999, Father Neil,' Fr. Duddleswell ordered, 'while I get me lamp.'

'I can't Father,'

'And why not? D'you think the health and salvation of Mr. Buzzle's last remaining pig does not merit the trouble?'

'But, Father—'

'Look you here, Father Neil. I once took a party of altar boys on a trip to Brighton. On the way back, I dailled 999 to enquire where the nearest fish and chip shop was and they sent me out a police escort.

Why in heaven's name do we pay our rates and taxes?'

I did as I was told.

A woman's voice answered. 'This is Emergency Services. Please state clearly which service you require: Police, ambulance or fire-brigade.'

'I'm not altogether sure,' I stammered.

'Well, sir,' the cool female voice said, 'what is the trouble?'

'It's a pig,' I said.

'Has this pig badly injured someone, sir?'

'Not this one. It's ill. Bess is ill.'

'Is this a hoax, sir? There are fines for—'

'No. Not a hoax. I'm a Roman Catholic priest.'

'Yes, Father.' She seemed reassured. 'Is this pig yours?'

I was perfectly aware of the crazy course the conversation was taking but somehow I couldn't stop it.

'No, she belongs to a neighbour of ours. Come to think of it, Mr. Buzzle might need an ambulance.'

'Where is this gentleman, Father? Is he lying in the road?'

'No, he's drinking tea in our kitchen.'

'May I suggest, Father, you call a vet. For the pig.'

'You couldn't give me a number, I suppose.'

She gave me two.

I rang them both but there was no reply. You can never get a blasted vet when a pig needs one, I cursed.

I reported back to Fr. Duddleswell just as he was about to leave for Billy's garden, armed with a torch and shod with gumboots.

'Me all, me dearest dear,' he sighed, 'me complete hero. Give *me* the bloody phone.'

He dialled Dr. Daley's number. 'Donal, 'tis me, Charles. Will you mix your legs and get over here in a hurry. Yes, with your black bag. Emergency. Tell you about it when you arrive . . . But you already know me address.'

95

Billy had circled the sty with paraffin lamps. Inside, lying on fresh straw, was Bess. She looked bloated, enormous.

'Have you been over-feeding herself, Mr. Buzzle? Giving her fizzy lemonade?'

'No, Father O'Duddleswell. She's been looking poorly ever since Porgy . . .' He broke off sniffing. 'Could be wind from those apples I gave her yesterday.'

We speculated scientifically on the cause of Bess' distress until Dr. Daley arrived five minutes later.

He took one look at Bess and said, 'Dear, dear, dear.'

'Is she dying, Doctor?' Billy asked.

'It's a straightforward case of 115 days.'

'Is she dying?' Billy repeated.

'She is about to give birth.' Dr. Daley touched his arm reassuringly. 'A simple case of the proliferation of pig.'

It was a clear night, no likelihood of rain. Billy, Fr. Duddleswell and I went indoors to muffle ourselves against the cold and I brought a chair for Dr. Daley who was fortunately clad already in an overcoat.

'Ah, Father Neil,' Dr. Daley said, as he sat down on the chair with a generous overlap, 'this takes me back to the days of my childhood in Connemara. Before we moved to the wicked city, it was. I reckon I wanted to be a doctor from the time I was present at my first farrowing.'

'Is there anything for us to do?'

'No, Father Neil. Sit and wait. It's a mistake even to put your hand in and help the poor sow. Risk of infection, d'you know? Let nature take her course.'

Billy said, 'So there's nothing you need, Doctor?'

Dr. Daley said there *was* one thing; and a couple of minutes later Billy returned with a bottle of Johnny Walker and a tumbler.

On his second glass, Dr. Daley said, 'I don't inhale the stuff into my blood stream, d'you know? It goes right through me.' He looked pityingly at Bess whose mighty form was tossing and swaying like a foam-crested sea. 'Won't be long before the show commences.'

Bess moaned as if to confirm his prediction.

After a quarter of an hour, a head appeared. Then the whole sticky piglet. At Dr. Daley's bidding, I picked up the small creature as soon as it severed its cord, wiped some of the ooze off it with a towel and put it on the ground. On very shaky feet, it immediately walked round Bess's hind legs, found an udder and sucked.

'It's drinking in colostrum,' Dr. Daley explained. 'Good for it. Like any baby, really.'

Things were not so good for Billy. The sight of the birth, after his earlier fright that evening, had upset him. He collapsed in a heap.

Fr. Duddleswell and I carried him into his house and up to his bedroom.

'Poor Billy,' Fr. Duddleswell kept gasping.

He took off Billy's outer garments and his shoes and put an extra pillow under his head.

I left him to attend to Billy and rejoined Dr. Daley. The second piglet had just arrived.

'How long is this litter likely to take, Doctor?'

'No idea. Sometimes a couple of hours, sometimes all night. Usually four to six hours.' He poured himself another. 'All females are unpredictable, Father Neil. That is their eternal fascination.'

He went on sipping contentedly and reminiscing, in a strange quaint tongue of the past, about his early years in Connemara.

'There was many a night like this, Father Neil. By firelight under the stars, telling stories often and often to each other. Family and friends. People used to come on a Connemara visit.'

'What's that, Doctor?'

'You never heard the expression? They'd come and forget to go home.' We laughed together. 'A hospitable people and so kind. We borrowed each other's troubles for days on end.'

'Nice,' I said appreciatively.

'This brings it all back: the light of candles and turf fires and cod-oil lamps.' He heaved a deep, sad sigh. 'I remember the morn my little brother was taken. Ah, do I remember. Six years old was I. Still in a petticoat with a cardigan over it and a cap on my head and me on only three pounds of potatoes a day.'

'Sounds a lot to me.'

'There was nothing else, y'see. And in summer late, before the spuds were in, not even that. Anyhow, little Johnny had the whooping cough. My mother, God be gracious to her, used to feed him ferret's milk, thinking it would do well by him. But it did not and what would? There still is nothing for the whoop once it's caught that I know of. And on this day, my father was down by the stream washing the sheep and feeding turnips to them and Johnny coughing and wheezing in the cold kitchen. When suddenly, all in a minute, silence. I look at my mother and she at me. Johnny is in her arms, his face as blue as the summer sky of evening, you know how it is, when the sun sinks over the sea. But he is coughing no more. "That's good, momma," says I. "For him," says mother. "But not for me. He's gone, Donal, me darlin'." "Ah," says I, for I was not so young I didn't know about these things. "Gone, Donal, and here am I hurted so me heart is killed." And I look at the little one asleeping for ever in her arms, in peace, the fingereens on him stiff already as winter twigs. "Bless his little heart," says mother, "the Almighty God only cut him a thin slice of life." And she stretches him out on two chairs like we used put a plank over two chairs in chapel to make an altar of it. "*They* have taken him," says she.'

'*They?*' I said.

'The people,' the Doctor explained, in a manner he

had never used with me before. 'The *Others*. *Them* as lives on the other side of the wall.' He saw my puzzled expression. 'The people live in the sea, Father Neil, multitudes of them. Or inside the mountains of which few know the door. You can't take a step but one of *them* has to move out of your way.'

'What do they *do*, Doctor?'

'Oh, they put the touch on the folk *they* want, the young and the handsomest, and it's highly dangerous to be *overlooked* by *them*.'

The lonely night, what with the quiet throbbing of the lamps and the shaky shadows, seemed dangerous all of a sudden and 'lived in'. I can't explain it.

'Little Johnny was taken by *them*.'

'He was?' I managed to get out.

Dr. Daley nodded. 'He was replaced by some old one of *them* they had no more use for, y'understand.'

'Did you ever see one of them?'

'Not me. But Mrs. O'Hea in our village, *she* saw *them*. She used to go away with *them* regular. And come back. And while she was away, she left someone just like herself behind so you couldn't tell the difference, unless you *knew*.'

'*How* did you know?'

'We *knew*,' he affirmed. 'Her man used to say to her, "Where have you been, Biddy?" "Nowhere," says she, "I have never left you." And Mr. O'Hea didn't doubt she was lying. "You wouldn't expect her to admit," says he to us on the side, "that she's been away, would you, now?" '

'I suppose not,' I murmured, as if the question was addressed to me.

'Then there were the dead folk used to turn up at wakes and funerals. No one would mention it, of course. We would talk to them as if we didn't know they were dead and they to us as if they didn't know we were alive. Why should we mention to them the fact of their being dead, anyhow?'

'Impolite, you mean.'

'Indeed. If you were dead, you would not want anyone drawing attention to it, now, would you?'

'No.'

'Jimmy's father died. He was my best friend, was Jimmy Keevan. And his father, after dying beautifully, sat up on his bed to tell his wife where his money was hid in the garden.'

'Are you sure he was dead, Doctor?'

'Shouldn't I know such things, being a doctor?'

'You saw him sit up, then?'

'I did not but they described it to me word for word. Then this nice gentleman, Mr. Keevan that was, stretched himself out again to save them the bother.'

'Amazing.'

'It was. Fr. McEntee didn't know whether he ought to anoint the man again when he heard of what happened. Jimmy often saw his father after that.'

'Exactly as he remembered him?'

'Not at all, Father Neil. Disguised was he so even Jimmy wouldn't recognize him. But he did, of course.'

'How did he do that?'

'Wouldn't a boy recognize his own father even though he didn't look like him?'

I nodded apologetically for not seeing something so obvious. 'But what about the priests, Doctor? Didn't they object?'

'They did. They told their people not to believe in *them* and not to talk to *them* either whenever they saw *them*.'

'So the priests didn't believe in these things.'

'Oh they did. They believed in *them* most of all. But they told their flocks not to believe in *them* so they wouldn't deal with *them* and come to harm or lose a cow or sheep. Now why am I telling you this?' He scratched his head. 'I remember now, it's because once I was waiting for a litter of piglets to come just like this night and Mrs. O'Hea was there watching like a star above. And before the piglets arrived she said to me, "Look you here and see this litter I have myself. Seven of them only." I looked as far as my eyes would let me and saw *nothing*. That was the strange thing, I saw nothing at all where she pointed. Then our pig gave birth and had seven little ones.'

'Fantastic,' I gasped, not sure if he was pulling my leg or his own.

'And every one of them dead as was the sow herself immediately after. Though why *they* took the old sow I never knew to this day.'

Since he had me under his eye I nodded to show I was as stupefied as he was.

'There are more horses, pigs, cows, on the other side than on this, Father Neil. And *they* had taken our pigs for themselves, you see.'

'Sad,' was all I could say to that.

He brightened up. 'But d'you know what is the saddest thing in the world?'

'No.'

'Seeing that little island coming out of the sea at you at the bottom of the whiskey bottle.'

I picked up the bottle and poured him another.

'Such kindness,' he said, 'you knowing it's very dry I am. You should have been born in Connemara.'

'That's a compliment,' I said with a smile.

'And meant to be. But don't breathe a word of what I've just told you or I will plaster-of-Paris your ears for you.'

We heard the sound of footsteps.

'Ah,' the Doctor said, 'here comes the great little jockey of the parish.'

Fr. Duddleswell was just in time to see the third piglet being born. There was evidently something wrong with it.

Dr. Daley sat up. 'It's not breathing, Father Neil.'

'Is it dead?'

'Not yet.' Sharply: 'Pick it up, Father Neil.' I

101

obliged. 'Now blow into its mouth.' He paid no heed to my hesitation. 'Go on, lad. Blow.'

I held the warm, chalk-white piglet in both hands and put my mouth to his. There was no feeling of nausea. On the contrary, I had a sense of exhilaration.

I did exactly what Dr. Daley told me. I slapped the piglet hard on the back and breathed down its throat.

I remembered how Ross, the gypsy boy, had described the newly delivered child, 'White all over with a black face,' and I prayed fiercely, 'God, let it live. No black face this time. Let it live.'

The piglet started to twitch in my hands. It seemed to yawn and I felt the convulsions of its lungs. It swivelled its face from side to side, its small eyes closed. Again I breathed into it and this time, when its heart beat, I felt like God breathing into Adam the breath of life.

After what seemed an hour but must have been nearer a minute, I gently set the piglet down. Dr. Daley told me to put it on one of the front teats because they produced more milk and were easier to suckle.

'Your nerves are in flitters, surely. A sip of the hard stuff for your brave self.'

I thought the Doctor was addressing me. In fact, he was offering Fr. Duddleswell a drink.

Even in that quivering yellow light I could see that Fr. Duddleswell had lost his colour.

'Not feeling so good meself, Donal. I reckon I had better . . .'

I helped him back to the house where Mrs. Pring took charge of him.

It wasn't until three o'clock that the eleventh piglet wriggled into the world. 'I was hoping,' Dr. Daley said, 'there would be a twelfth disciple. But it seems not.' Seeing the size of the litter, he added appreciatively, as he stroked Bess's flank, 'You're a good Catholic pig, there's no denying it.'

He picked up a stick, examined the after-birth to make sure no last piglet was there and then discarded it. Together we made Bess a feed of warm bran.

Dr. Daley's words to me, as he handed me an empty bottle, were:

'You know, young fellow-me-lad, you really ought to instruct those two gentlemen in the facts of life.'

'I tried it with Father Duddleswell not so long ago,' I said, 'but without success.'

'Dear, dear, dear, dear, *dear*. It is not healthy for old 'uns like themselves to be so unashamedly innocent.'

Billy burst into the breakfast room. 'Sorry to intrude,' he gasped, 'but I want you to know I'm dropping charges.'

Fr. Duddleswell rose to his feet. 'You are doing no such thing, you hear me?'

Billy was so grateful we had helped him the previous night, he felt it unneighbourly to continue with the case. Fr. Duddleswell did not agree. He had the death-wish of the self-righteous sinner.

'I had it coming to me, Mr. Buzzle, and I will not shirk me punishment. I intend seeing me humiliation through to the bitter end.'

Billy rang his solicitor, all the same. There was no reply. We offered him a lift to court where lawyers on both sides convinced him it was unthinkable to withdraw the action just before the Judge was due to give his delayed decision.

'All right, Father O'Duddleswell,' Billy promised, 'I want you to know that whatever happens in there, I won't take a penny from you.'

Judge Turnbull entered the courtroom with a black eye and walking with the aid of a stick. He resumed where he had left off. I hadn't noticed till then that he had teeth the size of camels'.

'There are many unusual features in this case,' he

began, hoisting his upper lip like the fire curtain in a theatre.

It soon became clear that the plight of Charles Clement Duddleswell, the distrainor of the pig, was far worse than I had imagined.

'He trespassed on the plaintiff's land,' the Judge said, baring his gigantic teeth, 'with intent to cause damage. Without any sense of guilt, he dared to cast not merely the first stone but several other stones at a window, thereby maliciously damaging it.

'Had the plaintiff sued for damages at the outset, the court would have had no hesitation in awarding them costs. As it was, the plaintiff did not ask for the cost of repairs. In his kindness, excessive I am inclined to think, he did not press charges, thus permitting the evil-doer to elude justice. Temporarily at least.

'As to the defendant, seldom in my years on the bench have I come across a more patently devious and untrustworthy witness. This man is not a credit to his cloth.

'I do not say the defendant lied. Only that he stretched the credulity of this court beyond the wide limits of tolerance.

'He had the affrontery to ask the court to accept that he impounded the said pig as a neighbourly prank, even though it broke the plaintiff's heart.

'He claims to have thrown bricks at the plaintiff's window without wishing to break it and carving knives at the plaintiff's pig in the assured conviction he would not harm it.

'Further, he asks the court to believe that he had a swift conversion from loathing to love of the said pig and, when it passed away, buried it hurriedly without feeling of guilt though not without pangs of sorrow like one bereaved.

'The plaintiff has every right to think that if the defendant is his friend he is indeed fortunate to have only one such.'

I was staggered. Fr. Duddleswell's transparent

honesty had completely baffled the court. The Judge found his testimony too childlike and innocent to be credible.

That was when I began to realize that not simply was Fr. Duddleswell going to lose his case, which was just enough. He was in danger of being sent to prison.

When next the Judge spoke he hooded his upper teeth with his lip to express benignity. 'As to the plaintiff himself, for him I have nothing but praise and sympathy. Praise for acting irreproachably throughout the noxious course of events; sympathy in that he has lost an animal most dear to him.

'For the record, the plaintiff built a regulation sty, doubled the height of his garden gate and erected an electric fence to keep his pet at home. What he could not anticipate was the keen intelligence and playfulness of his esteemed pet, Porgy.

'My role as arbiter in this case is not, however, to allocate praise or blame. Nor, regretfully, am I called on by the plaintiff to give judgement on a submission of trespass with malicious damage.

'The question before me is, Was the defendant legally within his rights to impound a pig which had damaged his fence, garden and motor car?

'The legal crux of the matter, and counsel for the defence was wise to lay such emphasis upon it, is this: the plaintiff as Tort Feasor did not tender any sum to the defendant.

'Because,' the judge concluded abruptly, 'the plaintiff not only paid nothing but tendered nothing to the defendant as damages, the plaintiff's case has failed and judgement is given against him. Case dismissed.'

And treading more warily this time, the Judge departed.

It seemed to me that the Judge's decision amounted to saying: 'Billy Buzzle, you have God, the angels, justice, my heart and everybody's heart on your side, but what does this avail you against the iron law of England?'

Who should I sympathize with first, Billy or Fr. Duddleswell? Fr. Duddleswell was nearer and more hurt. I sat down beside him.

He looked at me in a daze. 'Father Neil, to alter a famous phrase, I leave this court innocent but with every possible stain upon me character. And that, when I was guilty and altogether blameless.'

He was back to normal. I was pleased the judge didn't hear that. It would have reinforced in him the sense of Fr. Duddleswell's deviousness.

All the same, it was true, he had won his case and lost his reputation. 'I'm proud of you, anyway,' I said.

'Did I not always tell you, Father Neil, that the only way to get people to accept the truth is to hide the most of it from them? Oh, "the whole truth and nothing but" is a dangerous and wicked thing.'

I squeezed his arm and crossed the room to talk to Billy. He was equally confused. 'If the judge said I won so handsomely,' he was asking his counsel, 'how come I lost the case?'

A suspicion entered my mind when Flitch came up to Banks and shook his hand warmly. 'Seeing we both knew the defence had no case to answer, you did a splendid job.'

Banks smiled appreciatively. 'Yes, Flitch, but what a marvelous game I had in court.'

Both counsels rushed off to other business.

What did they mean: 'The defence had no case to answer' and 'a marvellous game'?

The answers were not long delayed. In the corridor outside the court room, Billy, Fr. Duddleswell and I were grouped around Josiah Tippett. Tippett said:

'Father Duddleswell, my deepest commiserations.'

Fr. Duddleswell tried to make light of his humiliation. 'At least I won, Josiah.'

'Ah, yes, Father Duddleswell, but there was never any question of you losing.'

'It seemed so,' Fr. Duddleswell said suspiciously.

'A legal illusion, Father.'

'Tell me more, Josiah.'

'Well, Judge Turnbull dealt with an exactly similar case a month ago when a donkey was impounded, just as you impounded the pig.'

'But, Josiah,' Fr. Duddleswell fumed, 'why did you allow me to be put through the mangle?'

Josiah adjusted his tie. 'But, Father Duddleswell, you were the one who insisted on fighting the case. I advised you to let the Registrar arbitrate.'

At that moment, the Registrar came to discuss costs. Fr. Duddleswell waved him aside and clasped Billy's hand.

'Billy,' he said, 'we may fight like a pair of Kilkenny cats but I want you to know . . .'

'And, Father O'Duddleswell,' Billy said, a tear trembling on his lid, 'I want you to know . . .'

'If that was justice, 'tis a very unfair thing.'

'And very expensive,' Billy said.

'Indeed, the Government was against us both, Billy.'

'You said it, Father O'Duddleswell. Believe me, you are sure of an Irish welcome in my house any time of the day.'

'Thank you, thank you, Mr. Buzzle. And may the divil fly away with the roof of the house that does not welcome you and me.' He put his arm round Billy's shoulder. 'One thing, Mr. Buzzle.'

'Yes?'

'You have now, how many is it? a dozen lovable pigs . . .'

'Not for long, Father. In two weeks time, when the little ones are weaned, I'm sending all of them away to a nice farm.'

Fr. Duddleswell beamed. 'You had a word with old Jed Summers?'

Billy nodded. 'On my oath. Last night was enough

for me. I couldn't go through that again. Not now that Porgy . . .'

'Do not grieve for him, Mr. Buzzle,' Fr. Duddleswell said tenderly.

Two weeks later, as Billy had promised, the pigs had gone. The sty was dismantled, the kiln and swill tub removed. Only an agricultural perfume, like a melody, lingered on.

When Fr. Duddleswell came to my room to tell me the good news, I thought it only politic to draw his attention to something in Billy's garden.

There, with his forelegs on our fence while he nibbled away at the lower branches of our apple tree, was a huge, tawny billy-goat.

Six

A BACK TO FRONT WEDDING

The date is unforgettable: Saturday, February 3rd, 1951. It was the day I first formulated Boyd's Law: 'At St. Jude's, what can go wrong, will.'

Apart from an early incident in the church which I hoped had escaped notice, it all began calmly enough, even cheerfully.

'First sitting for breakfast,' Mrs. Pring called out.

'Egg and bacon,' I said, sniffing delightedly. 'Sweeter than the odour of sanctity.' Fr. Duddleswell hadn't yet appeared and since his serving was much bigger than mine, I switched the plates round. 'He'll never notice, Mrs. P,' I said.

'Not notice, Father Neil? That man can see up his own nose.'

In steamed Fr. Duddleswell, his nostrils twitching. 'Afternoon.' It was a grunt but a good-natured grunt. 'From one breakfast to the next that woman has a full twenty-four hours warning and still she is late with it.'

He signed himself, blessed the food and, almost without looking, switched the plates back again.

Mrs. Pring muttered, 'He's only got little arms but a boardinghouse reach.'

'Keep quiet, woman,' he said, 'so you can hear yourself speak.'

When I complained that he had twice as much as me, Fr. Duddleswell declared it was very fitting seeing he was twice my age and had double my ration of brains.

'I demand my rights,' I said.

He tucked his tapkin firmly under his chin. 'As a curate recently ordained, Father Neil, the only right you have is to a decent Christian burial.'

He relented, stabbed a rasher with his fork and put it delicately on my plate. 'An extra piece of pig to pacify you, provided you do not breathe the fumes all over Billy Buzzle.'

'And half of that second egg,' I demanded, pointing.

Sadly, he put his fork down. 'What a pity, Father Neil. Eggs, lovely though they are to look at, are rich in cholesterol, if you're still with me. If you have heart trouble, eggs can sin very badly against you.'

'But I don't suffer from heart trouble.'

'And is not the chief reason for that,' he asked complacently, 'that I shield you from eating too many eggs?'

'What about *your* heart?'

'Ah, Father Neil, we have a saying in the Green Isle, "Eggs, if they are wise, do not quarrel with stones." '

Mrs. Pring humphed but said nothing as she poured coffee.

'D'you know, Father Neil,' Fr. Duddleswell said in a nostalgic mood that signalled happiness, 'oft' times when I am eating here, I imagine meself back in me student days. On vacation in the Italian Dolomites.' He paused to tell Mrs. Pring to put three spoons of sugar in his coffee not two. 'God is not deceived, Mrs. Pring.'

'No, God,' she replied.

'Indeed, Father Neil. I see myself in spirit lying on a thick carpet of grass under a lonely pine. The wind is sighing in the branches. Green leaves against an azure sky. And all the while I am gazing across a picturesque ravine to distant . . . snow-capped . . . mountains.'

He stopped speaking; his lips and jaws were still. He could actually see the scene.

'So you like my cooking, then,' Mrs. Pring put in.

He awoke with a start and began munching again. ' 'Tis abysmal but the scenery is marvellous.'

I guffawed but to prove his impartiality, he turned his guns on me. 'I appreciated your little sermon at Mass this morning, Father Neil.'

I had preached briefly about St. Blaise, an Armenian Bishop whose feast day we were celebrating. 'While he was being dragged to martyrdom,' I told the congregation of half a dozen, 'St. Blaise met a woman who was greatly distressed because her beloved pig had been carried off by a loathsome wolf. The Saint, who had a way with animals, spoke to the wolf and persuaded him to give the pig back to its rightful owner who had a broken heart.'

'You didn't have anybody particular in mind when you were telling the story about the wolf and the pig, Father Neil?'

'Of course not, Father.'

'And, Father Neil.'

Damn, I thought, he never misses a thing.

St. Blaise is the patron of sore throats. He won

this honour by curing a boy who had swallowed a fishbone and was choking to death. The Catholic ritual consists in crossing two candles and placing them round the necks of each member of the congregation, saying, 'May the Lord deliver you from the evils of the throat and from every other ill.' How was I to know you weren't supposed to light the candles?

'Did you really have to send Betty Ryder's best lace mantilla up in flames?'

'I only singed it, Father.'

'Oh, she got the message anyway, lad. She is sure to amend her life in the future.'

'I still don't know the reason for this lavish breakfast,' I said, changing the subject.

For answer Fr. Duddleswell said that the evening meal would be more festive still, and, with egg-yellow caking his lips, he softly sang a verse from *Trial By Jury*:

> You cannot eat breakfast all day,
> Nor is it the act of a sinner,
> When breakfast is taken away,
> To turn your attention to dinner.

When I thanked him for nothing, he said, ' 'Tis the feast before the fast.' He turned to Mrs. Pring. 'Bring the coffee in straight away if you would. Me throat, as St. Blaise would tell you, is dry as a cornflake.'

I had forgotten that Ash Wednesday was only four days away. To celebrate, he explained, he was taking me with him to a soccer match in the afternoon. This was why he had switched confessions that day from the evening to the morning.

'Everybody is celebrating today, Father Neil. 'Tis the last Saturday for solemnizing marriage with flowers and organ before Lent. I have three mixed marriages this morning, so you will have to hear all the confessions yourself.'

'And the same marriage address three times over,' I said.

'Well, lad,' he said in his defence, 'I had forty weddings last year and I cannot think up something fresh each time, genius though I am.'

I tucked into my egg and bacon. 'Mrs. Pring seems to like weddings, Father.'

'She does. Herself, poor soul, only had a penny wedding during the First World War, as I told you.'

Mrs. Pring returned at that point to say, 'Are you going to preach your wedding sermon again today, Father D?' She then mimicked him rather well: 'Me dear young couple, the one recipe for a happy and holy marriage is, Love God with all your heart and never spend more than you earn.'

He fixed her with his eye. 'I remember the first time you heard it, woman.'

Mrs. Pring turned to me. 'Twenty years and a thousand marriages ago.'

Fr. Duddleswell seemed a bit hurt at that. 'You said it reminded you of the love of God.'

'It still does,' she said. 'It never changes.' She began to pour for us. 'Didn't Peggy Barnes make a lovely bride last Saturday?'

'That she did,' Fr. Duddleswell said.

'Reminded me,' Mrs. Pring sighed romantically, 'of when *I* was a blushing bride.'

'Ping!' Fr. Duddleswell said.

I looked at him. 'What was that?'

'Sorry, Father Neil, me imagination just snapped.'

'Oh, you Philistine,' cried Mrs. Pring.

Fr. Duddleswell held out the milk jug to her. 'The cow is dry.'

Mrs. Pring grabbed it and went to her kitchen.

'Peggy Barnes,' Fr. Duddleswell whispered, 'happened to be three months gone.'

I was only half listening. 'Gone where, Father?'

'She is expecting, lad. A baby.'

'Ah yes. Which match are we going to this afternoon, Father?' I didn't much care for soccer but I could hardly say so when he was taking trouble to give me a treat.

'We are off to Highbury to watch Arsenal play Newcastle United. And in case your general education is woefully lacking, Arsenal, let me tell you, were once the finest team in the world.'

'I have heard of them, Father.' A modest statement but accurate.

We will leave at one-thirty sharp for a two-thirty kick-off. I want to park near the ground.

It was raining. That winter it seemed to be raining all the time. We paid three shillings extra, of my money incidentally, to stand in a so-called Enclosure. Tim Fogarty, one of Fr. Duddleswell's most trusted lieutenants and himself an Arsenal fan, had told him this was the best position in the ground.

Even so, the rain washed over us in mighty drifts. We were drenched in the first five minutes and so deep was the gloom I could scarcely see the big clock behind one of the goalposts.

What a preposterous way to enjoy ourselves, I thought, but Fr. Duddleswell was in such an effervescent mood, I agreed to follow his lead and cheer the Arsenal to the skies.

Next to us stood a belligerent, pasty-faced chap in a cloth cap and raincoat, sporting a black and white favour on his chest. His big nose was diagonal to his face so it looked as if it was made to smell round corners. In a meaty fist he was clasping a quart beer bottle.

The first team, in red and white shirts, emerged from the tunnel to tremendous applause.

'Boo,' Fr. Duddleswell cried with a blast only suppassed by our twice sodden neighbour. He nodded cheerfully to Fr. Duddleswell as if to say it was lucky for him they were supporting the same team.

'But that's the Arsenal, Father,' I said in his ear. Even I knew that.

113

'Father Neil, how many times have you been here before? Never. And you are trying to tell me—'

I pointed to the programme. 'It says here, Father, that Arsenal are playing in red and white shirts.'

He snatched the programme from me, lifted his glasses on to his nose, read the relevant line and, when the second team appeared, again cried, 'Boo.'

'Get shot of ye.' the Newcastle supporter said, 'or I'll scrunsh you wi' me teeth.'

I had no doubts that whatever that was he could do it.

Fr. Duddleswell immediately shouted out, 'Hurrah for Newcastle United.' which seemed to pacify the fellow for a bit.

'Treachery,' I mouthed to Fr. Duddleswell.

'Father Neil, Jesus said you are supposed to love your enemies.' He broke off to call out, 'Arsenal, boo, boo.'

'Jesus didn't say you had to hate your friends.'

'It amounts to the same thing, Father Neil.' He laughed merrily. 'This is not a contest between Satan and the saints. 'Tis only a game, after all.'

The Newcastle fan obviously didn't agree. Once when Fr. Duddleswell cheered at something I couldn't see, he roared, 'Enough o' that. Stop barkin' your heed off, man, or aa'll pay your backside.'

I must confess it took the edge off what little enjoyment was around.

At three-thirty, immediately after the interval, a voice boomed over the loudspeaker:

'A message for Father Charles Duddleswell of St. Jude's.'

A hush descended on the crowd.

'Will the Reverend Father Charles Duddleswell please return to his church where a bride and groom are waiting to be wed. Thank you.'

Even the players walking out of the tunnel on to the pitch were falling about. I guessed that for many spectators this was the only bright spot in a goalless afternoon. Certainly it received the biggest cheer.

114

Fr. Duddleswell nudged me, 'Jesus, Mary and Joseph. Mrs. Pring must have burned down the church.'

When the laughter had subsided, the message was repeated. Fr. Duddleswell did not budge. Out of the corner of his mouth, he ordered me to stay still for God Almighty's sake, by which, as Mrs. Pring would have said, he meant his own.

The Newcastle fan guffawed and asked Fr. Duddleswell if he were the guy.

'I ask you, would I be resting me feet here,' Fr. Duddleswell said, 'if I were this Father Duddleswhat?'

'Aa waddent put it past ye.'

Mercifully, at this point, he staggered off for another drink before the re-start.

As soon as the whistle went for the second half, Fr. Duddleswell tugged my sleeve and made a beeline for the exit. I followed him.

Unfortunately, I failed to notice the Newcastle fan's discarded beer bottle. I kicked it and it shattered on the stone step at the feet of the bystanders.

Hundreds of pairs of eyes swivelled away from the game towards us. Many, seeing our Roman collars, wished us, among other things, a very good afternoon. One said politely, 'Good day, Fathers.' It was Tim Fogarty.

'Father Neil,' Fr. Duddleswell complained, 'did you have to draw the attention of the whole stadium to me predicament?'

At the bottom of the terrace steps we ran into our Geordie friend carrying two bottles of beer.

'Newcastle United?' Fr. Duddleswell called out. 'what a shambles. Down with the lot of 'em. Boo, bloody boo!'

'Aa giovower,' the fan said, brandishing his second half nourishment, 'or I'll knock your heed off wi' a bleedin bottle.'

'You will not,' Fr. Duddleswell said, putting his skates on, 'me head is very attached to me.' For me, he changed his tune: 'Mind you, Father Neil, I *am* deserving of being beheaded.'

On the way out of the ground, he explained breathlessly:

'Wanda French and Richard Faber. A mixed marriage. A Jesuit from Farm Street did all the paper work. That is why it escaped me memory. It has never happened to me before. Dear sweet Jesus, what have I done?'

This last, a purely rhetorical question, was his constant refrain for the rest of the long day.

'Is the groom a Protestant, Father?' He nodded. 'At this moment, probably a very anti-Catholic Protestant.'

'Indeed,' Fr. Duddleswell said, 'he will not turn Catholic now. Not with me watching a soccer match while his bride is waiting to put her finger in his ring.' He groaned audibly. 'I should have remembered, seeing Dr. Daley is giving the bride away.'

As we huddled into a phone box to call Mrs. Pring, he was praying, 'Dear God in Heaven, will you not show me a bit of Christian charity?'

Mrs. Pring must have been sitting by the phone. She took the call immediately, the relief evident in her voice.

'You are there, Mrs. Pring?'

'Yes, why aren't you, Father D? The young couple have been waiting a whole hour since three. Can you hear me?'

'Mrs. Pring, I could hear you without a telephone.'

'Where are you?'

'You know perfectly well where I am. At a football match.'

'Which one?'

'If you do not know which one, how did the blessèd police contact me here?'

'They said they'd put out an announcement in every soccer ground within a fifteen mile radius.'

'Dear God in Heaven.'

My mind boggled at the thought of the same message being relayed at Fulham, Tottenham, Brentford, Charlton, Crystal Palace and God knows where else. We'd be lucky if our disgrace didn't make the Sunday papers.

'I'm very sorry about this,' I heard Mrs. Pring say.

'That is all right,' Fr. Duddleswell said soothingly, ''twasn't much of a match anyway.'

'I was thinking of the poor bride.'

'Never mind,' he rumbled, 'tell the wedding party I will be there in twenty minutes.' He slammed the phone down. 'Provided God is a good Irish gentleman.'

I was already in the passenger seat when Fr. Duddleswell's experienced eye noted that something was wrong with the car. The front tyre on the kerb side had been slashed.

Catching fragments of his colourful language, I got out to take a look. Vandals had run riot. Six cars, parked in a row along the pavement, had had their tyres slashed. Only one of ours was slashed, all four of the car's behind were in ribbons.

'Not the best time to get a puncture, Father.'

He expelled air from his lungs in a noisy stream. 'Pretend you are alive, Father Neil, and help me off with the bloody thing.'

In a couple of minutes, we were tugging it off together. In doing so, he lost his balance and fell heavily on his back with the tyre on top of him.

'Will you take the tyre off me belly, boy,' he called up. 'The rubber one only.'

After I'd helped him up, he went for the spare tyre, only to find it was flat.

'Shall I get your pump, Father?'

'If you would.'

'Where is it?'

He stamped his foot. 'Twelve miles away in me bloody garage. Oh, for three farthings, I'd break me head in six or seven halves.'

'Shall I thumb a lift, Father,' I said, 'and ask if anyone's "Going my Way"?'

'Dear Lord,' he sighed, paying no heed, 'me clothes are sown to me through perspiration. Listen lad, I will try and borrow a pump. You go ring Mrs. Pring and tell her God is an Englishman after all and we are further delayed.'

The phone was occupied so that the second call was almost half an hour after the first. When I got through, I spoke to Dr. Daley, who had retired to Fr. Duddleswell's study for a drink.

'Hello,' he said, 'I'm sorry Fr. Duddleswell is away at present.'

'I know that, Doctor.'

'So is his curate.'

'This *is* his curate.'

'Father Neil? Are you upstairs in your study? I didn't hear you come in.'

I explained that we were still at the football stadium.

'I thought you left there thirty minutes ago,' the Doctor said. 'It must be a great game.'

'Doctor,' I said, 'would you please tell the bride and groom to stay put till we arrive.'

I heard him pour himself a drink. 'Oh, I don't think they're going anywhere for a while. Your good health, Father Neil.'

'Father,' I said, on returning to the car.

'Me luck has returned to me,' he said, puffing away as he worked the pump. 'I borrowed this from a garage round the corner.'

'You didn't notice anything . . . unusual when you got back?'

'Father Neil, I have no time for I-spy-with-my-little-eye. Cannot you see I am in a tub of tar?'

He eventually stood up and followed the line of my pointing finger. The driver of the car behind must have started up in Fr. Duddleswell's absence and travelled a few yards before realizing his tyres were slashed. He had abandoned his car to get either a motor mechanic or a policeman.

'Jasus,' Fr. Duddleswell gasped, 'I must have parked me car on a nest of leprechauns. I cannot get out!' He fisted the door of the car that was hemming him in and received only sore knuckles as a result.

In complete exasperation, he kicked the car's bumper, doing his toes no good at all.

By now, masses of spectators were leaving the ground early because of the gloom and the rain.

'Bloody alive, Father Neil, what am I to do at all?' He came to a swift decision. 'I will leave you here, lad, so hooligans do not strip me car down altogether and I will take a taxi.'

Except there wasn't a taxi in sight.

Once more, we squeezed into the phone booth. Nearly twenty minutes had elapsed since the second call and we were not one yard nearer the church.

'Donal,' Fr. Duddleswell said, 'are you still there?'

'Indeed, I am, Charles. Half a bottle to go.'

'Listen here, what time is the reception?'

'Half an hour ago.'

'Of course,' Fr. Duddleswell whistled, 'it was fixed for four o'clock at Tipton Hall.'

'What a good memory you have, Charles.'

'Will you give the groom a message from me? To save time, start the reception at once.'

'Before the wedding?'

'That is right.'

'A back to front wedding. A brilliant stroke, Charles. I'll drink to that.' And he did. 'One thing, Charles.'

'The groom's mother is throwing her lightnings about, so when you come, see to it your little legs are well earthed.'

By the time we reached the car, spectators in their thousands were streaming out of the ground and jostling one another in the street. Two mounted police-

119

men acted as a breakwater against the human tide. No choice but to sit tight.

I had a brainwave. 'What about the parish priest of All Saints?'

'Monsignor Clarke? What about him?'

'Why not ring and ask him to officiate?'

'I am not sure I can delegate jurisdiction for weddings over the telephone, Father Neil.' He pondered for a few moments. 'Confessions are not valid over the phone, like.'

'They'd be more popular if they were,' I said.

'No,' he decided, 'I am not taking any chances. In questions of marriage, 'tis always better to be safe than sorry.' He bit his nails. 'Ah, but me nerves are frayed like a cow's tail.'

They were not improved by the sight of the Newcastle fan heading in our direction. We slid down our seats almost to the floor, hoping he wouldn't see us. His gait showed he was very boozed up by now.

Convinced he had passed us, I foolishly lifted my head. Only to find myself looking him straight in the eye.

'What are ye gauping at?'

He noticed my collar and Fr. Duddleswell's hat topping his squashed down frame. He lifted the hat. 'Are ye the mickle greet nit I was at the match wi?'

'Do I look like him?' Fr. Duddleswell asked anxiously.

'No, he was much taller than ye.' He put the hat back on. 'Lucky for ye. Aa'm goin to pay his greet fat backside.'

And he went swaying off on his holy mission.

It was not till nearly five that we were able to move off. Fr. Duddleswell drove at a mad pace, cutting every corner, while I kept a look-out for a patrol car. Whenever anyone attempted to cross in our path, he cursed and demanded to know why pedestrians were allowed on the street at all.

* * *

Mrs. Pring greeted Fr. Duddleswell with, 'At last. I never thought I'd be pleased to see *you*.' No response from him. 'It's a shame. Father Neil, don't *you* think it's a shame?'

Fr. Duddleswell, already pulling off his jacket, said, 'I can beat me own breast, thank you.'

'With a feather, by the looks of it.' After which she began her tale of woe with evident relish. 'The men came and took away the posh awning which the groom hired. And the red carpet. Mrs. Perkins, the organist, has gone home to feed her kids.'

'Tell me more,' Fr. Duddleswell said with total disinterest.

'The driver of the wedding car has had to leave for a banquet at the Mansion House.'

'Did they start the reception, that's the thing?'

'They had to, Father D. The bride and bridesmaids were frozen and in church it was like a funeral.'

'Thank you kindly,' Fr. Duddleswell said, brushing aside the hostility of bride-loving Mrs. Pring.

'Right,' she said, 'but never dare say to me again that one day I'll forget to cook potatoes.'

'Woman,' he grinded out, as he wiped his greasy brow, 'you are treading as close to the edge as a donkey on a mountain track.' He grabbed my arm. 'Two bits of luck, lad.'

I looked around. 'Where, Father?'

'I am meself an authorized Registrar of Marriages. Otherwise we would have to put the wedding off till tomorrow.'

'Second piece of luck?' I asked apprehensively.

'Having you, Father Neil. While I am making meself presentable, this is what I am wanting you to do.'

It was with feelings of belligerence that I walked to Tipton Hall as Fr. Duddleswell's advance emissary of peace.

It took me five minutes to summon up the courage

to enter the dining room. I went first to the Gents to pray and tidy up and pray some more. I was shocked to see myself in the mirror. My hair was a wet, tangled mess, my raincoat and trousers clung to me like the skin of an otter.

From a distance, the wedding guests, seventy or eighty of them sounded normal enough but as I passed through the main door, a hush descended. My loneliness at that moment was only matched by the loneliness I felt when I walked into the church to hear my first confessions and found the place deserted.

I went to the top table, past the uncut wedding cake, and took the groom's hand. It was cold.

'Mr. Faber,' I said for all to hear, 'I am so sorry for the delay. Father Duddleswell was in a mishap. In fact, a rather nasty accident.'

There was a sympathetic murmur from the Catholics present.

'Nothing serious,' I said, and wished I hadn't because sympathy immediately waned.

Mrs. Faber, the groom's mother, a waspish looking woman with butterfly-shaped glasses dangling from a cord, said bitchily, 'What a pity.'

'As soon as he's fixed up, he's coming round to apologize in person.'

'That is frightfully nice of him,' Mrs. Faber said.

'The least he could do,' I replied weakly.

Wanda French, the bride-to-be, plump, thirty-two years old, called out, 'Father Boyd, will you have a glass of wine?'

'Pour the Father a glass of wine,' the groom said.

I thanked them and secretly blessed Wanda for breaking the ice. Some of the guests even smiled at me in welcome.

The bride's mother, fat, red-eyed and unbelievably sad in her finery, stood up next to me. 'It was a cold meal, Father.'

'That's a relief,' I said.

Mrs. French, her handkerchief pressed to her nose, said, 'It was meant to be hot, Father.'

'Never mind, Mum,' Wanda said, 'what laughs we'll have in years to come.'

Dr. Daley rose to his feet amid cries of 'Shush,' 'The Doctor wants to speak.'

'Ladies and gentlemen,' he began, 'this is one wedding none of us will forget in a hurry.'

Mrs. Faber seconded that.

The Doctor scratched his head. 'I remember the day I brought the beautiful Wanda into the world.'

'Ah,' everybody cried, except Mrs. Faber.

'Three weeks overdue.' Smiles all round. 'Even then, y'see, the darlin' girl was learning to be late for important occasions.' He raised his hands as if he were a priest about to say *Dominus Vobiscum*. 'It was hands of mine, ladies and gentlemen, that helped Wanda edge into the light of day. Hands of mine that first held her. And now that her dear father has passed away, it'll be hands of mine—albeit a little shaky—that'll give her today into the safe keeping of her intended. So'—he picked up his glass—'I give you a toast.' The guests stood and raised their glasses. 'To the future Bride and Groom.'

The toast was followed by warm applause which petered out as Fr. Duddleswell walked in.

To my surprise, he hadn't washed the motor oil off his hands and face or changed his rain-soaked suit. The only difference I could see was that his left arm was in a sling.

'Forgive me all,' he said in a sort of whimper. 'I have been in an accident.'

A murmur of sympathy on all sides. Wanda said, 'Poor Father Duddleswell,' and Richard, 'Yes, poor fellow.'

Fr. Duddleswell winced but did his best not to. 'A motor accident.'

Mrs. French was very upset. 'Oh dear,' she cried, her hanky to her eyes.

Everyone was on his side by now, with the usual exception. What a performer, I thought.

Forgetting to mention that at the time his car was stationary and he was watching a soccer match, he said, 'The tyre of me car, you follow? Cut to ribbons.' He touched his wounded arm and gritted his teeth bravely. 'And the car behind gave me quite a hammering. I am so sorry.'

'Don't *worry*, Father,' Wanda implored.

He assured them that as soon as he was cleaned up the wedding would go ahead, whatever the cost to himself.

'Will six o'clock be soon enough for you?'

'Lovely, Father,' Wanda said.

'And after,' Fr. Duddleswell said expansively, 'everyone is invited to the presbytery for champagne, provided by St. Jude's. The bride and groom can cut the cake in me study.'

When he had finished his speech, Richard, nudged by Wanda, called for 'Three cheers for Father Duddleswell.' After which, the rogue withdrew to great applause, his left arm tucked into his side, his right hand waving gallantly.

Just before six, there were sounds of merriment in the street. Looking through the dining room window, I saw the guests making their way on foot to the church in the spirit of a carnival.

Wanda and Richard were carrying the cake themselves and a photographer from *The Kenworthy Gazette* was taking pictures. He had been at the local soccer match where the 'message' had been relayed over the loudspeaker.

Fr. Duddleswell and I, having been judged by Mrs. Pring to be as spruce as magpies, went into church where the ceremony passed without further incident.

Fr. Duddleswell, his arm still in a sling, preached a sermon, some of which was new to me.

'Me dear people, being somewhat wounded, I do

124

not intend keeping you for long. A brief comment on St. Paul's words which I have just read you: "Husbands love your wives and wives *obey* your husbands in all things."

'Some people today foolishly want to drop the word "obey" from the marriage service. Marriage is a matter of equality, they say. Life today is "democratic".' He sniffed. 'Let me just say this: Almighty God does not agree with 'em. Neither do I.

'God made the world and there is not much equality and democracy there that I can see. Yet which of us complains that the weed does not smell as fragrant as the rose or the worm look as regal as the lion or a sparrow sing as delightfully as the nightingale?

'No democracy even in our bodies. One side is always stronger than the other. And even on the same hand, me little finger would be well-advised not to get into a scrap with me thumb.'

The preacher looked around him challengingly. 'God did not build the family as a democracy, me dear Brethren. Let women, therefore, be subject to the stronger partners, their husbands. And let husbands respect their wives and treat them fairly. Which means above all not discarding them by the legal fiction called divorce.

'Not that bride and groom here are thinking of divorcing each other on a day like this. But 'tis as well to set out the long-term rules of the game clearly and fairly from the start.

'And now, Wanda and Richard,' he said, smiling paternally, 'may God bless you and keep you and turn His face of pity towards you. May He always bless you.'

A change to a drier tone as he gestured to the close relatives to follow him and the bridal couple. 'If you would like to come to the sacristy, we will hold the civil ceremony there out of sight of our Blessed Lord in the tabernacle.'

* * *

After the photographs, the guests came clamouring into the house. Fred Bowlby, landlord of The Pig and Whistle, had sent glasses and a crate of champagne.

The chief guests gathered in Fr. Duddleswell's study. 'Father Neil,' he whispered, 'since I am supposed to be wounded, I am wanting you to open the bottles.'

Gingerly, I started to nudge the cork off the first of them. Thirty seconds later there was a whoosh and the cork went across the room like a comet trailing clouds of champagne. The immediate bystanders, including bride and groom, were soaked as it pursued its path of devastation.

It brought down the Pope's picture dropped on to the clock which fell in turn on a tray of glasses smashing everything. Finally, the cork ricocheted off the ceiling and the metal cap landed in the eye of the groom's mother. Fortunately or unfortunately—opinion was divided—it had almost run out of steam by then. The lady was profoundly hurt but not in the least injured.

'Father Neil, are you not a menace with the bottles this day?' Fr. Duddleswell groaned. 'Take the bloody things and open them in the garden. And be careful with the stars, will you not? I do not want you giving *them* a black eye.'

Later that evening, Dr. Daley and we two priests sat chatting cosily with the remnants of drink and wedding cake all round us.

Fr. Duddleswell was trying to phone when Dr. Daley said, 'God, that was a powerful marriage address you gave us this evening, Charles.'

'You liked it, Donal?'

'So full of good sense. They'll never make you a Bishop.'

'Shush, Donal, 'tis the florist.' Fr. Duddleswell had got his connection. 'Jim, Father Duddleswell here. Sorry to bother you at this late hour but could you possibly get some flowers to a couple of friends of mine? . . . Tomorrow morning, first thing? That will be fine. Richard and Wanda Faber at—'

Dr. Daley helped him out. 'Hotel Excelsior, Bayswater,'

'Hotel Excelsior, Bayswater. Three pounds worth, Jim . . . A message? Oh, just put, "Heartfelt Regrets, Father Duddleswell". They will understand. A hundred thousand thanks.'

'Father,' I said, when he had replaced the receiver, 'did you have to put on that sling?'

'Sorry?' He was genuinely puzzled.

'Why didn't you give the young couple the truth straight?'

'Look, lad,' he said, 'you are still green as a bloody leprechaun. Truth, y'see, is like a ladder. Unless you give it a generous, charitable slant, you will fall thud on your bum. Did you not know that? Besides,' he added, 'look what happened once before when I told the whole truth and nothing but.'

'It was noble.'

'The noblest disaster ever seen in the County Court.'

I had to say it. 'Father, don't you think you may be letting yourself off rather lightly?'

He was amazed. 'I did not play-act to save me own face, Father Neil.'

'No?'

'Not at all. Do you not realize, me strong sinful inclination was to rush into that banquet, fall on me benders and say, "I am a heel and a skunk. I have ruined the happiest day of this young couple's life through me crass stupidity." I would have felt much better after that but what of them?'

'What *about* them?'

'That delightful group of people would have gone into church to celebrate the sacrament of holy matrimony in the most un-Christian frame of mind.'

'As it was,' Dr. Daley said, 'we went in joyful and forgiving.'

'You agree with him, Doctor?' I asked.

Wide-eyed for effect, he pointed to his glass of whiskey. 'Do you want me to lose my oldest and dearest friend?'

Fr. Duddleswell said, 'I do not doubt, lad, that your way is the noblest and the best. Except it makes the world an impossible place to live in.'

'Everyone has his own way, Father Neil,' Dr. Daley said, 'and our Charles has a hundred ways.' He stood up and, indicating that the bottle had given its last, said, 'Well, there's nothing to keep me here.' He placed the empty bottle in my hand. 'Be sure to give it a good Christian burial, Father Neil.'

At the door, he ran into Mrs. Pring and wished her good night.

'I'm just off to Bedford,' she said to us.

'Wait, Mrs. P,' I called out, 'what did *you* think of Father Duddleswell wearing a sling?'

She looked at me solemnly. 'Even God can't get by without a little help from His friends.'

' 'Tis important, y'see,' Fr. Duddleswell said, 'that you do not leave the laity with the right impression, like.'

I waved his interruption aside to concentrate on a woman's point of view. 'So you agree with him, too, Mrs. P?'

'Of course I do, Father Neil. It was my idea.' She left and I heard her laughing outside the door.

'It's a conspiracy,' I said, grinning.

'I tell you, Father Neil, if and when I come to die, I will remember the doings of this day.'

'That's two of us.'

'Do not sigh like that, lad. After many crooked windings, you must admit things turned out well for everyone.'

'Apart from the groom's mother.'

Fr. Duddleswell took out a gold fountain pen. 'See this, lad. I borrowed it from *her* to fill in the register.'

'And forgot to give it back.'

128

How we laughed.

'When you struck her in the eye with that cork, Father Neil, she nearly went up on her hind legs to you.'

'She didn't exactly take to you, either. I heard her say to Richard, "I knew we should have hired a Jesuit." '

Through tears of mirth, he managed to say, 'Beside that one, Mrs. Pring herself seems like St. Bernadette or The Little Flower.'

'No wonder Richard's father divorced her.'

He tried to look serious. 'A heinous sin, mind.' But hilarity overcame him. 'Which if I were God I would not find it hard to forgive.'

'Just before she left,' I roared, 'just before she left, she said, "We came for a three o'clock wedding and it takes longer than *Gone With The Wind*." '

We both shook uncontrollably until Fr. Duddleswell suddenly froze and his face turned white as an altar bread.

'Father? Something wrong?' I thought perhaps he had forgotten to lock away the marriage registers or lost the fee paid up by the best man.

Fr. Duddleswell was already across to his bookcase, flipping through a volume. After a few seconds, he closed it and slumped down again in his chair. 'Father Neil, I have miserable intelligence for you.'

'Oh yes,' I said pleasantly, draining a glass of leftover champagne.

'They are not married.'

He wasn't joking. 'How . . . ? What . . . ?'

'The rules for registrars. According to the Marriage Act of 1949, marriages can only be lawfully celebrated between eight in the morning and six in the evening.'

'And the civil ceremony started over fifteen minutes late.'

'Dear sweet Jesus. In all the hurry-burry, it escaped me mind altogether.'

129

I joined him in silent sympathy.

'They are married in the eyes of the Church, Father Neil, but not in the eyes of the State. That is the fat and thin of it, the this and that of it.'

'If God is happy,' I said, with a feeble attempt to console him, 'why worry about Caesar?'

'Dear sweet Jesus,' he groaned. 'I am all abroad and no mistake.' He held his head tightly in his hands as if to stop the contents splashing out. 'Richard Faber is a Protestant. If ever he should want to rid himself of Wanda he will not even have to divorce her.'

'His lawyers will just have to prove they were never married according to law in the first place?'

'Wanda's children will be disinherited and I—'

'The Tower for you, Father.' A remark not well received.

'Dear sweet Jesus, what have I done? What have I done?'

'More to the point, what're you going to do?'

He looked at me pathetically. 'What hour is it? Eleven? I can hardly ring them and tell them to stop what they are doing immediately, can I?'

'Especially as they might be fast asleep,' I said, taking an optimistic line. 'Any way, why do anything if they're married in the eyes of the Church?'

He nodded, 'I will leave badly alone for tonight. 'Tis not till four tomorrow afternoon they are catching their plane to Las Palmas.'

He thought long and hard. Then those words again:

'Now, Father Neil, this is what I am wanting you to do.'

Next morning, I celebrated the first two Sunday Masses. After a hurried breakfast, I took a taxi to the Excelsior Hotel.

The middle-aged receptionist ran his finger down the list. 'Faber, yes. Here they are, sir. Mr. and

Mrs. Checked in last night. Room 101.' He glanced up in surprise. 'That's the bridal suite.'

'Well, they *are* supposed to be married.'

The receptionist smoothed his brush moustache. 'Are you a relative, sir? Brother or something?'

'Father,' I said, 'Oh, I see what you mean. Um, not exactly.'

'Are they expecting you?'

I put on a pleasant smile. 'It's a kind of surprise visit.' An inspiration. 'I'm their spiritual adviser and there's something they've got to know.'

The clerk shrugged, dialled the number and handed me the phone. There was no reply for some time. This was, after all, the morning after *some* night before.

Eventually Richard's voice came on the line. 'Yes?'

'Mr. Faber,' I said, completely embarrassed, 'I'm glad I found you in.'

'I didn't ask for a call.'

'This is Father Boyd.'

'Who?'

'Father Boyd. We met yesterday at St. Jude's.'

'I remember.' He said to Wanda. 'It's Father Boyd.'

'I was wondering if I might come up and see you.'

'Come up? Where from?'

'Downstairs. I'm at reception.'

'Can't it wait? Until we've had breakfast, for instance.'

I turned my back on the receptionist. 'It's rather, er, a delicate matter.'

'Delicate?'

'And urgent.'

Richard sounded alarmed. 'Has someone died?'

'I don't think so. That's not why I'm here, anyway.' I really wasn't any good on the phone.

I heard Wanda say, 'Somebody's been in an accident?' to which Richard replied, 'It's nothing seri-

131

ous, darling.' He made sure. 'It's not serious, is it, Father Boyd?'

'Nothing that can't be put right.'

'Very well.' His deep sigh made the bed creak. 'I presume you can give us a few minutes to put some clothes on.'

I allowed them a full fifteen minutes for decorum's sake, then climbed the stairs.

Outside Room 101 were Richard's shoes, a copy of the *Sunday Express*, a silver horseshoe and a wreath. I thought for one mad moment that someone *had* died until I saw the tag on it. 'Heartfelt Regrets. Father Duddleswell.'

I removed the card and put the wreath in a firebucket.

Wanda was smoothing the bedspread as I entered.

Richard coughed. 'Come in, Father Boyd. You're very welcome.'

'Mr. Faber,' I said, taking his hand. 'Wanda.'

Wanda said, 'Nice morning, Father.'

'Yes, thank you.' I handed Richard the newspaper.

'You haven't just come to deliver the *Sunday Express*?'

I felt awkward and couldn't escape the conclusion he regarded me as some sort of crank.

I cleared my throat. 'I'm terribly sorry to have to tell you, Mr. Faber, *and* you, Wanda, that according to the law of England . . .'

'Yes?' Richard said.

'You are not yet . . .'

'No?'

'Not *quite* . . . married.'

'Tell me more,' he said, dropping like a stone into a chair.

I sat on the bed. 'I realize this must be something of a shock to you.'

Richard was in a daze. 'How can I be an unmarried husband?'

I explained. 'We celebrated the wedding outside the hours permitted by law.'

He was too stricken to reply.

'Believe me, Mr. Faber and Wanda, this isn't a crime. In my view, what you've done, in the circumstances, isn't even a sin.'

'What *we've* done,' Richard cried, 'it's what *you've* done that's landed us in this mess.'

I looked across to Wanda, expecting tears. Instead, she was helpless with mirth.

'Richard,' she laughed, 'Richard, we started life together with the reception and now the honeymoon before the wedding. Our children are going to love this.'

Richard was not yet able to see the funny side of things. 'Are you in the habit,' he asked testily, 'of sending bridal couples away from your church unmarried?'

'Very, very seldom,' I assured him, without thinking.

'But it's hilarious,' Wanda shrieked, her plump body vibrating all over.

'I was under the impression,' Richard said, 'that the Catholic Church disapproves of . . .'

'Sex before . . .' I said.

This time, Richard laughed, too, and said to Wanda, 'Darling, will you marry me?'

Wanda, still overcome, nodded acceptance. I thanked God for that. If she had refused him now, we would have been in a terrible fix.

Eventually Wanda was able to splutter out, 'It can't have been easy for you, Father.'

'Rather, like being sent into the lions' den to eat the lions.'

'What is St. Jude the patron of?' Richard asked.

'Hopeless cases,' I said.

More laughter before Richard said. 'Tell us what to do.'

'The marriage licence is valid for three months. If you'd like to take a taxi to St. Jude's, I'll take

133

another. The cab drivers can be the witnesses at your wedding.'

'It *is* lawful on Sundays, I suppose' Richard said.

'Of course, Mr. Faber. Father Duddleswell wouldn't make a mistake like that. I mean, would he?'

The door to the sacristy was left open, according to regulations, so that the public could have right of access.

'But if you let anybody in,' Fr. Duddleswell whispered to me, 'I will bloody murder you for a start.'

Red-faced, he went through the civil ceremony. In two minutes it was over. 'Bless the pair of you,' he said, 'and may you be as prolific as the fern.'

I paid off the taxi drivers, Fr. Duddleswell made a few alterations to the civil register and handed Wanda a new marriage certificate. 'Tear up the one I gave you yesterday, me dear.'

'Father Duddleswell,' Wanda said, 'will I ever be able to forgive you?'

'Wanda, darling,' he said gently, going on his knees, 'name me punishment.' He touched his face. 'As red as blood is me cheek and I am positively melting with shame like a cheap candle.'

Richard took his bride in his arms and kissed her. 'Third time lucky,' he said.

I put something in Wanda's hand. 'A wedding present from me.'

'You shouldn't have, Father.' She opened her hand and smiled. 'A champagne cork.'

Richard was delighted. 'Just what we needed,' he said.

Fr. Duddleswell turned to the groom in his most efficient manner. 'I want to atone for all the trouble I caused you.'

'We hardly noticed, Father.'

'All the same, I just want to say you do not have to worry about getting to the airport in time.'

Richard looked apprehensive. 'No?'

'I intend driving you there meself.'

Already, Richard had taken his bride's hand and they were backing towards the door.

'That's very kind of you, Father Duddleswell,' Richard said, 'but really and truly there is no need to put yourself out.'

The couple were at the door when Mrs. Faber burst in. 'Father Duddleswell, I have come for . . . my . . . fountain . . . pen.' She glared at her son out of one good and one black eye. 'Richard, why aren't you on your honeymoon?'

'It's a long story, Mother.'

Fr. Duddleswell improvised at a furious rate. 'I think Richard may be thinking about becoming a Catholic.'

Mrs. Faber nearly exploded. 'A *what*?'

Richard surprised even his bride. 'That's right, Mother. As a matter of fact, ever since I met Wanda'—he held her closely for support—'I've been trying to summon up enough courage to ask.'

Wanda stretched up her face for a kiss.

'But I'm a Protestant,' Mrs. Faber said.

Exactly,' Richard said. 'I mean, we all have our different roads to tread.'

Fr. Duddleswell didn't want a family squabble in his own back yard. 'Run along, Richard,' he urged, 'and have your honeymoon first. Come and see me after.'

The three of them departed, Mrs. Faber having snatched her gold fountain pen out of Fr. Duddleswell's hand.

Left alone, Fr. Duddleswell and I looked at each other and shook our heads.

I was first to speak. 'God's ways are certainly mysterious.'

' 'Tis true, Father Neil. Ah, but 'tis a grand relief to know Himself comes from Tipperary, after all.'

Seven

IS THE CORPSE A CATHOLIC?

'He is one of us, I am telling you, so 'tis meself who will lower him into his grave no matter what Fatty Pinkerton says.'

Fr. Duddleswell's reaction to the news I brought from "Fishermen's Rest" was as predictable as belly-ache after little green apples.

Had he know then what it would cost him to fulfil his pledge he might have insisted on his rights a good deal less.

'How are you making out at "Fishermen's Rest," Father Neil?' Fr. Duddleswell noticed my unease. 'A problem?'

There was. Earlier that Friday afternoon I had visited the rest home-cum-hospital for retired fishermen and merchant seamen on the edge of our parish. The Director, Captain Andrew Kent, told me that of four new crew members one had died within twenty-four hours of coming aboard.

'A new inmate, Father,' I said. 'As soon as he came in, he, um, went out.'

'Died you mean. God rest him.' And Fr. Duddleswell signed himself.

Mrs. Pring came into his study, brandishing an empty tray. 'For the last time,' she said in an exasperated tone.

'Will you be quiet, woman, so I can hear the church bell.'

'Didn't you hear me say tea's ready?'

'I keep a special pair of little ears for what you say.'

Mrs. Pring turned to go. 'I'll not call you any more, God is my witness. You'll have to go without.'

'This seaman who died, Father Neil, you did give him the last sacraments, of course.'

'That's the problem. I'm not sure if he's a Catholic or not.'

'Didn't he have a card?'

'All yellow and faded. He brought it with him from the Seamen's Home at Shelwell which has just closed.'

'And?'

'Well, the entries were made originally in the 1930's and never brought up to date. I could hardly read a word of it.'

'What was his name?'

'According to his card, James Driscoll.'

Fr. Duddleswell snapped his fingers. 'He's Irish. Driscoll is a Cork name. He is a Catholic, all right.'

'Um, Pinkerton says he's C of E. And he wants to bury him.'

Fr. Duddleswell snorted. 'An Anglican curate is not qualified to bury a dead sausage.'

'No, Father.'

'Listen here, no Driscoll is shipmate of a C of E parson,' he said, coming over nautical, 'and I will not have an Old Soak of ours voyaging to the other side, save in the Barque of Peter.'

I nodded agreement.

'Blasted Anglicans,' he said. 'First they pinch our churches and cathedrals and now they are scheming to pinch one of our Catholic corpses besides.'

'I told Pinkerton that, Father. Not exactly in those words.'

Fr. Duddleswell was on his feet, peeling off his

cassock. 'Let us go see Captain Kent and sort this thing out.'

Mrs. Pring returned. 'Where are you off to, Father D? The tea'll be cold.'

'Holy Moses,' he said. 'There is a Catholic corpse in mortal peril and all that woman can think of is that the tay will get cold.'

'Jasus, Father Neil, this tay is stone cold.'

We had parked ourselves on a wooden bench outside Captain Kent's office. A tea-lady had supplied us with refreshment and I had bought myself a doughnut.

'You did give Driscoll absolution at least?'

I played for time. 'Pardon, Father?'

'Indeed, pardon for his sins.'

I gulped. 'No, Father. He was as dead as Porgy the pig.'

'And who, pray, said so, the Angel Gabriel?'

'Captain Kent. And a doctor signed the death-certificate.'

Fr. Duddleswell put down his cup with a clash. 'I do not doubt Driscoll is medically dead and will not breathe again. Is he *theologically* dead, that is the thing.'

'You mean, has his soul yet left his body?'

'Correct.'

'He was stiff and cold.'

Fr. Duddleswell took another sip of his tea. 'At this moment, so am I.'

'He looked dead to me, Father.'

'God help us, every time I preach a sermon, I see what looks like rows of the departed. Eat your doughnut, lad, while I tell you some basic facts about corpses.'

That so took away my appetite, I put the doughnut down on the bench beside me.

'Did you know,' he began, 'that the muscles of a corpse continue to respond when you touch them? Like this.' He made a clawing gesture at my arm which nearly made me drop my cup and saucer. 'And the hair and nails keep growing.'

'I've never noticed, Father.'

The tea-lady came belatedly to offer me sugar. I was about to put a spoonful in my cup when Fr. Duddleswell said:

'Also a corpse's liver goes on manufacturing sugar.'

'Sugar?' I put the spoon back in the bowl and the tea-lady, bemused, went away.

'This shows you, lad, that something is still alive inside dead people, does it not?'

'I never thought of that.'

'Well, as a priest, you should. Furthermore, many people have been given their death-certificates, been buried and *still* they proved the doctor wrong.'

In my amazement, I put my thunb to my mouth. 'How did they do that?'

He put on his Edgar Allen Poe look. 'By biting through their thumbs in their coffins.'

I hastily removed mine from the vicinity of my teeth.

'So much for medical opinion, Father Neil.' He winked knowingly as if the priesthood gave him secret sources of information denied even to scientists. 'Now 'tis true, lad, that after a long lingering death, the soul of an old person may leave the body in a grand haste, but you should not have presumed on it.'

Nor should I. I knew the drill. A dead person is entitled to the benefit of every possible doubt. The normal procedure is to give absolution from sins, Extreme Unction and the papal blessing, all conditionally. 'If you are alive, I absolve you . . .' The death of Mr. Driscoll and the dispute about whether his corpse was a Catholic or not had made me negligent.

Fr. Duddleswell was maintaining that the only incontestable proof of death, theologically speaking, is decomposition. Not even decapitation or being blown to smithereens guarantees the soul has left for God.

'It may still be hanging around somewhere for a few hours at least, Father Neil, if you're still with me.'

'I am, Father. I am.'

'The largest lump of smithereen remaining should be absolved and anointed. What about someone who has been guillotined?'

'The biggest bit, Father?'

'Not at all. That was a catch question, lad. In that special case, you would go to work on the head.' He proudly tapped his own. 'The noblest part of the body.'

'Even when it hasn't got a body?'

He glowered at me. 'This is where the soul most intensely resides.'

'In England, Father . . .' I tried to tell him.

'The English hang murderers, that I know. But I had in mind the case of someone losing his head in a motor accident or in wrath over his curate's inefficiency.'

My soul began to stir uncomfortably in my stomach as well as in my noblest part. I stood up.

'What the divil are you up to, lad?'

'Father, I'm going back to St. Jude's straight away to get the Holy Oils.'

He restrained me. 'Tut-tut, O me baby sparrow, me lambling, me green young twig, finish off your tay first. D'you think the corpse will run out on you that you are in such a fanatical hurry?'

Captain Kent came out of his office. A small, broad-shouldered man in a black blazer with brass anchor buttons. His reddish-blue face, topping a bushy ginger beard, was like a three-dimensional map with pock-marks and protuberances all over it.

'Come aboard, gentlemen,' he said, a twinkle in his eyes.

Adorning the walls of his office were sepia coloured pictures of ancient schooners and steam boats.

On his desk was a glass boat in a bottle. And there, seated comfortably, was the treacherous John Pinkerton.

Fr. Duddleswell managed to whisper in my ear, 'Fatty has come to steal a march on us.'

'You know each other already, I believe,' the Captain said, as he sat behind his desk.

Pinkerton didn't let our presence interrupt his flow. 'You were saying, Captain, that Mr. Driscoll has no next of kin.'

Captain Kent, his left hand cupping his beard, shook his head.

Fr. Duddleswell, on the way, had given it as his opinion that sailors, in spite of their salty tongues, are generally a pious, sentimental lot. He asked:

'Was there a string of beads on him, by any chance?'

'No.' The sound stayed in the air like the boom after a wave pounds the cliff.

'A miraculous medal? A picture of the Sacred Heart?' Receiving no for an answer each time, he muttered something about the poor feller dying naked as a Protestant.

'There was a Bible in his case,' the Captain said.

Fr. Duddleswell looked pleased. 'With an *Imprimatur*?'

An *Imprimatur* is the Bishop's permission to print a book after a theological adviser has assured him it is free from heresy.

Another contented shake of the head from Captain Kent.

'Of course, Andie,' Fr. Duddleswell hastened to add, 'there are Bible societies as would drop a Bible free of charge into the Kremlin or Hell itself if they only could.'

'Is that so?' Captain Kent said disconcertingly.

Undaunted, Fr. Duddleswell said, 'Driscoll, now. Did any of you gentlemen ever hear of a Protestant by the name of Driscoll?'

Mr. Pinkerton, puffing away furiously at his cig-

141

arette, said in his high-pitched whine, 'Could have been a convert.'

Fr. Duddleswell obviously forgot he had often said to me, 'There are some in our congregation as would turn Protestant to get a potato.' He rounded on Fatty.

'Do not be insulting to the Catholic Church, Mr. . . . Mr. . . .'

The fact that he couldn't remember his adversary's name rather took the edge off his rebuke.

Pinkerton, who knew how to look after himself, pointed out that many Protestants, even Anglican clergymen, sometimes mysteriously converted to Catholicism, and 'Where's the harm in that, Father . . . Father . . .?'

'There is none at all in *that*,' Fr. Duddleswell retorted.

One of his favourite stories, I remembered, was of a Catholic priest who, on leaving the Church, was asked if he intended to become an Anglican. 'It's my faith I've lost,' the apostate priest replied, 'not my reason.'

'Gentlemen,' Captain Kent broke in, 'we have as yet no information on our deceased shipmate. But his corpse will be walking out of here on its own unless one of you padres does the honours.'

'Let's leave the matter entirely in God's hands,' Pinkerton drawled, with more in his cheek than his cigarette.

'What does that mean?' I said.

'We'll toss for it, old sport.'

'Andie,' Fr. Duddleswell said, paying as much attention to Pinkerton's intervention as to a dog barking, 'have you tried the "Fishermen's Rest" where Driscoll was before?'

Captain Kent dialled a number and held up the earpiece for us all to hear the whine.

'Disconnected?'

Captain Kent, for reply, smiled with his eyes. With his reddish beard, he looked like a mischievous schoolboy, up to no good, peering over an autumn hedge.

I reminded the Captain that Driscoll had arrived from Shelwell with three other ex-sailors. 'Couldn't we see them, Captain?'

Without a word, Captain Kent rose and beckoned us with a horny hand to follow him.

In a dormitory awash with murals of seas, rocks and lighthouses were the three men lying in a row.

The first was clearly dying. Fr. Duddleswell was about to ask what his religion was when Captain Kent spoke one word, 'Methodist.'

The second man was propped up against pillows, his beard and hair were long and yellow.

'Can't read nor write,' the Captain said.

Fr. Duddleswell wasn't put off by his illiteracy. 'May I have a word with him, Andie?'

'Deaf as the sea.'

The third man, dishevelled and wild-eyed, began to sing sea shanties as we approached his bed. I did my best not to listen to the lyrics of this pious and sentimental Old Salt but they had little to do with 'Rock of Ages'.

'D.T.'s,' the Captain said.

When we returned to his study, Captain Kent held up a crumpled document. 'I found this in his wallet. An insurance policy.'

'For?' Pinkerton asked.

'Driscoll took it out forty-five years ago for his funeral. A modest premium.'

I asked how much it was worth today.

'An actuary tells me that it could be worth £400.'

James Driscoll was of my grandmother's generation. Her constant wish was to be buried in style, owing nobody a farthing. Each week, she made a small contribution to a provident society to pay for her coffin, wreaths, hearse and grave stone with enough left over for the priest, grave digger and pallbearers. There was an old world courtesy about such arrangements.

Before bidding us good evening, Captain Kent said, 'I'll give you gentlemen twenty-four hours to come to some sort of agreement. Otherwise'—a final touch of mischievousness—'I shall have to ask the Salvation Army to bury him, shan't I?'

'One last question, Captain,' Fr. Duddleswell said. 'Which doctor was it signed the death-certificate?'

'Dr. Daley,' he said.

In the car park, Fr. Duddleswell and Mr. Pinkerton fell to debating the theology of the Hereafter.

'You do not believe in Hell,' Fr. Duddleswell challenged, harking back to a Clergy Conference we had attended before Christmas. 'I take it, then, you do not believe in the resurrection of the dead.'

'Not if you mean bits and pieces being stuck together on the Last Day with celestial glue,' Fatty retorted. 'Besides, have you never read about cannibalism?'

'So?'

'Well, if one chap eats another, you get two people in one, so to speak. Perhaps a Catholic inside a Protestant. Which of them will God raise at the Last Day?'

'God will unscramble them,' Fr. Duddleswell muttered, giving no indication how.

'Oh, yes?'

'After all, He made you out of *nothing* and that is quite a feat.'

Fatty was not perturbed. He blew out a huge column of smoke to prepare for his next argument. 'What about cremation?'

'We do not believe in cremation,' Fr. Duddleswell snapped.

'Whether you believe in it or not, some people get cremated against their will in burned out houses, planes and cars.' He asked me to confirm it. 'Don't they, old sport?'

'Yes,' I admitted, feeling like a traitor.

'And that includes Catholics,' Fatty said.

144

'D'you think, Mr. . . . Mr. . . . , that the Almighty God will have difficulty shifting through the ashes?'

'Why should He bother, tell me that.'

'In your case, Mr. Pinkerton, a very good question. But surely He who makes a human being out of an invisible seed in a woman's womb can remake him out of a finger nail, if it so pleases Him.'

'After an atom-bomb drops on *you*, there won't be even that much left.'

Fr. Duddleswell turned away in disgust. 'Oh, what can you expect of somebody born blind?' In the same Biblical vein, he pretended to spit on the gravel and grind it in with his shoe.

'What're you doing?' Pinkerton growled.

'Making a paste for your eyes, that is what.'

'If I'm blind, then you are stone deaf.'

'What did you say?'

'You heard.'

Pinkerton squeezed into the driving seat of his red MG sports car, an ancient model with spoked wheels and the spare tyre attached to the back like a life belt.

'I admire your faith, Father . . . Father . . . ,' he said insolently, as he pressed his starter.

Nothing happened. He tried again without success and then put his head out of the window. 'Care to give me a tow?'

'I will be pleased to give you me entire foot,' Fr. Duddleswell barked.

'Charity used to be kind,' Pinkerton mumbled. 'I only need a gentle pull to get this thing going.'

Fr. Duddleswell walked over to him with a concerned look. 'So your battery appears to be dead, young sir.'

Pinkerton again tried unsuccessfully to start the engine.

'Never you mind, young sir. 'Twill surely rise again at the Last Day. Or so me admirable faith tells me.'

With that, he pushed me into the car and climbed in himself.

He drove round the block for the fun of it but returned immediately, backed his car in front of Pinkerton's and tied a rope around the bumper.

'An Anglican parson in tow,' he laughed, as we drove off. 'He is as validly ordained as a can of beans.'

That I couldn't deny.

'I will not have a heretic like that burying a Driscoll. Why, at the Last Day, poor Driscoll may be resurrected in the wrong way. One of his legs conjumbled with a Protestant's and he condemned to spend his eternity walking like a crab.'

'That'll never do,' I said, praying hard for him to keep his eye on the road. Another example of unanswered prayer.

Fr. Duddleswell was so impressed by his own joke that he didn't see a dog in our path till the last moment. He jammed on the brakes and Pinkerton, taken by surprise, ran into the back of us. My head nearly jerked off my shoulders with the impact.

Fr. Duddleswell leaped out, furious. He stood gesticulating in the Italian fashion first at the big dent in his chromium-plated bumper and then at Pinkerton who was peering in a daze through the window.

He banged his hat on the bonnet of Pinkerton's car. 'Am I to lose me no-claims bonus for being Christ-like towards a fat lump of an Anglican curate?'

He only calmed down when he saw that Pinkerton really was shaken up.

I sat next to Fatty for the rest of the journey to lend him my support and, this time, Fr. Duddleswell drove more carefully.

To no purpose.

We had reached the crossroads where busy Penn Avenue joins the High Street when there was a tremendous clonk and clatter as Fr. Duddleswell's rear bumper, shaken in the collision, broke off completely. Our small MG drove over it and came to a halt, stranded in the middle of the junction. Buses and cars whizzed all round us in the rush-hour melée, hooting madly.

A policeman arrived to direct the traffic. 'Funny place to play at dodgems, Reverends,' he called out.

Pinkerton and I walked to a nearby garage which sent a breakdown truck to fetch the MG. A few minutes later, Fr. Duddleswell met up with us, a twisted bumper sticking out of his rear window.

Pinkerton had a new battery fitted which Fr. Duddleswell paid for, a mechanic promised to straighten out the bumper.

After that, Anglican and Catholics decided it was best for both parties if we followed the centuries' old tradition and went our separate ways.

On the journey home, I said to Fr. Duddleswell, 'Pinkerton may still have no faith in the resurrection, Father, but you've done something for him.'

'What is that?'

'Made him a very devout believer in death.'

Next morning at breakfast, Fr. Duddleswell said, 'We *must* do it, Father Neil. Not for the money, though if something is left after expenses are paid, St. Jude's may benefit a little. But Driscoll went off at such a fine speed, not even greased for death, 'twould be sinful not to give him a full Catholic send-off. He has a good right to it.'

But how could we prove we were best qualified to bury him?

I tried calling Fr. Blundell, the curate of Shelwell. He had been chaplain at the Home where Driscoll was an inmate before. His parish priest told me that Fr. Blundell was making a week's retreat with the Carthusians at Parkminister and the monks didn't even have a telephone.

'Did you go back and anoint the deceased?' Fr. Duddleswell asked.

'I did, Father.'

'Fine, fine.'

I had slipped into the Seamen's Home in the dark and anointed the marble body of James Driscoll with two provisos: that he had been baptized a member of our flock and was still alive.

Shortly before ten, Dr. Daley arrived.

'Donal,' Fr. Duddleswell said, 'I hear 'twas yourself that signed the death-certificate of a feller at the Seamen's Home.'

'It was,' the Doctor replied. 'I signed both certificates.'

'I never heard that two died.'

Dr. Daley nodded. 'Two of 'em, side by side.' He blinked to clear his vision. 'At least, I think it was two.' He put his forefinger first to his right eye, then in his left. 'Perhaps it was only one, after all.'

'When you have finished joking, Donal, I would like some information about the Catholic one, name of Driscoll.'

Dr. Daley held up his right arm and made a pouring motion once or twice. 'I'm yours if you can afford me, Charles.'

Fr. Duddleswell looked across to me as if to say there was no hope. 'No liquor this morning, Donal. The tide is out.'

'I can smell it, Charles, and it with the bottle and six cupboards round it.'

'Shall I, Father?' I said.

'Jasus, haven't I enough on me plate already with Mrs. Pring's cooking on it?' He nodded towards me. 'Fetch me the mischief, lad.'

'You are so thoughtful, Charles.'

'Donal, I should not be doing this at all. Already your eyes are glassy as a teddy bear's.'

I handed Fr. Duddleswell the bottle and a glass.

Dr. Daley brightened up. 'Driscoll, you say. I did attend him before he set sail for sunnier climes.' He broke off. 'God, where's your sympathizing eye,

Charles? Can't you see my lips are sticking together so I can't speak another word?'

The cue for Fr. Duddleswell to pour.

'My daily prayer for you, Charles, is, May your holy hand never suffer from cramp.' When he saw the economy-sized drink he'd received, he sighed, 'Ah, but you are a small little man when it comes to carving the joint.'

'Driscoll, Donal. Did he say something at the last, something that gives us a clue to the sort of man he was?'

Dr. Daley, careful not to spill a drop, motioned to Fr. Duddleswell. 'Come here close and lend me your ear.'

Fr. Duddleswell listened to the whisper, wide-eyed. 'He said *that*?'

'He did.' Dr. Daley drained the glass to erase the memory. 'And also.' Another whisper to his friend's even greater astonishment.

I was intrigued. '*What* did he say to you, Doctor?'

Fr. Duddleswell wouldn't let him answer. ''Tis none of a curate's business what an Old Soak says in his fatal delirium.'

Dr. Daley winked at me. 'It was not only his prayers he was saying. I tell you, the swear words was thick as grass.'

'One thing, Father Neil. Driscoll may not deserve a Catholic burial but he certainly needs one.'

I urged the Doctor to finish his story.

'Oh, I said a Hail Mary for him, naturally, and put a glass of whiskey in his trembling hand, like this.' He lodged his glass with Fr. Duddleswell. 'A waste really, what with him so near the end.'

'You meant well, Doctor.'

'You are too kind, Father Neil. D'you know, the poor feller was dead for two drinks before I even noticed.'

'Ah,' Fr. Duddleswell said, 'didn't you do your best for him?'

'That I did. I even folded his arms and drained his glass for him.'

'There's not many as would have done that, Donal. One last query for you. Did he speak with a brogue, like?'

Dr. Daley pointed at the empty glass but got no response. 'Charles, Charles, sometimes I think that if you were a hen you'd lay hard-boiled eggs.'

'A brogue, Donal?' Hearing the front door bell ring. 'Quick, now.'

'My memory has paled with my glass.' He received a fresh splash to colour it. 'Wait a bit, now. It's coming miraculously back into focus. Indeed, I'm quite certain he spoke with a brogue.' His glass suddenly tuned pale again. 'At least, I think he did.'

Fr. Duddleswell slapped his knee and rose. 'Good. You will be wanting to get to your surgery, Donal.'

Mrs. Pring led in Pinkerton as Dr. Daley, at the study door, turned to say, 'D'you reckon, Charles, that when we rise from the dead you and I will have a fresh head of hair?'

Fr. Duddleswell beamed at him. 'May you be as hairy as a caterpillar, me faithful old friend.'

'Been discussing the resurrection of the dead again?' Pinkerton asked in a relaxed way.

'I suppose,' Fr. Duddleswell said irritably, 'you are wanting to cremate Driscoll and put him in a pot.'

'No.'

'Dr. Daley, who attended the deceased in his last agony, assured me Driscoll was a good practising Catholic. He gave all the signs, any way.'

'As a matter of fact,' Pinkerton says, 'after the way you treated me yesterday, I've only come to tell you I'm bowing out.'

Fr. Duddleswell started in surprise. 'You are handing the body over to me.'

Pinkerton nodded. 'He's probably a Catholic, if his name is anything to go by. And, anyhow, St. Jude's will give him a marvellous send-off, I'm sure.'

Like myself, Fr. Duddleswell must have been thinking his recent brush with death had something to do with this transformation. 'But this is surprisingly generous of you, Mr. Pinkerton.'

'Not at all,' Pinkerton said modestly. He took a note out of his top pocket. 'A quid towards his memorial.'

Fr. Duddleswell waved the money aside as he showed him courteously to the door. 'No need, kind sir. St. Jude's will be privileged to take care of all the funeral expenses. God go with you.'

He came back into his study chanting, 'Though God be slow His grace is sure.'

'Heavens,' I said, 'Pinkerton's not such a bad chap, after all.'

'He is really rather splendid,' Fr. Duddleswell chuckled, 'seeing he has little or no religion to sustain him.'

' 'Twill please you to know, Andie, that I personally will lodge Mr. Driscoll beneath the sod.'

The Captain examined a mast of the ship in the bottle on his desk. 'Afraid not.'

'You mean I *cannot* bury him?'

'You can.' Fr. Duddleswell relaxed. 'On one condition.'

'Name it only.'

'That you bury him at sea.'

Fr. Duddleswell and I echoed together, 'At sea.'

'Last night, I went through Driscoll's effects. A gold watch that don't work. A compass that points due south. And a scrap of his will. He wants to be buried as he should. At sea.' The Captain looked wistfully at the vessels on his wall. 'Must have loved the sea.'

'I like it as little as the divil likes Sunday,' Fr. Duddleswell said, and I seconded him. Why Driscoll had saved over all those years was now made plain.

'Want me to call Pinkerton back?' The Captain asked.

'Not at all, Andie. 'Tis me solemn duty to do it.'

Fr. Duddleswell swallowed painfully. 'Driscoll was too poor to strike a match, yet he had the piety to arrange a powerful funeral for himself. A great and good man.'

The Captain handed over a card. 'Here's the address of a funeral firm in Greenwich. They specialize in burials at sea. Should use 'em if I were you.'

'Thank you, Andie. One thing, though.'

'Yes?'

'Did, er, Mr. Pinkerton know of this will, by any chance?'

'I told him on the phone first thing this morning.'

'Thank you, Mr. Drabble.'

Fr. Duddleswell was in his study, telephoning, when I walked in.

'If you could get that headstone done for James Driscoll as soon as possible I'd be much obliged. . . . The inscription? "Rest in Peace" will do fine. Goodbye, now.'

'You're putting a memorial to him in our cemetery here?'

'That is the idea. In the sea, 'twould sink, you follow?'

'Looking forward to your little boat trip, Father?'

'A voyage to the mouth of the Thames will do me no harm. Besides, I will be getting the worth of me trouble.'

'I hope you will.'

'Why should I not? Driscoll's people are all dead, else they would be crawling out of the woodwork now demanding shares in the money.' He shook his head complacently. 'St. Jude's will surely get the balance of £400 by me self-sacrifice.'

The bell rang.

'That is the funeral director now, Father Neil. We are going to his place to discuss details. Care to come?'

'All the way to Greenwich?'

'Not at all. I intend using the local Co-op.'

I sensed problems ahead. 'Any particular reason?'

'There is. The Co-op gives dividend trading stamps.'

Fr. Duddleswell's spirits had revived sufficiently for him to sing for us the opening chorus of *HMS Pinafore*:

> We sail the ocean blue
> And our saucy ship's a beauty;
> We're sober men and true
> And attentive to our duty.

Mr. Freddie Williams, tall, stooping, elderly, with blue lines like major roads running down his nose, slowly shook his long lugubrious head. 'Very jolly, Father. Come, if you please, into my parlour.'

He opened the glass door for us. The place, not unnaturally, smelt of death.

'Business good these days, Freddie?'

'Much the same as usual, Father. It doesn't vary much. Unless we get a good cold spell.'

Fr. Duddleswell pointed to a line of coffins. 'Not exactly like a fun-fair in here, is it?'

'There aren't many laughs,' Mr. Williams conceded.

'A nice envelope, this one,' Fr. Duddleswell said, stroking a gleaming oak coffin.

Mr. Williams' eyes glistened. 'That is a beaut, all right. Isn't it a beaut? My Doris has got her sights on that one.'

'For herself?' I asked.

'For me,' Mr. Williams said. 'She says when I go, she won't spare any expense. She's like that, my Doris is.'

'It certainly looks expensive,' I said.

'Costs in general are going up every day, Father. Soon people won't be able to afford to die.'

'About this burial at sea, Freddie.'

'To be honest with you, Father Duddleswell, the

153

Fairwater Co-op's had very little experience of burials at sea.'

'Then you have had some.'

'None at all.'

'That is very little, indeed, Freddie.'

'Mind you,' Mr. Williams said with a solemn shake of his head, 'we're always willing to learn.'

'Have you worked out the cost yet?'

'I've got a quote here, Father, for £300.'

'Jesus, Mary and Joseph,' Fr. Duddleswell whistled. 'What do you intend hiring, The *Queen Mary*?'

'No, Father, but not a rowing boat either. Need something reliable.'

'It still sounds steep to me.'

Mr. Williams assured him the Co-op's charge was a modest £40 for pallbearers and a hearse to transport the deceased to the docks.

'What have you arranged, then, Freddie?'

The only vessel available at short notice was a Thames Barge Tug, the type that carried freight from the Port of London to the East India docks.

'Lucky to get it,' Mr. Williams said. 'There's a lull in cargo traffic at present because of heavy storms in the Channel and the North Sea.'

M.S.C. *Edding*, he assured us, was a sturdy ship of 85 tons. Anything bigger would have cost the earth and the sea. He read out its statistics :

'Diesel and spray. 140 Brake Horse Power.'

'What the divil does that mean?'

Mr. Williams sighed and looked up to Heaven as though he expected a downpour. 'Don't rightly know, Father, but it sounds reassuring.'

Fr. Duddleswell still hesitated to close the deal. 'Surely, Freddie, you could have hired a pleasure steamer and saved me well over a hundred pounds. Why a tug just to cruise down the Thames?"

Mr. Williams jerked his head back in surprise. 'A cruise down the Thames,' he said. 'But didn't someone tell you, Father, he's got to be buried outside the twelve-mile limit?'

Eight

ALL AT SEA

Wednesday morning began unpromisingly. It was dark, damp and wet.

Fr. Duddleswell and I were standing inside the church porch, vested, awaiting the hearse. The church was empty save for Mrs. Pring and a handful of regular Mass-goers.

'What's the weather forecast?' I asked out of the corner of my mouth, in the best priestly manner.

'I am not worried, Father Neil. God looks after His own.'

'Whoever *they* are.'

'You are coming on the boat trip afterwards, Father Neil?'

'No, Father.'

'You are a stiff-necked curate and no mistake.'

I rubbed my neck where it still hurt. 'Put that down to your driving,' I said.

'Do you want me to think of you as a gutless coward?'

'Yes, please.'

'Very well, lad,' he sighed, 'but do not say I didn't ask you before I made you.' He stamped his feet. 'Now, where is the blessèd hearse?'

I told him I'd heard the car drive up a couple of minutes before.

Mr. Freddie Williams came into view, his top hat under his arm. He advanced in front of only two

155

pallbearers who were carrying the Big Sack. On a stretcher.

'What in the name of God . . .' Fr. Duddleswell groaned. 'Is that the body or a hundredweight of coal?'

Mr. Williams motioned his men to stop for the blessing and I handed Fr. Duddleswell the sprinkler.

'I am not sure,' he whispered, 'if 'tis dead or merely wounded.'

He sprinkled the Sack with Holy Water in the form of a cross and while the pallbearers proceeded up the centre aisle he made signs to Mr. Williams that he wanted a word.

'Why no coffin, Freddie?'

'You know it's not needed for a burial at sea, Father.'

'Surely you could have boxed him up decent, like, for the Requiem Mass.'

'Father,' Mr. Williams pointed out, 'you gave me strict orders to economize in every possible way.'

Fr. Duddleswell put on a grieved expression. 'You could have loaned me a coffin for an hour or two.'

Mr. Williams looked shocked. 'We don't hire them out, Father. It's not hygienic, you know. I mean to say, how would *you* like it?'

He followed his men up the centre aisle to where the catafalque, surrounded by six big yellow candles, stood in front of the High Altar.

'Only two pallbearers, Father,' I said softly, 'and you don't have to pay a grave-digger. That's what I call economy.'

'But what Christian was ever buried without a coffin, tell me that.'

'Jesus, Father?'

He gave me one of his special looks. As we walked round the catafalque to begin the Mass, he said, 'God Almighty, this one looks like something out of Tutankhamun's tomb.'

* * *

We travelled in one hearse to the docks. The two pallbearers were in front. The rest of us sat in the back around the Sack.

'Sorry it's a bit cramped,' Mr. Williams said.

'There'll be a bit more room on the way back,' I said.

Mr. Williams appreciated that. 'You *are* a cheerful lad, I like that happy approach. Do you know, I can't recruit young chaps like you any more.'

'No?'

He shook his head sadly. 'They've got this funny idea that somehow the job is morbid. I can't think why. I employed a lad once who even had ideas about jogging trade along.'

'How exactly?'

'Half-price for pensioners. I ask you, a hearse isn't exactly a bus, is it?'

'Your customers only travel one way, you mean.'

'You *are* a cheerful lad.'

Fr. Duddleswell was sniffing suspiciously in the direction of the Sack. 'What is this funny smell in here, Freddie?'

'Only my shaving lotion, Father. My Doris bought it me for Christmas.'

' 'Tis a wonder your beard manages to grow again after a dose of that.'

'It must help a lot in your job, Mr. Williams,' I said.

He confirmed it with a nod. 'Especially at cremations when the wind's strong.'

'Freddie,' Fr. Duddleswell said, 'I hope you have read up about burials at sea.'

'I was in the Forces during the War, you know.'

'The Navy, Mr. Williams?'

'The Army Catering Corps.'

'How does that help, Freddie?' Fr. Duddleswell asked.

'I don't suppose it does, really.' He lifted his eyebrows optimistically. 'Anyway, dropping a body in the sea can't be so different from dropping it in the ground, can it?'

'He'll get a bit wet, of course, Mr. Williams.'

'I do *like* that happy approach,' Mr. Williams said glumly.

The wharf was desolate. Cranes and derricks cobwebbed in mist. Overhead, gulls wheeling and crying in search of food. In the air, a sickening smell of diesel oil and dead fish.

M.S.C. *Edding* had a black hull and a red and black funnel. Its Captain was there to greet us with his two mates.

'Welcome aboard, Padre,' the Skipper said to Fr. Duddleswell.

'Thank you kindly. 'Tis always a quiet sea for the funeral barge, or so they say.'

'Oh, yes?' The Skipper didn't seem too sure. 'No need for wreaths, at any rate. Plenty of white flowers in the fishermen's garden today.'

'Make yourselves comfortable, gentlemen,' one mate said.

He gave no indication how this could be done and there was no cover that I could see.

The Sack was placed on a kind of platform at the stern, strapped down with leather thongs and covered by a Union Jack which rose and fell in the wind.

As soon as the pallbearers had disembarked, the Skipper said, 'We'd better cast off if we want to be back by dark.'

There was barely a blink of sunshine all day. As soon as the boat moved off, we felt the cold steel of the wind run us through.

Fr. Duddleswell, understating the case, said, ' 'Tis not such a very soft day, after all. There is a little breeze of wind hereabouts, that's for sure.'

The first part of the voyage was not too bad. Mr. Williams pointed out a few familiar landmarks.

158

From then on, it was one long, lost battle with the elements.

The three of us huddled together at the rail for comfort. 'It's a bit chilly, you know,' Mr. Williams commented unnecessarily.

'Me nose,' Fr. Duddleswell confessed, 'is as icy as a marble altar.'

'My teeth,' I said, 'are going like a sewing machine.'

Mr. Williams gulped in a heroic draught of ozone. 'But the air's nice.' Another gulp that nearly drowned him. 'Isn't it nice?'

'Better than your shaving lotion, Freddie, that's for sure.'

A gust of wind blew Mr. Williams' topper off and it went from him like a bullet. We watched the gulls inspect it before they squawked and lifted in disappointment.

'Oh dear, oh dear,' the undertaker said, as if he'd just lost a friend. 'I'll have to charge that up to St. Jude's, you know.'

I shouted in sympathy but the wind rammed the words back down my throat.

'My Doris was very fond of that hat. She often used it for a tea cosy. Very wrong of her, I realize that.'

The farther up the estuary we sailed, the shaggier the water, the more snarling the wind. A faint yellow glow in the clouds above was the only sign of where the sun was.

We reached the last of the docks at Tilbury, opposite Gravesend. By then, I had lost all sense of time. It was as if the clock inside my head had frozen up. Here the Thames was nearly half a mile across and still widening in the last northward reach.

Below Gravesend, I glimpsed factories and mills and, after them, tidal marshes flanking the river. The grey-brown estuary was opening even more alarmingly. Huge ships belching black smoke seemed to come too near us and waves from them pounded the hull of our pitifully small craft like blows from a huge hammer.

On high ground on the north shore, oil refineries, cement works, paper mills and power stations appeared out of the mist. No need now, I felt, to keep promising myself that one day I would read Dante's *Inferno*.

At this point, only the cry of gulls, curlews and wild geese winging above us, and on our flanks mud flats, misty saltings and an old sea wall overlooked by an occasional wooden shack. Then the grey arms of the land ceased to shield us. Ahead was nothing but the North Sea. Next stop, Holland.

Almost at once, the prow of the boat took off like an aeroplane for about twenty feet before plummeting down. Sometimes I felt as though I was gazing down a thousand foot ravine and sometimes as though my head was craned to watch a high-wire artist, without a safety net, balancing crazily before a fall.

I leaned over the rail and started to heave, though at first nothing came.

I heard Fr. Duddleswell say, 'I told him not to have any breakfast. What doesn't go down, cannot come up. I told him.' And I felt him pat my back.

'My Doris,' Mr. Williams said, 'gave me a packed lunch but I couldn't eat that even on land.'

'The only time I ever tried eating on board boat, Freddie, there was more on me plate after than before.'

That was more than enough. I threw up. The centre of my spinning skull was anaesthetized. The rest of my anatomy became fluid. The geezer began in my toes, was swollen into a flood at my stomach and sped up me until it all gushed out. With each monumental heave, I wondered where all the stuff was coming from. I must have lost several pounds. Having parted with so much ballast, would the wind lift me off deck and deposit me in the deep? Not that I cared.

Eventually, my convulsions ceased. As I turned about, Mr. Williams said kindly, 'How are you, lad?'

'Inside-out.'

'I do like that happy approach in adversity,' he said. 'Mind you, Driscoll's the lucky one. He was dead when he came on board.'

Fr. Duddleswell came close to shout in my ear. 'I am mightily afraid for the corpse, Father Neil.' I nodded to show I'd heard. 'In case 'tis sea-sick. Promise me one thing.' I nodded again. 'After the committal, drop me in the briny. No life-jacket, mind.'

The Skipper, seeing we were not dressed for the part, invited us to the bridge house.

We battled our way there with buckling knees. Across the deck, water seethed to and fro like driven snow.

My legs were like a baby's, the water from my eyes had frozen so my cheeks were as brittle as glass. I now knew why the last book of the Bible promises the Blessèd that in Paradise there will be no more sea.

The bridge house was more like a chicken coop. Everything was in disarray: sextant, maps, weather charts. The radio was spluttering and the wind came whistling through large cracks in the woodwork. The Skipper's pipe didn't help. It was wedged in his mouth and the bowl of it gave off thick black smoke like a ship's funnel.

The Skipper pointed through his home-made fog to a cupboard where oil skins were stored. 'Get yourselves kitted out.' he said.

We went through them till we found something that more or less fitted.

'How do I look?' Fr. Duddleswell wanted to know.

'Like something out of the Wizard of Oz,' I said.

Once, I went outside for a breath of fresh air. When I returned, Mr. Williams and Fr. Duddleswell were leaning against each other on a bench. When I opened the door and the wind struck him, Fr. Duddleswell lifted his cowelled head pathetically from between his knees.

'I feel giddy-headed as a woman, Father Neil.'

'Is it that bad?'

He nodded. 'Me face must be white as a duck's something or other.'

I patted his cheek for him.

'I cannot be dying, Father Neil, because God has promised me a happy death.' He tried to joke some more but his great spirit was not up to it. He ended by clasping my shaking hands in his. Then down with his head again.

The throb of the engines and the thud of the waves on the hull hurt my ears. The steep rise and fall of the rolling boat meant a continuously changing pattern of boat-sea, sea, sea—boat, boat—sky, sky. And then the same pattern in reverse as the stomach dropped in advance of the rest of the body which promptly raced to catch up.

There was nothing left but prayer and abandonment to divine providence, especially after I heard the Skipper curse and say, 'A force 8 gale on the way. Christalmighty.'

Mr. Williams, too, had heard the message over the radio. 'I don't suppose I could contact my Doris,' he asked.

The Skipper looked at him sympathetically. 'Not unless you've got a very loud voice.'

I was beyond laughter and tears, time and space, good and evil, life and death. There was no God, no family or friends, no reality. Nirvana!

After incalculable ages, the Skipper tersely summed up the situation: 'We're beyond our limits.' And he handed over to his mate.

Fr. Duddleswell rose to his feet and struggled to get his ritual out of his overcoat pocket. The three of us hung on to one another and, stung by the spray, staggered to the stern.

The Skipper cupped his hands and yelled, 'We'll

162

make this short, shall we?' He wrapped a rope around each of us and tied us to the white and rusted rail with a long lead to prevent us being whisked overboard.

Fr. Duddleswell, with frozen fingers, opened his book. The pages flapped wildly like birds in their last agony. Eventually, he found the scripture passage he had chosen: Mark's Gospel, the end of chapter four.

His lips moved but no sound reached me. Looking over his shoulder, I saw the words:

'And there arose a great storm of wind, and the waves beat into the ship so that the ship was filled. And Jesus was in the hinder part of the ship, sleeping upon a pillow; and they awake him, and say to him: Master, doth it not concern thee that we perish? And rising up, he rebuked the wind and said to the sea: Pease be still.'

I glanced sideways at Fr. Duddleswell. We had topped a crest and were about to plunge to the depths. I could tell he had reached the words, 'Peace be still.' He lifted his head and said again, 'Peace be still,' as if it was an imprecation for now and he half-hoped his prayer would work a miracle. His head then dropped and I found he had placed the book in my hands. Looking like some animated garden gnome, he was *en route* to the rail to unload.

The Skipper gestured to the sky as if to say the light was fading fast and he volunteered to complete the ceremony for us. I declined the offer.

After five minutes, Fr. Duddleswell returned, trailing the umbilical cord that bound him to the rail, and finished the Gospel reading with the words, 'Who is this (thinkest thou) that both the wind and sea obey him?' The *De Profundis* followed and a brief committal prayer.

The Skipper and a member of the crew untied the leather straps. One end of the platform was tilted and the large canvas bag slipped under the flag and over the side as Fr. Duddleswell was saying, 'I commit the body of Thy servant James unto the deep and his soul into Thy keeping, O merciful God.'

With a last envious glance in the direction of the corpse, I joined in praying, 'May his soul and the souls of all the faithful departed rest in peace.'

'Now that 'tis all over,' Fr. Duddleswell cried, 'I am about to follow the example of Our Blessed Lord and get some shut-eye.'

The heavy stamping of the Skipper demonstrated that things were far from over. He was leaning widely across the rail shouting angrily at his mate and pointing towards the foam.

I looked over and saw that the canvas bag, instead of sinking, was floating like a wreath. I tugged Fr. Duddleswell to the side.

' 'Tis not fair,' he groaned, 'the departed is not living up to his name.'

'Christ,' the Skipper said to his mate, 'the corpse looks as if it's got water wings. Jack, tell Tony to start circling while I get the grappling hook.' He turned on us landlubbers. 'Who the hell weighted that body down?'

'Me, sir,' Mr. Williams admitted.

'What did you use, a threepenny bit?'

'My old army belt.'

'Another economy,' I said to Fr. Duddleswell.

'You . . .' the Skipper said, 'you are a very silly man.'

'That is perfectly justified from your point of view,' Mr. Williams conceded. 'But, believe me, we're always willing to learn at the Co-op.'

The next forty-five minutes were worse than what had gone before. The tug, dipping and rolling in the heavy sea, circled the Sack repeatedly until the Skipper and his mate were able to get the grappling hook in it and haul it aboard.

The Skipper was afraid, apparently, that the corpse would be washed ashore or picked up by another boat. As a result, a bather on a quiet beach might suffer a heart attack and Scotland Yard launch a murder hunt.

Naturally, this is a free translation of what the Skipper actually said.

He ordered his mate to fetch some chains. 'Thirty quid,' he yelled, 'these chains cost me and *I'm* not footing the bill.'

'Of course not,' Mr. Williams said understandingly, 'why should you?'

Down goes Fr. Duddleswell's profit margin another peg, I thought.

At length, the corpse was trussed up and weighed down. 'Rest in peace,' Fr. Duddleswell pleaded, as the body was dropped overboard for the second time. '*Please* rest in peace.'

This time, James Driscoll did the decent thing and sank as he was supposed to do.

'Thank you kindly, God,' I heard Fr. Duddleswell say.

The return journey was not so bad. Had we not already given our all and more to the sea?

I sat next to Fr. Duddleswell on the bench in the bridge house and closed my eyes. I did not think a thought or utter a word. From time to time, I may even have dozed off.

It was pitch dark when we docked. I got to my feet. They felt like someone else's borrowed for the occasion. Someone shook my hand. A voice that sounded vaguely like the Skipper's said, 'Never again.'

I was bundled into a car and it moved off. I wasn't sure who was driving. If we crashed, did it matter? You don't have to face a firing squad like the young Dostoievsky to grasp the futility of all things human.

'Will you come in, Freddie?'

'Just for a minute, Father.'

'They're back,' I heard Mrs. Pring say as we walked in, frozen.

Dr. Daley was sitting by the fireside, sipping away.

Seeing him there, Fr. Duddleswell said, 'Be with you in the turn of me hand, Donal.'

'God, Charles,' Dr. Daley exclaimed, 'I'll light my next fag off the tip of your nose.'

Mr. Williams gave Fr. Duddleswell an envelope. 'The bill, Father.' A shivering hand took it. 'I've altered it to £335.'

'But we agreed three hundred.'

'Thirty pounds for the chain, Father.'

'And?'

'Five for my hat.'

Fr. Duddleswell rubbed his hands together. 'Mrs. Pring, will you pile some more turf on that fire and give it a good blow.' To Mr. Williams: 'I will write you a cheque tomorrow when this'—he held up his right arm—'is thawed out.'

'The dividend stamps are in the envelope too.'

'Fine, Freddie, fine.'

'To the value of £40.'

That shook him. 'Only *forty*?'

'That's all the Co-op charged for the funeral,' Mr. Williams explained. 'Be fair, Father. You can't expect divi stamps for the hire of a tug.'

'Nor for a top hat,' I said. For some reason, it made me feel much better.

'You *are* a cheerful lad,' Mr. Williams said. 'Now I'm off home to my Doris. If I'm late she'll tell all the neighbours I've drowned, and when I turn up, she'll blame me for ruining her story.'

'Give her my love, Mr. Williams,' I said.

He stopped by the door, all sad. 'It's hard enough giving her mine, Father.'

As Mrs. Pring went to show him out, she winked at Fr. Duddleswell. 'Thanks for the stamps, all the same.'

Fr. Duddleswell madly fanned the fire with his hat, muttering that the fireside is the only safe port and never would he be able to take a tub again without recalling this cantankerous day.

'Dear, dear, dear, Charles,' Dr. Daley said 'you look as full of misery as an empty bottle. Shall I call a priest to read over you?' No answer. 'I don't suppose I can pour you a stiff'un.'

'You can. It will suit me condition.'

'You *are* a wild card, Charles. The trip's done you good, I can see.'

'You'll catch Daley's Disease,' I said.

'Turn your back if you are scandalized, Father Neil. I have a chill on me that is not meagre.' He hunched his shoulders like a cat. 'Jasus, that wind would have skinned a dogfish.'

'Ah, it's well for you, Charles, that the corpse didn't have you killed. Still, you did your duty by him as you saw it.'

'That I did. I was ordained to consign Catholics to eternity and I would do it again any day of the week.' He swigged his drink. 'And you, Father Neil?'

I hugged a blanket Mrs. Pring had provided. 'Any day of the week, Father. Except Sunday to Saturday inclusive.'

'Remind me to tell Mrs. Pring,' he said, 'I forbid her to shop at the Co-op in future.'

'Has the whiskey lessened the shock for you?' Dr. Daley asked.

Fr. Duddleswell took a deep breath. 'I am over the worst of it by now.'

'Indeed you are not.'

'What d'you mean, Donal?'

'I was at the Seamen's Home at midday today and Captain Kent asked me to give you the bad newses.'

'Tell it me all, straight *and* crooked.'

'Driscoll's insurance company went broke forty years ago.'

'God help us. That's the crookedest thing I ever did hear.'

'God help us say I also.' Dr. Daley raised his glass for a toast. 'Cheers to the divil.'

'I will drink to that, Donal. He has buffeted me all over today like Billy Buzzle's goat.'

'No matter, Charles. Driscoll was one of your flock, however wayward, and you owed it him to have him buried according to his heart's wish.'

'True.'

The telephone rang. Fr. Duddleswell answered it and handed it to me.

I spoke up for Fr. Duddleswell's benefit. 'Fr. Blundell, the curate of Shelwell . . . Yes, Father, I did ring you a few days ago about a James Driscoll . . . Really? His name wasn't Driscoll at all?'

'Oh?' Fr. Duddleswell said.

'But Dris*cott*.'

'Oh?'

'What did you say? When you asked him if he wanted you to hear his confession, he hit you over the head with a what? . . . A bottle? Was he drunk? . . . Perfectly sober.'

Dr. Daley said, 'That fits.'

'You mean,' I said down the phone, 'he wasn't a Catholic at all but a *what*?'

Dr. Daley was shrinking in his chair. 'An Orangeman. He did have a brogue of a sort, you see.'

I thanked Fr. Blundell and said goodbye.

Fr. Duddleswell was in a daze. 'You may as well wash me, I am done for.' He looked up. 'Not Green Irish at all.'

'A Prod,' Dr. Daley said.

'Jasus, 'tis meself not Pinkerton who is guilty of body-snatching. Fancy, burying an Orange Irish.' He was shaking all over again. ' 'Tis bad enough having to love your enemies, without risking your bloody life dropping 'em in the ocean during a storm.'

'Dear, dear, dear,' was all Dr. Daley could manage.

'Imagine, Donal. The first pap he sucked was

hatred of papists. His one ambition to silence the harp of Old Ireland.'

'God rest him,' I said.

'Indeed, Father Neil. God rest him. The dead are all brothers. They even look alike.' Yet still his mind turned to the theological gravity of the situation. 'Mark you, Father Neil, there was no sin on our part. We did not know he was not one of us when we buried him.'

'I think you're very lucky, Father.'

'How so?' he said, as he picked up the phone and dialled.

'You might have buried him in consecrated ground. Then you would have had the bother of getting him exhumed and planted where he belonged.'

He smiled. 'You are a great wit, you know that, Father Neil.' He got his connection.

'Jack Drabble?' he said. 'Good. That headstone you are doing for me. I've changed me mind about the inscription. Instead of "Rest In Peace", I'd like you to put "God Bless Our Pope".'

Nine

THE PIOUS PRISONER

Mrs. Nelly Grourke, a widow in her mid-sixties, lived in a sixth-floor Council flat with a budgie and a tabby cat. 'A lovely lady,' was all Fr. Duddleswell had told me about her. 'She has two five shilling Masses said for the Holy Souls each week.'

After Benediction one Sunday evening, she asked

me to visit her as a matter of urgency, so I fixed up to have tea with her the next day.

At four, she drew back the latch to let me in. A slight, bowed woman was Mrs. Grourke, always in black from her shoes to her shawl and lace mantilla. A kind of professional widow.

'Come in, Father dear,' she whispered in a soft, attractive brogue, 'it is an honour you are doing us.'

She dipped her fingers in the Holy Water stoup by the door and brushed them against my fingers. From her left hand dangled a large olive-wood rosary.

Her modest well-kept living room was like a shrine. There were statues of the Sacred Heart, Our Lady of Lourdes and Sainte Thérèse of Lisieux on separate shelves, each with a red votive lamp burning in front of it.

On the wall there was a picture of Our Lady of Sorrows. It seemed to me that Mrs. Grourke was not unlike the figure of Our Lady in the painting: the same grey hair, intelligent eyes and fine distinguished nose.

'It's my boy, Father dear.'

I nodded, not sure what her tone denoted.

'I was into my forties when he came along. And after all that time, he was born six weeks premature, if you would believe that. A tiny wee mite he was, so my husband, God rest him, and I called him Zachary. Like the feller in the Gospel who was so small he had to climb a sycamore tree to see our Blessèd Saviour.'

'A nice name,' I said.

'And a nice lad, too.'

From a table beside her, she picked up a photo of a young man with sleek black hair parted in the middle, admired and kissed it. 'A nice boy, Father dear, a sweet boy.'

'He looks it,' I acknowleged, not able to see too well in the February half-light.

'It warms my widow's heart to hear you say that, Father dear.'

'Is he married, Mrs. Grourke?'

'Married?' The thought had never struck her before. 'But he's only twenty-four years old.'

I had obviously put my foot in it. 'He seems so mature for his age,' I said.

'Indeed, but with his entire life ahead of him, why should he plunge headlong into matrimony?'

'Does he live with you?' Mrs. Grourke had said, 'It is an honour you are doing *us*.'

She touched her heart. 'I have him locked in here. All the time.'

'Where's he living, Mrs. Grourke?' I pointed to her chest. 'Apart from in there, I mean.'

'At the moment, my Zachary is living in Wormwood Scrubs.'

I knew Wormwood Scrubs was a prison but I wasn't sure if it was a district as well like Dartmoor and Brixton.

'Oh, yes,' I said non-committally, 'does he, um, like it there?'

'He is not a Carthusian, Father dear. No, he is lonely as the big bead between two decades of the rosary.'

Thinking he might be in a bed-sitter, I said, 'A warder, Mrs. Grourke?'

'A prisoner, Father dear.'

'I *am* sorry,' I said.

'That's all right. I know you didn't mean to give offence.'

I chose my words even more carefully. 'What is he doing there, Mrs. Grourke?'

'Six months, Father dear.'

I loved old Mrs. Nelly Grourke. She was a daily communicant and, though she never seemed to speak to anybody in the parish, she spread about her an atmosphere of kindness and good will. All the same, my guess was that Zachary had had a long experience of being locked up. His mother's story didn't bear this out.

Zachary dealt in cars. Buying and selling. From the age of ten, soon after his father died, he had shown an interest. He left school at fourteen and now, ten years later, he was running a nationwide business.

'My Zachary is always wanting to buy me a grand house in the suburbs, Father dear, but I operate better here.' She explained what she meant by 'operate'. 'Being near my church, you see that. I was wed here and my Zachary was dipped in the Holy Well here.'

As she toasted muffins and served tea, I fell to wondering how such a pious youth as Zachary came to be behind bars.

She read my thoughts. 'Jesus was condemned and crucified though *He* was perfectly innocent, isn't that so, Father dear?'

'He was.'

'My boy, too, is as honest as the day is long.' Not an apt image for an early afternoon in winter. 'As guiltless as Father Duddleswell himself.'

'Uh huh. How, then, did Zachary . . .'

'Get into trouble?'

'Um, yes.'

'A frame-up, Father dear.' That didn't sound quite right coming from Mrs. Grourke, nor did the rest. 'Two filthy crooks gave false testimony.'

The parallel with Jesus was closer than I'd thought.

'Wait a little minute till I tell you.' She brushed a tear away. 'They said my sweet darling boy had broken into their car.'

'Sad, sad,' I murmured.

'My Zachary is in good circumstances. He doesn't need to break into cars these days, Father dear. He told me *on his Catholic's honour* he did not break into those cars.'

'It's a scandal,' I said sympathetically.

'They just wanted to get him striped. Behind bars,

that is. But with full remission for good conduct, he will be out in less than a month.'

'Would you like me to see him after he comes out?'

'*Before,* Father dear. I'd like the prison authorities to see my Zachary has a holy priest for a friend.'

'I don't know about the "holy" bit,' I said modestly.

'Tell my boy that every day I am reciting his favourite hymn here before the Virgin's statue.'

'Which hymn is that?'

'*Sweet Saviour Bless Us,* Father dear.'

'One of my favourites, too, Mrs. Grourke.'

'Who wrote it?'

'Faber, I think.'

'Ah yes, Father Frederick Faber. Beautiful hymn. Be sure to tell my Zachary I bless the very year the writer of that hymn was born. And please don't breathe a word of this to Father Duddleswell.'

'No?'

'My Zachary was once his favourite altar server and Father Duddleswell taught him all he knows. It might break his priestly heart.'

'Mustn't risk that,' I said.

'There was a time,' Mrs. Grourke went on, 'when my Zachary was tempted by Satan and a brand new car. Thank the dear Lord, Father Duddleswell spoke up for him.'

I lowered my gaze. 'A fine priest in many ways.'

'Then do not break his lovely heart.'

'I'll go next Sunday afternoon, Mrs. Grourke.'

'Tomorrow, Father dear. It's not a regular visiting day, that I know, but they're bound to let a holy priest in, are they not?'

'I hope so.'

She went to the sideboard, took two half-crowns out of a chipped china bowl and handed them to me. 'Five shillings for a Mass for my Zachary's imminent release from the nick, Father dear.'

'Thank you,' I stammered, embarrassed at having to take the widow's mite.

'When you get to the Scrubs, Father dear, be sure to ask for Emilio Zaccharone.'

I blinked.

'He changed his name by deed-poll, you see that, Father dear.'

Getting to see Zachary out of hours meant not only a check of my credentials but a body-search as well.

They flipped through my breviary to make sure it wasn't hollow and examined the spine, I presumed, for a file. They even gave me a receipt for my rosary and held on to it till I left.

If Zachary was such a sweet, good boy, why all this fuss? There's more to him, I thought, than his poor old mother is aware of.

I had never been inside a prison before and I looked forward to it very much. My expectation was heightened by my reading of Dostoievsky. I had worked my way laboriously through *Crime And Punishment*, ten pages at a stretch, and was currently in the middle of his prison experiences in *The House of The Dead*.

An extraordinary world was opened up to me. It was peopled, perversely it seemed to me at first, with honest crooks and villainous saints and some characters ten times life-size. On reflection, very like the parish of St. Jude's. There a bookie fell madly in love with a pig, a rich respectable Catholic widow was a kleptomaniac, a former convict was the only person I could entirely trust and Fr. Duddleswell was . . . Fr. Duddleswell. I was so 'wised up' by now, I wouldn't have been too surprised if Mrs. Pring turned out to be a call-girl.

I was led through four enormous iron gates, each of which had to be unlocked and clanged to before the warder accompanying me and I could proceed. The place reminded me of the seminary.

Emilio Zaccarone sat opposite me behind a small-meshed grill. Under his black greasy hair, the roots and first two inches of which were ginger, was an unmistably Irish, freckled face.

'Thanks for coming, Father.' The accent was London, not Irish except in snatches, and certainly not in keeping with his assumed name.

I gestured around me. 'What's it like in here, Emilio?'

'Like a prison.'

'Not as nice as home.'

'Wouldn't go so far as to say that.'

I gave Emilio his mother's message about the hymn and repeated her tribute to its author.

'Nice, real nice. Tell her from me, I'll recite that hymn for her every day and twice on Saturday, Our Lady's day.'

When the warder on duty momentarily turned his eyes away, Zachary slipped a card under the grill. There was only a fraction of an inch of space. Nothing thicker would have made it.

I was about to protest that this was against regulations when I saw he had handed me a holy picture.

'For my mum,' he whispered. 'In your book with it, Father. Quick, for God's sake.'

Before putting it into my breviary, I just had time to notice that it was a picture of Pope Pius XII, his aquiline face in profile. He was clad in scarlet with a white skull cap and his hands were joined in prayer. Above his head the papal insignia and, at the bottom, in crude handwriting, 'Thou art Peter and upon this Rock I will build my Church.'

'Your mother will like that,' I said softly. 'Would you like absolution?'

'Please, Father.'

'Right, Emilio, you can make your confession without the warder overhearing.'

'Just absolution will do, Father. No confession.'

'I can't give you absolution unless you confess your sins.'

175

'Sins?' he asked hoarsely. 'What sort of facilities for sins do you think they provide us with here?'

I declined to speculate. 'I'll give you a blessing.'

'Thank you kindly, Father.' And he bowed his head.

Before I left, Emilio said:

'Tell my mother to remember me and Dev in her prayers.'

'Mr. de Valera?'

'Yeah. A family joke. I think he's some sort of Irish geezer. My mother's potty about him.'

When I gave Mrs. Grourke the messages, she sat gazing at the picture of Pius XII and said, 'God bless him,' whether referring to his Holiness or Zachary or Mr. de Valera I could not tell.

The middle-aged gentleman was wearing a fawn raincoat and fingering a brown trilby like a rosary. As soon as he entered the sacristy after Sunday's nine o'clock Mass I knew it meant trouble.

I had removed my vestments and the altar server was extinguishing the candles when the stranger flashed his identification in front of my nose.

'Scotland Yard. Is there somewhere a bit more private, sir?'

In my room, he introduced himself. 'Detective Sergeant Chinnery of C.I.D. You, sir, I gather are Father . . .'

'Neil Boyd,' I said, offering him a chair. I hadn't the slightest doubt he had come about Emilio.

'The church notice board says the priest in charge is a Father Duddleswell.'

'He has nothing to do with it.'

He stared at me. 'With what, sir?'

'With whatever you're going to say.'

'What *am* I going to say, sir?'

'I don't know.'

'You only know he's innocent of what I'm going to say.'

'Yes.'

He looked at me coldly as he took out his notebook. 'Have you by any chance seen today's papers, sir?'

'No.'

'Or listened to the wireless?'

I shook my head. 'I've been saying Mass all morning.'

'Good. It's better that way. For everyone concerned.'

I was on the point of asking what this was all about when it flashed through my mind that, in films, guilty people always said that. I decided to act as if this was a friendly call. The act didn't last long.

'Emilio Zaccharone,' he began, testing me. 'Ah, I see the name means something to you, sir.'

'Well, yes. I've met him. Once.'

'Last Tuesday afternoon between three and three-thirty'

'Wormwood Scrubs.'

'You knew I'd come about Zaccharone, didn't you, sir?'

'Yes.'

'Even though today you've not read a paper or listened to the radio.'

'That's right.'

'Can you explain this?'

'Sixth sense, Officer.'

'You're psychic?'

'No, Sergeant, just inclined to get into a fix.'

He nodded as if to signify he didn't believe a word I said.

'He hasn't escaped, has he, Sergeant? He's not dead?'

Detective Sergeant Chinnery lifted his head like a patient ox from his notebook. '*I* ask the questions, sir.'

'I'm sorry.'

'But I do not know the answers,' he admitted, 'and that's why I'm here.'

Odd, I thought. If he doesn't know whether Emilio has escaped or not, is alive or not, why doesn't he call Wormwood Scrubs and ask them to look in his cell? They'd tell an officer from Scotland Yard, surely. Why is he interrogating me?

I hadn't read my Dostoievsky for nothing. Perhaps this plausible chap in my chair wasn't from Scotland Yard. I'd better answer cagily.

But if he *was* genuine, my caginess would make matters worse for me, especially if Emilio had done something silly in prison like killing a warder. Besides, the Sergeant knew too much about me already to be an imposter, even the date and duration of my visit to Wormwood Scrubs.

'When you visited Zaccarone on Tuesday, sir, did you pass him anything? Metal objects, for instance?'

'He has killed someone,' I blurted out.

'Has he, sir?'

'Hasn't he?'

'Not to my knowledge. Not recently anyway.' He allowed himself a smile. 'Answer my questions, please.'

'No metal objects.'

'Wax or anything like that?'

'Wax what?'

'Just wax.'

'Sergeant, I couldn't pass him anything. There was a grill between us and a warder was on guard.'

'Did you convey any messages to him?'

'No. Well—'

'Yes, sir.' He looked up. 'Details, insignificant to you, could be important.'

'I told him his mother was praying for him.'

'That's nice, sir. Did Zaccharone mention, um, weightier matters?'

'He didn't make his confession, Officer, if that's what you mean. And even if he did, I wouldn't be able to repeat it to you.'

'Understood, sir.'

'Not even to a judge.'

'Did he give you a message for anyone outside?'

178

I repeated Emilio's request to his mother to pray for him and Mr. de Valera.

He sucked the end of his pencil for a moment or two. 'Is Zaccharone an I.R.A. sympathizer, then?'

'He's alive,' I blurted out.

He shot up. 'Thank you, sir. But how do you know that?'

I hesitated. 'You just told me.'

'I did?'

'You said, *Is* he an I.R.A. sympathizer? not, *Was* he?'

He sank down again. 'That is very brilliant of you, sir.'

He put his pencil on his lap as if it were suddenly a burden too heavy to bear.

'Did Zaccharone, sir, give you the impression that some party or other was leaning on him?'

I felt like saying, Only his mother, but thought better of it. 'No.'

'The warders, perhaps? Members of his own Organization? A rival gang?' He must have seen a glazed look in my eyes. I certainly saw one in his. 'You only discussed . . . spiritual matters?'

'Yes.'

'Why did you have to go to Wormwood Scrubs to do that and by chance immediately before this . . . incident?'

'Incident?' He gave no clue as to his meaning. 'Sergeant, his mother is a devout Catholic, a daily communicant if you must know. She wanted me to persuade him on his release to go back home to live. But he prefers prison.'

'You didn't get the impression on the way to and from the Scrubs that you were being watched?'

'No. That's one thing I am sure of.'

'Thank you, sir. You've been most helpful.'

'*Have* I?'

'Yes, sir. You've eliminated one suspect from our enquiry.' He put his notebook away and stood up. 'You're in the clear. I'd be grateful if you kept this

179

to yourself. This investigation has been instigated at the highest level.'

As he was leaving, Chinnery suddenly faced me. 'So you've no idea where Zaccharone is?'

It was clever. A last question when you are relaxed, thinking it's all over. Fortunately, I had nothing to hide.

'Isn't he in prison?' I asked with deliberate naivety, knowing I was safe.

'This job isn't easy, you know, sir.'

'His mother will want to know. What's happened to him?'

'What's happened to him?' As the Detective Sergeant climbed wearily into his car, he called over his shoulder, 'I'd waste a lot of coppers to know the answer to that, sir.'

At lunch, Fr. Duddleswell asked me if I'd read about Nelly Grourke's son in the paper.

'He's in it, is he?' I said, to put him off the scent.

'At six last night, he was in a special security wing. At six-thirty, his cell was empty.'

'The lock was picked?'

Fr. Duddleswell shook his head. 'That's the strange thing. *And* the door was locked after him.'

'Tidy,' I said.

'According to the paper, the Home Office has ordered an enquiry.'

'The highest authority,' I gasped.

'Indeed. It seems Zach Grourke needed four keys to get out of that prison.'

'And his mother says he's such a good boy.'

'Ah, Father Neil,' he laughed, 'if the divil had a mother, she would say the same about *him*. But 'tis a strange business, all right.' He handed me the paper. 'Cast your eye over that.'

What I read explained why the C.I.D. man was so enigmatic. A journalist was questioning whether Emilio Zaccharone had really escaped at all. What motive could he have for engineering such a brilliant break-out when he was due for release in three weeks time?

One suggestion was that a rival gang had sprung him and killed him. But if so, why not rub him out in his cell? Why bother to take him with them? In any case, Zaccharone would have known it wasn't his Organization that had come to get him and put up a hell of a fight. Instead, complete silence at the time of his disappearance.

Zaccharone's Member of Parliament, it was reported, was tabling a motion asking the Home Secretary why it was that a constituent of his was no longer guaranteed safety in one of his Majesty's prisons.

When I'd finished the article, Fr. Duddleswell said, 'D'you know, Father Neil, Zach had a hundred wiles from his earliest years. At fifteen, he pinched a car from right outside the front door here and sold it.'

'A parishioner's?'

'Much worse.'

'Yours?'

He nodded. 'An Austin seven. His mother thrashed him within an inch of his life for that.'

'Did you report him?'

'I did, not realizing, of course, who had stolen it. I went to court. But for his dear mother's sake I pleaded for him, suggested he may only have been borrowing it.'

'Borrowing it!' I exclaimed, laughing.

'He got off with a warning.'

'He didn't show any gratitude, I suppose.'

'Oh, he did. He stole me another just like it.'

'What did you do with it?'

'The only decent thing I could in the circumstances. I had to drive it all through the War.'

'Mrs. Grourke did tell me once you were a lovely priest.'

'Well she might, the dear soul. I tutored that lad

181

of hers meself, made him an altar boy and used his services at the parish bazaar.'

Fr. Duddleswell then told me that Zachary had changed his name to get into the big time and, in spite of his thick headedness, made a fortune in the car-trade, buying and selling.

'He went straight, then, Father?'

'As straight as a pig's tail.'

Mrs. Pring burst in. 'Father Neil.'

'Yes, Mrs. P?'

'There's a gentleman to see you.'

'Tell him,' Fr. Duddleswell snapped, 'to wait till we have finished lunch.'

'He's from the Home Office,' Mrs. Pring said.

The visitor was a florid-looking man with salmon-hued cheeks. I took from him his fawn, officer's overcoat and bowler hat. Underneath, he had on a pepper and salt hacking jacket, fawn waistcoat and fawn bow-tie with pink spots.

He held out a card. 'Clark, Father. Jonathan Clark from the Home Office.' It was a smooth, pleasant voice. 'A very informal confabulation.'

'Is it about Emilio Zaccharone?'

He nodded. 'A bizarre business, *mon père*. I'm surprised you have such a keen interest in the chappie in question.'

I motioned him to be seated. 'I already told the Detective from Scotland Yard everything I know.'

'The Yard's been on to you?' As he sat, he lifted the tail of his jacket like a toilet top.

'Earlier this morning.'

'*Très curieux*,' he mused. He spoke the occasional French phrase with exaggerated Englishness as if to show what he thought of the foreigner across the water. 'What was this chappie's name?'

I told him.

'Chinnery. Mind if I use your blower.' I heard him mutter 'Whitehall 1212' as he dialled.

'Scotland Yard? Give me extension 3063. *Merci*

182

bien. . . . Jimmy, Johnny C. here. Listen, got anybody with you on the Scrubs job called Chinnery, Detective Sergeant? . . . No? Anybody of that name on attachment from one of the beastly provinces like Leeds or Nottingham? . . . You're sure? Thanks *beaucoup.* Be in touch.'

Mr. Clark turned to me. 'Describe him to me, Father.'

I tried without much success. Mr. Clark didn't seem very interested in a raincoat and trilby.

'Was he tall or short, Father?'

'Medium, I think.'

'About my size.'

'Yes.'

'But I'm short, five feet six.'

'Sorry. It's difficult to tell when you're sitting down.'

'But when I came in, I was standing up.' He waved his hand forgivingly. 'Did he wear glasses?'

'I'm not absolutely sure.'

'Not sure whether he did or didn't?'

'Both.'

'Any distinguishing features? Him, I mean. Birth marks? A moustache?'

'He might have had a moustache.'

'Might he?'

'A small one.'

'Barely visible.'

'That's right.' He was having me on, I could tell.

'Did he come by car, *mon capitaine*?'

I was glad to be able to assure him of one thing. 'Yes, he did.'

'Which make?'

'I didn't notice.'

'But you did see him get out of a car.'

'No, I saw him get into one. As he was leaving.'

'And you inferred he had arrived in the car he was leaving in. *Un esprit sage.* Colour of car?'

'No particular colour.'

His eyes opened wide. 'No . . . particular . . . colour.'

'I mean it wasn't bright yellow or anything like that.'

'That's useful,' he murmured. 'Car not bright yellow. You wouldn't have taken the number, I suppose.'

'Mr. Clark, I assumed he was a police officer and it *was* before breakfast.'

'Of course,' he said soothingly, 'of course. I understand because I haven't had breakfast myself yet.'

Detecting a trace of mockery in his tone, I said, 'I don't suppose you'd care to close your eyes for a few moments.'

'Why not, *mon ami*?' And he complied.

'Mr. Clark, you have been with me for about as long as I was with that bogus policeman. What have you learned about me?'

'All right,' he smiled. 'Do my best. You are approximately six feet two inches tall and weigh in the region of, say, um, 155 pounds. Good looking, black wavy hair parted on the right. Your eyes are brown with a green tint and you have a scar about one eighth of an inch at the right corner of your mouth.'

'Above or below the lip?' I asked, impressed.

'Above. You are left handed.'

'I am?'

I guessed firstly from your handshake. Apart from that, whenever there was an alternative you used your left. You closed the door with it. You took my coat with your left and transferred it to your right. You put my hat on the peg, you pushed the chair towards me with your left. In fact, the whole room is a left-handed room. A simple example, your pen and pencil are to the left of your blotter.'

'It's so easy,' I laughed, expecting him to stop.

'It's a Parker pen, by the way. It's strange,' he continued, 'how you can tell a left-handed person in a thousand ways, even from watching him clap at a concert. *Mais peiner toujours*. You don't drive.'

'I don't?'

'Unlikely. If you drove a car, you would probably have noticed the make and age of Chinnery's car and compared it with your own. Vanity and all that. Also, on your desk is a key ring. Only three keys. Plenty of room for a car key on it but there isn't one. Besides, your trousers give it away.'

I looked down them. 'They do?'

''Fraid so. They bulge alarmingly at the knees and the bottoms, I regret to say, have creases going in opposite directions, all of which indicates that you regularly ride a bicycle and wear cycle clips.'

'Correct,' I said.

'Shall I go on?'

'Please.'

'You don't smoke. Usually when I appear and say where I'm from, people take out a cigarette at once. In fact, three smokers who had given up the weed immediately resumed it on meeting me. No, you don't smoke. No nicotine on your fingers, no ash tray to hand, no fug in the atmosphere. I noticed immediately I entered the house that nobody smokes here. Of course, cigarette fumes do not prove you smoke. Could be visitors. The absence of such fumes proves you do *not* smoke. Finally, and this is quite common in non-smokers, you forgot to ask me if I'd care to smoke.'

'I'm sorry. Please go ahead.'

Without opening his eyes, he held up his left hand, splayed his fingers to show they were free of nicotine stains and said, 'You didn't notice, then?'

I sniffed as a substitute for no. A flash of inspiration. 'Chinnery didn't smoke.'

'Not while he was here. I realized that long ago. But that doesn't mean he's a non-smoker unless you happened to . . .'

'I didn't look at his fingers.'

'Why should you, *mon vieux*, before breakfast?' He went on, 'You use an electric razor. *Difficile à*

185

comprendre. Your eyesight is good. No glasses. No dents on the bridge of your nose. You look at things and people, focusing correctly. You don't use a table lamp, but'—a solicitous touch—'you won't be young for ever and I would advise . . .'

'Thanks,' I said.

'Though you have good eyesight and are serious-minded—'

'I am?'

'Not one light novel on your shelf, yesterday's *Times* on your window ledge next to Dostoievsky's *The House of the Dead*—not the best translation by the way—your radio tuned in to the Third Programme. In spite of this, you are not very observant and are easily duped.'

'How did you gather that?' I asked.

He smiled. 'All this combined with your housekeeper's protective attitude towards you, her saying, "You want *our* Father Neil", indicates strongly that you are simple, direct, truthful, vulnerable—and unlikely to provide me with any viable information.'

'But this is fantasic,' I cried. 'Please, that's quite enough.'

'Pity. *La leçon est seulement à moitié finie.* I was hoping to astound you with my detective powers. You are an anxious person, for instance.'

'I am.'

'Your clock and your wrist watch are both five minutes fast.'

'So I shouldn't be late for—' I broke off with a laugh.

Patting his thinning locks, he said, 'You are fortunate in that you won't go bald.'

'Consoling, but how can you tell at my age?'

'Your father there in your ordination photo has a thick mop and that's the one thing in which a son is sure to take after his father. Lately, you've put on quite a bit of weight.'

'I have but—?'

'Look at yourself in the photo next to your father.

But it was obvious to me *au premier coup d'œil.*
Your collar is making a red ridge under your chin
and you keep fingering the collar to ease the pressure.'

'I hadn't noticed.'

'No charge. But beware of acquiring mannerisms,
mon père. Bad as birthmarks. Make you too easy to
place. And, by the way, your hyacinths are badly in
need of watering.'

I begged him to open his eyes. 'You really learned
all that in a few seconds?'

He looked at me and blinked. 'Good God, no, I read
most of it in your file before I left the office.'

'You have a file on me?' I gasped.

He froze and bit his lip. 'You are also a trifle gul-
lible.'

'I'm sorry,' I said. 'There's a gentleman in this
house you really ought to meet.'

'I'd hate you to think I've been snooping. I honestly didn't realize I knew most of that stuff until
you started grilling me. It's a bit obscene, really.' He
straightened up. 'Enough of the party games and
back to business.'

'So, Mr. Clark, my last visitor was an imposter?'
He nodded. 'How did he know about my involve-
ment?'

'You *are* involved, then?'

That made my stomach jump and reminded me
that Jonathan Clark wasn't a vaudeville artist but
an official from the Home Office.

'All I meant was, how did he know I visited Zaccharone in Wormwood Scrubs?'

'A tip off from inside probably and then he or one
of his gang must have watched you go in and out
and trailed you.'

'Is he Zaccharone's enemy?'

Mr. Clark shrugged his shoulders. 'Sorry to use a
cliché, Father,' he said pleasantly, 'but *I'm* asking
the questions.'

The repetition of that phrase made me remember

again my resolution, 'Wise up'. How could I be sure this man was genuine and his predecessor an impostor? What if this one was the impostor? Or they were both impostors? At St. Jude's, everything was possible.

I gulped. '*You* wouldn't be an impostor, Mr. Clark.'

'Cross my heart,' he said, 'I'd tell you if I was.'

'May I see your identification, please?'

'I showed it to you once already.'

'So did he, the bogus detective.'

'Be my guest.'

He handed me his Home Office card again. It bore his photograph, his name and number and an official stamp.

'Satisfied?' he asked.

'I don't know. I've never seen one before.' Politely: 'It's not a forgery, is it?'

He snatched the card from me and examined it anxiously. 'Hope not. That's the only one the Home Office supplied me with.' He eased up. 'You're learning fast, *mon élève*. I've always thought myself that ninety-nine per cent of means of identification are of no use whatsoever.'

He dialled for me and before it had stopped ringing handed me the phone.

'Scotland Yard,' a woman's voice said. 'State your business, please.'

I asked for extension 3063 and was put through first to a secretary then to Chief Inspector James Bourne. Reluctant to speak to me until Mr. Clark had verified my predicament, he confirmed the authenticity of my visitor. 'Which doesn't mean, sir,' he said with a laugh, 'that you should trust him an inch.'

'For future reference,' Mr. Clark said afterwards, pointing to his left eyebrow. 'I have a tiny mole, invisible to the naked eye, right here.'

I was leaning forward to examine it before I realized it was meant as a joke.

'This Chinnery chappie left you no address where you could contact him?'

'No. Would you like to examine the room for fingerprints?'

'Why should I do that, why not go straight to your fingers?'

'Perhaps this bogus policeman left *his* fingerprints somewhere.'

'Only the genuine article do that. Bet he never even opened the door for himself.'

'He didn't,' I admitted.

'Neither did I, come to that,' he said, smiling. 'Tell me one thing, Father. Is that plump priest who nearly jumped out of his skin at the table a friend of yours?'

'*Very*. In an unfriendly sort of way.'

He grinned. 'I've got a boss like that. Why didn't you tell *him* about the Scrubs or the visit from Scotland Yard?'

'How do you know I didn't?'

'From the look he gave you I suggest that *Monsieur le Curé* will be swift to have words with you when I've gone.'

I repeated to Mr. Clark everything I had told Chinnery. He, too, seemed satisfied that there was no connection between my visit to Wormwood Scrubs and Zachary's escape.

Seeing he had relaxed, I said, 'How do you think he got out, Mr. Clark?'

'Various theories in the press. The first is he never left prison.'

'No?'

'He's still in his cell hiding under the bed. Second, he dug a hundred-foot tunnel with a soup spoon. Third, he wrapped himself in laundry linen and carried himself out in a wooden horse. Fourth, like Jesus, he walked through the wall. The fifty theory, which I am inclined to prefer to the rest, is that he or his accomplice had a set of keys.'

'Keys,' I repeated.

'Things you put in locks to open doors. Damned clever. Who'd ever have thought of using keys to unlock prison doors?'

As he was leaving, I noticed he was almost as tall as I was. He advised:

'Shouldn't mention this to anyone, *mon ami*, if I were you.' He handed me a card. 'Give me a tinkle if you come across anything you think might be useful to us. And in future, don't forget to look for the mole, old chap.'

I smiled in relief. 'Right.'

He took out a cigarette case and put a cigarette in a holder while he called after him, 'I drive an ancient Wolseley, by the by. Black, *d'un certain âge*. The number plate, the cubic capacity . . . Ah, *mon petit*, but why should such trivia be of concern to you?'

He climbed into a new Sunbeam Talbot, ten-horsepower green saloon and drove off.

He was a funny one.

As soon as I closed the front door, Fr. Duddleswell pounced on me and drew me into his study. 'Now what the divil is after coming over you, lad?'

I apologized for my secretiveness, explained my promise to Mrs. Grourke and outlined the two interviews I had already given that morning.

The phone rang. Fr. Duddleswell answered it and handed it to me.

A woman said, 'John Smith to talk to you.'

John Smith's voice was unmistakable.

'Zachary,' I said.

'Emilio. That feller from the Home Office, you didn't tell him anything?'

'Tell him what? I haven't anything to tell.'

'You're a brick, Father. But I knew Clark wouldn't suspect you of anything. He's a Roman himself.'

'How do you know that?'

'He went to Holy Communion at Father Duddleswell's last Mass.'

'So he hadn't had breakfast, then,' I said. 'Hold the line, please.'

I hurried to the bathroom, opened the window and looked out onto the street. I returned and picked up the phone.

'Emilio, would you mind telling your man in the windcheater opposite our house to shove off.'

'Windcheater?' Emilio said. 'He's not my man. But thanks for the tip, Father. I'll sort him out straight away so he won't bother you any. Received my little gift yet?'

'Gift?'

'It's on its way. I only rang to say I'm hoping to invite you to a meal one evening.'

'You're alive,' I said inanely.

Zachary laughed. 'See you, Father, and thanks a million.'

'I'm relieved to know he's not dead,' Fr. Duddleswell said. 'Else his lovely mother would have had me celebrating a Requiem Mass for the repose of his soul three days a week.'

'I'll pop along and tell her the news.'

'She *knows*, Father Neil. She would bite Zach's ugly head off for him if he did not contact her first.'

Mrs. Pring came in with a stout parcel which had been delivered to the side door. Fr. Duddleswell and I opened it to find a carton with a dozen bottles of Johnny Walker and an envelope with a hundred pounds in notes. There was a typed card attached: 'With the compliments of John Smith. In gratitude for your visit to my Hotel.'

'Once more, Father Neil.'

Unlike the bogus policeman and Jonathan Clark, Fr. Duddleswell was convinced there was a connection between my visit to Wormwood Scrubs and Zachary's escape. The token of gratitude clinched the matter. I had to go into every detail of the story.

'What was that hymn again, Father Neil?'

I told him, with a yawn. This third grilling was easily the worst.

He snapped his fingers. 'The first line in full reads, *Sweet Saviour bless us 'ere we go.*'

I couldn't deny its aptness for a gaol break.

He went to his bookcase and was drawing out *The Westminster Hymnal* when he said, ' 'Tis Number 172. I have called that out in church often enough.'

Before he opened the hymnal, he was repeating, '172, 172.' Insight the second. 'What is today?' he asked.

'Saturday.'

'No, the date. February 18th.'

'It is,' I said, nonplussed.

'18th of the second month. 18—2.'

I got the point. 'Yesterday was 17—2, 172.'

He drew in a deep breath and nodded. He scanned the hymn for any more clues.

'If this is an elaborate code,' I said, 'Mrs. Grourke must be behind his escape.'

He was shocked. 'Father *Neil*. A gracious lady like Nelly who has two five shilling Masses said each week for the Holy Souls.'

'I'm convinced,' I said.

'Did she not say anything else, Father Neil? *Think.*'

I scratched my head and came up with her strange remark about blessing the year of Faber's birth.

'That is it,' he crowed. 'Look.'

Underneath the hymn were Faber's dates, '1814—63'.

'You can bet your bottom dollar, Father Neil, that Zach was sprung last night, Saturday February 17th, at exactly 18.14 hours, fourteen minutes after six o'clock.'

'But how was it done?' I whispered.

'I am working on it,' he said excitedly.

He was struck by Zachary handing over the picture of the Pope and his curious request for prayers for Mr. de Valera. But for the moment, inspiration failed him.

When he had given up guessing for the day, I said off-hand, 'I'll ring up the Home Office and get in touch with Mr. Clark.'

He looked at me sourly. 'Father Neil, d'you reckon the high and mighties of the Home Office will be interested in the hunches of an amateur sleuth like myself?'

'No, Father,' I said, and saw his jaw drop. 'I'm only going to let them know that Zachary telephoned.'

'Whatever for?'

'It'll save the police a lot of work if they know that Zachary's alive.'

'You leave the police to do their job, lad, and get on with your own.'

'All right, Father.'

'One last thing, Father Neil. When Zach rings up to invite you to dine, ask him if you can bring along a close friend.'

'Who?'

'Me,' he said.

Ten

THE DINNER PARTY

Fr. Duddleswell hated interruptions. He had reached the point of saying, 'I have worked it out that Zachary never broke out of prison at all,' when Mrs. Pring came in.

'Woman,' he cried, 'get away, 'way, 'way.'

Mrs. Pring looked around her calmly. 'I hear the bark,' she said, 'but where's the dog?'

'Jasus. She could bite the head off the Pope and him with his tiara on.'

'What do you mean, Father?' I asked, intrigued by his previous remark. But, as often happened, once his concentration was broken he refused to continue, out of pique.

'Tell you another time, Father Neil.'

Mrs. Pring announced, 'Mrs. Grourke for you, Father Neil.'

Again a transformation on the face of Fr. Duddleswell. 'Nelly,' he said, as Mrs. Grourke came in wearing a white mantilla, 'God prosper you and yours.'

' 'Tis a friend would say that, Father dear.' And after her friend had shaken her hand and departed, she said of him:

'On the outside he's as cold as a dog's nose but really he's so kind he would put his arm around your cow.'

I coughed to avoid the need for comment.

'Father dear,' she began, beating her breast, 'it pains me to have to tell you, you were unwittingly deceived. You did know that, I suppose.'

I nodded and said I was sorry in my turn that Fr. Duddleswell had found out about my visit to Wormwood Scrubs.

'And he was not—?'

'Broken-hearted? If he was, he didn't show it,' I assured her.

She shook her head in admiration of Fr. Duddleswell's detective powers. 'So many clever people in the world. And here is myself just a black pawn in the midst of it all, doing as I am told and not knowing what is for the best.'

'Your son must be clever,' I said, 'to have got out of prison.'

'A brain as big as my thumb, Father dear. He is

not in the least intelligent like your holy self. It was the work of the world learning him his A—B—C when he was eleven years old.'

'The Press seem to think he's very bright.'

'He will be bright, come the Feast of Nevermas,' she said. 'No, my Zachary is but a puppet.'

'Isn't he the head of his Company?'

'Only nominally. Above him is someone he calls The Boss. My boy is terrified of this person. He will not reveal The Boss's identity to anyone.'

'Not even to you?'

'Not to *anyone*.'

'The car trade he's in *is* perfectly respectable?'

'I would decorate his eye for him, Father dear, if he did anything in the slightest bit dishonest, would I not?'

Keen to put all the pieces together before Fr. Duddleswell, I said, 'You don't know how Zachary got out, I suppose, Mrs. Grourke?'

'Indeed I do.'

'How?'

'A miracle, Father dear. To be precise, the fruit of your holy Mass.'

'But,' I broke it to her, 'I haven't celebrated it yet.'

'Is that so? Then it is more of a miracle than I even thought.'

I delved into my pocket. 'Since your son is already free, perhaps you ought to have your five shillings back.'

She stayed my hand. 'Keep it, Father dear, and,' she said ambiguously, 'offer up a Mass for the release of another Holy Soul.'

Reluctantly I agreed. 'I'm having dinner with Zachary tomorrow evening,' I said.

'That's why I'm here. I want you to tell him to go back to prison as soon as possible. In this instance at least, *I* am The Boss.'

* * *

195

John Smith had telephoned the day before to say he had booked dinner at 'The Gay Lords', a club in Thrace Street, Soho. Of course I could bring a friend. He would follow suit and make it a foursome.

Fr. Duddleswell and I parked outside St. Patrick's Church in Soho and walked the last two or three hundred yards, past sleezy bars and dimly lit night clubs with life-size pictures outside.

'Keep the custody of the eyes,' Fr. Duddleswell said, his head erect. 'Butchers at least have the decency to put sausages in skins.'

A notice in the window of 'The Gay Lords' said 'Closed For Repairs' and the shutters were drawn.

'What a joint,' Fr. Duddleswell said. 'I tell you, rather than eat here, St. Patrick would have preferred to visit Kerry.'

As we approached, the door was flung open and a bear of a man, with shoulder length brown hair and gold earrings, hoisted us inside.

A much slighter man in a blonde wig and dark glasses said, 'Thank you, Zom,' to the bear and advanced to meet us, his right hand extended.

'Zach,' Fr. Duddleswell called out with obvious delight.

'Father, *please*,' Zachary pleaded, 'it's Emilio.'

Fr. Duddleswell said, 'Ah, yes. Emilio Zaccharone. I mistook you for someone very unlike yourself.'

Emilio dismissed his bodyguard and led us into a small private room where a table was dressed for dinner and lit by silver candelabra.

Emilio introduced us to his girl friend, Rosy. He must have been unpleasantly surprised to see who my close friend was.

Emilio, stooge or not, had influence. To entertain me he had taken over the whole night club for the evening and cancelled the floor show out of respect for my collar. The food, served by discreet Spanish-looking waiters was superb, as were the wines. 'A meal for a hundred,' Fr. Duddleswell called it.

The only brainless thing about Emilio was Rosy.

Moon-eyed and big-breasted, she had garish tastes in clothes and was constantly giggling and saying of Emilio, 'Isn't he a one? Isn't he something? Isn't he something else?'

Once the waiters had left, Emilio undid the top button of his shirt. 'Mind if I smoke?' he asked.

'Not at all,' Fr. Duddleswell said. 'Get in some practice for when you are dead.'

'Don't be mad at me, Father. We don't steal cars. My Organization just borrows them on a permanent basis.'

'Get your balance back,' Fr. Duddleswell said, 'and talk some sense.'

'No, straight up, Father. A car's not exactly something that can be stolen, you see that.'

'Isn't he something?' Rosie said.

'What d'you mean?'

'You learned me my trade, Father. You said in church once that stealing's wrong because someone gets hurt as shouldn't.'

'Indeed.'

'There you are, then. When you borrow a car, no one gets hurt, do they, not really? The insurance pays up. That way, the cost of the car's spread over half a million people or more.'

'No-one even notices, you mean,' Fr. Duddleswell said. 'Jasus, isn't this one a stray potato?'

'Why are you doing this, Emilio?' I wanted to know.

'To help criminals go straight.'

'Hold tight, Emilio,' Fr. Duddleswell cautioned him, 'else you will be taken up like Jesus into the clouds.'

'We only take ex-cons,' He turned to face Fr. Duddleswell. 'You know how it is, Father. If you've got a record, no job for you, mate. "Once a crook" and all that. I know.'

'Oh,' Fr. Duddleswell said, 'you are just a has-been that never was.'

'Be fair, Father. Remember that one small lapse when I was a kid of fifteen?'

'That was no small lapse.'

'Sorry,' Emilio said, grinning, 'I forgot it was your car. Anyway, nobody wanted me on the payroll after that. Even though I've never been in the nick before my recent stay in the Scrubs.'

'Isn't he something else?' Rosy said, giggling.

'Shut your potato hatch, Rosy.'

'Stealing cars sounds violent to me,' I said.

'That's rich,' Emilio said with a laugh.

'Presumably,' Fr. Duddleswell said, 'your man uses a magnetized plate between window and frame and lifts the catch that way.'

Emilio gave him a knowing wink. 'Drive away in sixty seconds. Any make of car. Don't even scratch the paintwork.'

'You must upset a lot of innocent motorists,' I said.

'No, no, Father. Not innocent ones. Take our little operation in Hyde Park. One of our girls shows a leg and the lecher passing by stops sharpish, like. A little trip to the bushes, a kiss and a cuddle.' He stopped to look at Fr. Duddleswell. 'That's not really company keeping, is it, Father?'

Fr. Duddleswell turned his head away.

'Anyway,' Emilio continued, 'if this lecher asks for more, the girl screams and slaps his face. Meantime, our man is driving off the, um, abandoned car.'

'There must be quite a number of cars lost in Hyde Park,' I said.

'Sure are,' Emilio said, filling my glass. 'Sometimes the drivers don't even report it to the police. Awkward questions, you see that. Yeah,' he added proudly, 'we stop an awful lot of vice in the Metropolis.'

Fr. Duddleswell leaned forward. 'I suppose you concentrate on the smaller cars.'

'The size and make of car make no difference, Father. Listen. First, one of our men hires a Rolls and books a room in advance in a swish Hotel. On the actual day, he parks the hired Rolls near the Hotel. When he sees another bit 'un, a Rolls or Daimler, about to drive up to the Hotel, he nips in front of it smartish. The doorman opens his car door. And straight away, our mans falls ill with a stroke or something like.'

'Whatever for?' I said.

'Wait for it, Father. There's a ripe gefuffle. The doorman rushes into the Hotel to get help. Meantime, the car we want to acquire stops. Another of our men puts on a peaked cap—'

'That's all it takes,' Fr. Duddleswell mused, 'a peaked cap. Jasus, you could steal the butter off hot toast.'

'Yeah. Our man tells the gent inside the Rolls we've got our eye on that the guest in front has just had a heart attack in the Hotel lobby. He offers to park the car for him.

'So, the rich nit leaps out, leaving his key in the dashboard. He can't wait to have a butchers at another rich nit like himself having a heart attack.' Emilio roared with laughter. 'People *are* wicked.'

'And,' Fr. Duddleswell said, 'your man in the peaked cap just drives the new Rolls away.'

'Right. And cheap at the price.'

'Very good, Emilio,' Fr. Duddleswell said, 'but wouldn't the doorman immediately call a doctor?'

'Sure,' Emilio grinned, 'except we have our own doc loitering in the lobby for just such an emergency.'

'An impostor?' I said.

Emilio tried to look hurt. 'Give over, Father.'

'Struck off the Register,' Fr. Duddleswell said.

Emilio nodded. 'One who can't get a job anywhere, poor feller. Wicked world, i'n't it?'

'One thing,' Fr. Duddleswell asked, 'how in the name of Beelzebub do you dispose of a Rolls?'

'The bigger the car, the easier to get rid of.'

'Even a Rolls? Now there you have me.'

'All up and down the country, Father, there are car-hire firms for weddings, receptions, banquets, that sort of thing. They're lining up to replace one of their old crocks with a new model.'

'You mean, 'tis not easy spotting a new Rolls in a respectable fleet of 'em.'

'Right. Only the other day, our Organization sold one to a Funeral Director in your parish.'

Fr. Duddleswell blinked. 'Bottesford?'

'Can't name names but the Co-op refused to deal with us, I tell you that for nothing. Naturally, part of the service we provide is selling the replaced cars on the legitimate market.'

'Surely,' Fr. Duddleswell said, 'your dear mother always did say your Organization runs a perfectly legitimate business.'

'Books correct, income tax paid up on the nose, the lot.'

'But,' Fr. Duddleswell said, 'are not some of your customers afraid the police will charge them with receiving stolen goods?'

Emilio touched his shoulder. 'Want a job, Father? You always did think of everything. First, the Organization and the customer agree a fair price for the acquired car, then we put an ad in the paper—'

'That *is* clever,' Fr. Duddleswell murmured, anticipating the outcome.

Emilio smiled vainly. 'The customer cuts out the ad and keeps it so if he's picked up he can say—'

'And quite truthfully,' Fr. Duddleswell interrupted him.

'Yeah, quite truthfully, that he bought the car on the open market. But our final safeguard for the customer is, he actually pays the full market price for the car.'

'But if the customer's paying the full price,' I said, 'why does he risk buying a car from you?'

Emilio winked at Fr. Duddleswell. 'Well, he does pay the full price and he doesn't. After we agree the price, usually half the trade price, we give him cash equivalent to the remainder.'

'Give us a for instance,' Fr. Duddleswell said.

'Well, we charge a customer £400 for a car worth £800. We give him four hundred quid in cash. He puts this in his bank and makes out a cheque to our temporary company for eight hundred. Besides the ad in the paper, he now has his cheque which his bank returns to him as proof that he is a *bona fide* buyer who paid the market price for the car.'

'Even though he hasn't,' I said.

'The point is, the cops can't accuse him of purchasing stolen goods at a price so low he must have known the car was nicked.'

'You are a brawny sinner and no mistake,' Fr. Duddleswell said. 'There must be a power of competition in your line of business, I am thinking.'

'Too true, Father. It's a rat race. Which reminds me. It was one of the opposition that leaned on Father Neil the day after God in His mercy let me out of gaol.'

'He told me he was a policeman,' I started to say, but Emilio interrupted me.

'Charlie Ripley that was, though he obviously used a different name.'

'Chinnery. He said he was a Detective Sergeant from Scotland Yard.'

'I promise you one thing, Father. That nutter won't be bothering you no more.'

'You're not going to rub him out,' I asked anxiously.

'You've been watching too many Jimmy Cagney films, Father. No, while Ripley was in your place, one of our lot went through his car. Didn't burglarproof it. Probably because it was knocked off. Careless. On our file now is the info' that he likes Peter Cheyne novels. Uses Brylcream and Ozec aftershave. Size nine shoes.'

'How——?' I said.

'He keeps a pair of pumps in the pocket by the

driving seat for break-ins. But I won't go on except to say our man got a perfect set of prints from the driving wheel. I'm sending the details on a memo to Ripley's boss and after that—'

'No more work for Charlie Ripley,' Fr. Duddleswell said.

'I'm insulted they put a creep like that on to me.'

'And the Home Office chap?' I asked.

'Clarkie? He's genuine all right.'

'Of course,' Fr. Duddleswell said. 'He's Emilio's second-in-command.'

'My Sales Manager, to be precise,' Emilio said. 'An old Etonian. But how did you find that out?'

'I rang the number on the card he gave Father Neil.'

Emilio smiled appreciatively. 'I sent Clarkie to check that Ripley didn't get anything out of Father Boyd.'

I swallowed my last mouthful of dessert. 'Why are they so keen to know your whereabouts?'

'To put me out of circulation for a few weeks, so I can't complete vital Organization business.'

'And that's why,' I said, 'you were sprung less than a month before your release.'

'Yeah.'

'You won't elaborate on that?'

'Nope.'

'Nor on how you escaped from Wormwood Scrubs?'

Fr. Duddleswell leaned on the table and whispered, 'Emilio, I will tell you *how* you got out of Wormwood Scrubs, if you tell me *why*.'

For the first time, Emilio lost his cool. He turned to Rosy who had just stuffed her mouth with trifle and said, 'Go powder your nose, Sweetheart.'

Still trying to swallow, Rosy jumped up and went to the ladies' room.

'You won't tell my mum about Rosy, will you, Father?' Emilio pleaded with Fr. Duddleswell.

'And why should I break your dear mother's

heart, Zach, by telling her you are living with a woman?'

Emilio looked really hurt. 'I don't shack up with Rosy, Father. I'm a good Catholic, I am.'

'Like the butcher's dog, Emilio.'

'Eh?'

'You never touch the meat.'

'It's just that—well, Rosy is a Protestant.'

'What about my proposition?'

'I dunno, Father.'

'I won't mention Rosy.'

'Okay,' Emilio said. 'Agreed.'

'What I had to unriddle, Zach, was why your gang instructed your dear mother to send me curate to visit you in prison and not meself. Father Neil was obviously chosen because he is too green to twig what I might. And did.'

'Thanks,' I said.

'The clue, Father Neil, lay in the picture of the Holy Father and the request for prayers for Mr. de Valera.'

'I'm sure you're right, Father,' I said, not knowing what he was talking about.

'You told me, Father Neil, that above the Pope's head was the papal insignia.'

'Yes, the crossed keys.'

'Indeed. You can bet your bottom dollar that those keys were drawn on both edges to Emilio's specifications.'

Emilio looked as if someone had whitewashed his face.

'As I told you, Emilio never broke out of prison at all. One of his gang had the keys made up outside and broke in.'

There was a long pause before I said, 'What about de Valera?'

'That was how Eamon de Valera got out of Lincoln Jail in 1917. Except he was clever enough to file his own keys in prison from impressions he made on the wax of an altar candle.' One look at Emilio confirmed that Fr. Duddleswell was right in every detail.

'Now, Zach.'

Emilio gulped before beginning.

'Nothing to it, really, Father. There's a new tool-kit on the market designed by Biondi of Zurich. The rumour was that Ripley's crowd had first option. Many of ours were leaving us and going over to them.'

'And every day was precious.'

'Yeah, Father. That's why The Boss decided to spring me. So I could sort things out.'

Fr. Duddleswell took his hand. 'The Boss?'

'If I told you who The Boss is,'—he made a slicing movement across his throat—'I wouldn't see tomorrow's dawn. I'm the only one in the Organization who knows who The Boss is and the only one who needs to know.'

Fr. Duddleswell, hearing the Sweetheart twittering outside, gallantly stood up, saying, 'I will call Rosy back so she can finish off her trifle.'

As he left the room, Emilio jerked his thumb at the door. 'My mum always wanted me to be a priest, Father. There but for the grace of God go I.'

Rosy came back shrieking, 'Isn't he a one? Isn't he something else?'

Outside 'The Gay Lords', we shook hands with Emilio and Rosy and thanked them for an entertaining evening.

'Want a lift, Fathers?'

'Thank you kindly, Emilio,' Fr. Duddleswell said, 'but I have parked a bit further on.'

'You're not still driving that old twenty horse power Chrysler?'

Fr. Duddleswell nodded.

'I could get you a replacement for that old banger, if you like,' Emilio said, not expecting the offer to be taken up. He gave me a specially warm pat on the back. 'My mum has really taken to you, Father.'

Suddenly Emilio became very agitated. He turned back to Zom who was five yards behind. 'Where's the car?'

The Big Bear stopped in his tracks and jerked his hairy head in all directions. 'Dunno, Mr. Zaccharone.'

Emilio took us by the shoulders. 'Fathers, would you mind stepping back into the Club.' To Zom: 'Find out. Quick.'

We retreated into 'The Gay Lords' where we sat and ordered more coffee.

Fr. Duddleswell touched Emilio's hand sympathetically. ' 'Tis not stolen, I assure you of that. Only borrowed, wouldn't you say?'

'Ripley's crowd have swiped it.' Emilio thought about that before asking aloud, 'But how *could* they? And how did they get wind I was here?' He rounded angrily on the Sweetheart. 'Rosy?'

'It wasn't me, Emmy. Honest to God, it wasn't.'

'Sorry, Sweetheart. It can't have been Zom, he's as faithful as a dog, and we didn't tell the owner of this joint *who* was coming. Their intelligence is better than I gave them credit for.'

Five minutes later, Zom returned. 'It's okay, Mr. Zaccharone, sir.'

'You found it?'

'No, sir. The cops towed it away. You were in a non-parking zone.'

'Thank God for that.' He thought the matter through. 'We've got to get it back fast or The Boss will roast me alive.'

Fr. Duddleswell glanced at his watch and stood up. 'Sorry, Emilio, Father Neil and I have to be home before eleven. Glad to know your car is in safe keeping.'

'Father,' Emilio pleaded. 'Don't leave me. You got me off the hook once before.'

'And a lot of good it did you.'

'Father, I was wondering if you and Father Boyd could go along to the nearest police station and ask where my car is, pay the fine and drive it back here.'

While Fr. Duddleswell hummed for a bit, I said, 'It's not stolen, is it?'

'Do me a favour, Father.'

'I'm sorry,' I said, 'I didn't mean to accuse you of doing anything dishonest.'

'Use your nut, Father. How could anyone in my line of business risk driving around in a nicked car? Especially when I'm absent without leave from one of his Majesty's prisons?'

'All right, Emilio,' Fr. Duddleswell said. 'On one condition.'

'Name it, Father.'

'When your present business is complete, you give yourself up.'

Emilio smiled with relief. 'You sound just like my mum. I think, Father, you'd better tell the cops the car is yours.'

'We're not going to lie for you,' I said.

Fr. Duddleswell waved me to silence. 'Steady, Father Neil. A cool head untangles the thread. There is no need for lies.'

'No?'

'Indeed not. Emilio here will sell the car to me.'

Emilio was on Fr. Duddleswell's wave length. He smiled crookedly. 'John Smith's the name. How much am I bid?'

'Two bob, John Smith.'

'And how much will you sell it back for afterwards?'

'Half a crown. Me hand and me word to that.'

'Done,' Emilio said and forked out a florin. As he started to give us basic facts about the car, I realized we were in for a torrid time.

Emilio handed over the key and needlessly annoyed his saviour by wishing him 'the best of British.'

* * *

At Tottenham Court Road police station, Fr. Duddleswell held up the car key in front of the Sergeant's nose. 'I have lost the other bit of this,' he said.

The Sergeant, in his middle years, with a plump red face and sleek black hair parted in the middle, smiled benignly. 'Had your car pinched, have you, sir?'

Fr. Duddleswell said he was led to believe it had been towed away.

'Where were you parked, sir?'

'Thrace Street.'

The Sergeant raised his round, black eyebrows. 'Visiting a parishioner, sir? Been to the cinema, p'raps?'

Fr. Duddleswell decided to be straight with him. 'No, we had a meal.'

'In any place I know?'

' "The Gay Lords".'

'Oh, yes,' the Sergeant said. 'In your collar?'

'And the rest of me clothes, Officer.'

Without a flicker of a change in his features, the Sergeant dipped his pen in the ink well. 'The make of your car, please, sir.'

'Rolls-Royce.'

The Sergeant relaxed into a smile and put his pen down. 'Tell me more, sir.'

'Silver Wraith Limousine by Park Ward.'

'Ha, ha. Sure it's not a Rolls Phantom III Sedanca di Ville by Wendover?'

'Quite sure,' Fr. Duddleswell said.

'Come on, sir,' the Sergeant said, losing some of his good humour. 'It's been a busy night. What've you lost, a Ford Anglia, Hillman Minx, Morris Oxford, what?'

A Silver Wraith—'

'All right, sir, go on.' The Sergeant bit his lower lip. 'Colour?'

'Midnight blue with black wings.'

207

The Sergeant leaned his elbow firmly on his desk as if he were planting a tree.

'Heater and demister. Picnic tables.'

'Not for "The Gay Lords"?' the Sergeant asked.

'Cocktail cabinet, radio, telephone.'

'To keep you in touch with your Bishop, sir?'

'Bumpers with over-riders, front and rear. And ladies' and gentlemen's compacts.'

The Sergeant ran his eye malevolently over Fr. Duddleswell's old suit to suggest his clothes didn't exactly match his motor car. 'Car number, sir.'

'LMT 41 . . . 413.'

'412,' I said.

Fr. Duddleswell confirmed that I was right. The Sergeant wrote something on a piece of paper and handed it to a young Constable before asking pleasantly, 'Colour of upholstery?'

'Blue, I think.'

'Brown,' I said, 'Browny-blue. More accurate to say brown.'

'I suppose you could say 'tis brown.'

'Had this car long, sir?'

'Not long at all.'

'*How* long?'

'I bought it only very recently, really. Which is why me curate knows some of the details better than meself.'

'May I see your key again, please, sir?'

Fr. Duddleswell handed it over.

The Sergeant examined the leather tag and said, 'Do you buy all your cars from Godfreys of Hampstead, sir?'

'Not all. In fact, as far as I can recall, this one only.'

'It says on the tag, sir, "Goddards of Hounslow".'

'Does it, now? Well, to be perfectly honest with you—'

'I'd like that very much, sir.'

'I bought it this very evening on the spur of the moment.'

'Off the peg, so to speak.'

'Off a feller called John Smith.'

'We should be able to trace him easily enough, then shouldn't we, sir? You know his address, of course.'

'I am afraid—'

'This car cost you a bob or two, I should say, sir.'

'It did, Officer. You are exactly right.'

'I don't suppose, sir, you'd care to let me see your cheque book. No obligation, mind.'

Fr. Duddleswell's hand went instinctively to his inside pocket. 'I must have left it at home.'

'You paid in pound notes, did you?'

'In silver.'

'May I see the bag you carried the money in?'

'No bag. I used me pocket.'

'Which pocket sir?'

Fr. Duddleswell turned round and showed his back pocket which was big enough to hold a medium-sized apple.

'Where did you study, sir?'

'For the priesthood? Rome, of course.'

As soon as he said 'Rome', it struck me that this was exactly the kind of reply you would expect from a bogus Catholic priest, especially one with a brogue. That's why I said, 'St. Edward's.'

'Which is it, sir?' the Sergeant said in a tired voice, as if he had long ago despaired of getting anything approaching the truth from us.

'*He* was trained in Rome,' I said, 'and *I* was trained at St. Edward's in this diocese.'

The Constable returned and handed the Sergeant a note. After reading it, he said, 'It may interest you two Reverends to know that the owner of that car happens to be a lady.'

Oh my God, I thought, Emilio has sold us down the river.

'Rose Dollerby is the lady's name. Lives in the Uxbridge area.' There was a smirk on the Sergeant's face. 'You don't know her, I suppose, sir?'

209

'Oh, indeed,' Fr. Duddleswell said. 'Delightful young woman, Rosy.'

'John Smith's girl friend,' I said.

The Sergeant squared his jaw. 'I'm going to book you two crooks.'

'Whatever for?' Fr. Duddleswell said.

'For stealing a car and impersonating, very *badly*, two gentlemen of the cloth.'

As soon as the young Constable was replaced at eleven-fifteen, the newcomer greeted me with a loud cry. 'Neil. What on earth are *you* doing here?'

Johnny Downes had been a fellow student in the seminary until he had left at the end of his first year. I had met him only once since then.

When I had explained our situation, Johnny vouched for my honesty and I, in turn, vouched for Fr. Duddleswell who informed the Sergeant, hand on heart, 'I have not told you the word of a lie all evening.'

As the Sergeant wrote us out a ticket and told us to collect our car at the police pound in Ende Street, he scratched his head. 'Jesus Christ! Just shows how mistaken you can be. I'd have sworn my badge away that you two Fathers were a couple of con-men.'

We hurried to the pound, paid the fine and drove off.

'The gods were on our side, Father,' I said.

Fr. Duddleswell smiled. 'Ah, lad, the lucky man has only to be born. Stick with me and you will be all right.'

Emilio had left 'The Gay Lords' in a taxi with Rosy to be on the safe side but Zom remained to express his master's gratitude. After Fr. Duddleswell had claimed his half-crown, we almost ran back to Soho Square in high spirits.

Our car was gone.

'Jesus wept,' Fr. Duddleswell said. 'This has been a dirty day and no mistake. You would think I had met a red-haired woman this mornin'.'

210

A notice said parking was restricted to three hours and our car had been standing there for four and a half.

Fr. Duddleswell made a face. 'I can hardly go back to the Station and claim a second car within half an hour.'

'You're not going to sell me your car for two bob,' I told him, backing away.

'Indeed not,' he said. 'You unfortunately cannot drive.'

I mentally resolved never to learn.

'We will leave it so till tomorrow morning when I will be selling it to Dr. Daley. He is all the friend I have left.'

We took a taxi home. On the way, he said that Dr. Daley was employed by the police to examine suspected drunks, rape victims and the like.

'He will be able to walk into the Tottenham Court Road police station in the morning, flash his card and get the car back without even a fine.'

Touching, I thought. Such optimism in an old campaigner.

Next morning, before I celebrated the early Mass, I heard Fr. Duddleswell talking to Dr. Daley on the phone and negotiating the sale of his old Chrysler.

At eleven, Fr. Duddleswell came to my room. 'Strange,' he said. 'Dr. Daley has parked me car outside and did not even ring to collect his half-crown.'

Mrs. Pring brought us mid-morning tea. When he asked, she said that no car key had been put through the letter box.

The phone rang. It was Dr. Daley. He apologized for carrying out his assignment so late but he had arrived at the Station to find that the car was not in the pound and nobody there had heard of it.

The Doctor can't have been well briefed. He apparently said there was a Sergeant at his elbow who knew my parish priest well and wished to be remembered to him.

'Never you mind, Donal,' Fr. Duddleswell said in conclusion, 'bring back the car key I dropped through your letter box this morning. A hundred thousand thanks for doing your best.' He put the receiver down. 'The blitherin' idiot,' he barked. 'Wait till he tries to hitch a drink from me again.'

'How did the car get back?'

'The fairies must have brought it,' he said.

Still puzzled, he left for his parish rounds. I took the phone call half an hour later. John Smith wanted me to convey to Fr. Duddleswell his deepest regrets. One of his Organization had had the bad taste to steal his car the night before.

'Lucky I read the report on it, Father. If I hadn't, the car would have been torn apart.'

'Really,' I said, breathing heavily, 'life is very complicated.'

'Sorry to hear that, Father,' Emilio said. 'What seems to be the trouble?'

'It'll pass,' I said.

'Take my word, Father, you and Father Duddleswell saved me a lot of sweat last night. What I couldn't tell you was that in a secret compartment of that car were our Organization's entire plans for the next six months.'

'Is that all?'

'Not quite. Also the prototype tool-kit I bought from Biondi. With a piece of metal the size of a rolling pin, we can remove an ignition switch in fifteen seconds.'

'Congratulations,' I said fiercely.

'Thanks, Father.'

I thought it was about time I acted like a priest. 'I presume, Emilio, you are ready to go back to prison now.'

'I'll put it to The Boss,' he said, 'and let you know. If I need your help—'

'Just give me a call.' I had said it before it occurred to me it might land me in another fix.

* * *

A week later, the *Daily Sketch* ran an exclusive on Emilio Zaccharone. He had decided to 'make a clean breast of his innocence,' and explain to the fair-minded British public, who had the right to know, why he had made his breathtaking escape from Wormwood Scrubs.

With only a few days of his sentence to run, he broke out simply to draw attention to the injustice he had suffered.

He intended to give himself up freely. He had made his stand selflessly on behalf of all innocent men wrongly accused. He would pay Society in full the debt he did not really owe as a token of good faith.

He exonerated the Governor and warders of Wormwood Scrubs from any collusion in his escape. He did not need their help. He even thanked them for their inspired and charitable concern for the prisoners.

He intended giving himself up the next day in the company of a young priest adviser who had always believed in his innocence and stood by him in this, the greatest crisis of his life.

'Just like Zach Grourke,' Fr. Duddleswell said, 'to slip away in a blaze of publicity.'

I grunted. 'Who's his script-writer, Winston Churchill?'

'Oh, but 'twas nice of him all the same to describe me as his young priest adviser.' He laughed merrily. 'But he is a sly one and no mistake.'

'He had the best teacher,' I said.

He laughed again. 'D'you know, even the authorities must be convinced that if Zach can escape that easily from Wormwood Scrubs, he has no need to steal cars. If he wanted to steal anything, he would start with the Crown Jewels.'

'I'm warning you, Father. I've had my fill of double-dealing. Emilio is going home to prison on his own.'

'Do not snap at me like an otter, lad.'

'Why does he want me there anyway?'

'Ah, me suckling lamb, me little green apple. The Boss has decided you are Mr. Clean and Zach may have need of your services again.'

'Well, count me out. I'm not playing any more.'

He looked mournfully into my eyes. 'I suppose you cannot draw blood from a turnip.'

'Pardon?'

'What're you trying to do, Father Neil, break his poor mother's heart and herself one of Patrick's people?'

Next morning, when I saw Mrs. Grourke reciting her rosary during my Mass, my resolve, as usual, cracked. She did not come up to me or even look my way. But how could I refuse the unspoken request of such a dear old lady? 'A widow,' Fr. Duddleswell reminded me, 'for whose sort our Blessed Lord opened wide His Sacred Heart.'

At nine-thirty, a Daimler drew up at the presbytery. Zom was driving. He jumped out and opened the door for me.

I sat in a stubborn silence next to Emilio throughout the journey. As we approached the prison gates and saw the horde of reporters and photographers, Emilio said, 'Don't take it so hard, Father. We're both in favour of the fallen.'

He took my hand and squeezed it in a brotherly way.

'Show me your good faith, Emilio.'

'Anything, Father. But for you, I'd be a dead duck now.'

'I promise to keep it as close as a confessional secret.' He nodded trustingly. 'Who is The Boss?'

'That, Father,' he said, 'is the one secret I can't reveal. Not even in confession. One thing, though. The Boss gave me this envelope for you in token of heartfelt thanks.'

He winked, stepped out of the car and was immediately swallowed up by press men. A few photographs were taken of me through the window. I put my hands in front of my face when I saw someone I knew in the crowd. An old mac covered his uniform but there, without a doubt, was the police Sergeant from Tottenham Court Road Station.

'Zom,' I ordered, 'get us out of here quick.'

I rushed triumphantly into the presbytery.

Fr. Duddleswell waved me into his study. 'How did it go, lad?'

'Fine,' I said, and gave him a brief account of what had happened, ending with, 'And I have discovered who The Boss is.'

He looked at me doubtfully. 'Careful, Father Neil, you are out of your depth, so may the divil hold your face up.'

I showed him the envelope. 'The answer's in here. A present from The Boss for services rendered.'

'Open it, then, lad.'

'No.'

'Why ever not?'

'I'm not such a fool as to suppose The Boss has signed his name. But I'm handing this over to the police for fingerprinting.'

He drew back with a start. 'Jasus, lad, you are getting high notions like the poor man's cabbage. Are you wanting to betray Zachary, me former altar boy?'

My turn to be shocked. 'Father!'

'Are you wanting to betray a lad with a lovely mother like Nelly Grourke and leave her lonesome as a cow bereft of her calf?'

'That's blackmail, Father, and you know it. I think you admire and almost approve of what Zachary does.'

He lowered his gaze. 'You misjudge me sorely, Father Neil, like that Sergeant at the Station.'

'I'm sorry, then. But, look, we lost the chance of turning over the plans of a gang of thieves to Scotland Yard. Let's hand the police this envelope so at least they can arrest the ringleader.'

'Have you been with me all these months, lad, and still you have no idea what a priest is?'

'Father?'

He snapped his fingers. 'The very word: "Father". And what sort of father is it would deliver his son to the police, whatever he's done? Give the police The Boss and you give them Zach Grourke.'

'We're citizens, too, Father,' I said with feeling.

'We are. But a special kind of citizen, the kind that judges no one. The keys God gave us, y'see, were not for locking crooks up in prison but for opening to everyone, including crooks, the Kingdom of Heaven.'

I went to speak but found I had nothing to say.

'A priest, you follow, is like Jesus, a window into the Heart of God. Can you imagine Jesus, now, betraying Judas, whatever his crimes?'

'No,' I said, thinking for one wild moment that Jesus doesn't half complicate matters.

'That is why we cannot even reveal what thieves and murderers tell us in confession or in strict confidence. That is why we alone can win their confidence and stand in the place of God. So they may know, if only at their last gasp like the thief on the cross, that the God to whom they go is love and forgiveness and nothing else.'

I was silent for a while. I recalled how, when Emilio was running through all the people who could have betrayed his presence at 'The Gay Lords', he never for one moment thought it might have been Fr. Duddleswell or me.

I handed over the envelope. 'You open it, Father.'

He gave me the gentlest look. 'Ah, Father Neil, if you had not given it me, I would have knocked your blessèd block off.'

He opened the envelope, examined the contents and whistled through his teeth.

'Know what's in it, lad?'

'No idea.'

He smiled enigmatically. 'Five shillings and a note: "A Mass for the Holy Souls".'

Eleven

FATHERS AND SONS

'I'd be very grateful, Father, if you'd keep an eye on my wife while I'm away.'

Don Martin, a dapper young executive, was off on a fortnight's trip to Cairo. He didn't want to go but he was in the export trade and, had he turned it down, he might have lost his job.

His wife, Jane, in her mid-twenties, was expecting their third child in three weeks time. The first two, Don explained, had been difficult births.

Francis, now three-and-a-half, had been wrongly presented. Jane had been in labour for twenty-four hours before the doctor was able to turn the child by Kielland's rotation in the birth canal and deliver him by forceps.

Just over a year later came Danny. When Jane was X-rayed, they found he was so contorted in the womb, the hospital kept the picture as a prize exhibit. The doctor in attendance afterwards admitted he thought he was dealing with a case of spina-bifida. Fortunately, after the Caesarean, Danny was found to be a perfectly normal child.

'The Kenworthy General is a progressive hospital, Father,' Don said. 'I was hoping to be present at the births but because of the complications, they threw me out at the last minute. Both times.'

He gave me a grim look. 'I saw enough to know why we call God "Father". If He were a Mother, He would have planned some things differently.'

'You'll be back for the birth, Don. Let's hope you're in on the next one.'

'Hope so, Father. My sister-in-law, Diana, is standing by to lend a hand if Jane needs it.'

Don merely wanted me to be on the alert so that if there was an emergency I would administer the sacraments to Jane and baptize the baby.

'I promise you, Don, I'll call on Jane every day you're away.' Easy enough to say, seeing the Martins lived opposite the presbytery.

As Don shook my hand in farewell, his eyes misted up. 'Thanks, Father. It means a lot to me to know you'll stand by my wife if anything happens.'

I gripped his hand as firmly as I could. 'Don't worry, Don. It'll be no trouble at all.'

Four days later, Dr. Daley visited Jane Martin and ordered her into hospital immediately. Her ankles were swollen and she had high blood pressure.

As soon as I heard, I phoned Diana Martin. She was very upset to hear the news because she wasn't in a position to help out. Her husband, Don's brother, had gone down with 'flu complicated by long-term bronchitis. She couldn't leave the house.

I told Fr. Duddleswell and he consulted Mrs. Pring about what to do with Francis and Danny. He reminded me of Monsignor Ronnie Knox's definition of a child: 'A loud noise at one end and no sense of responsibility at the other.'

'Where's the problem?' Mrs. Pring said. 'I am a mother myself, you know. I'll take over the house opposite. And it'll do the pair of you the world of good to see how the other half lives.'

Jane thanked Mrs. Pring for offering to look after her home, including the boys. Mrs. Pring, she knew, was already very fond of them and was often dropping in with gifts of chocolate and home-made cakes. Mrs. Pring was looking forward to the challenge.

She arranged for us to eat at the Martins and Fr. Duddleswell took on a young woman, Jill Bennett, to answer calls at the presbytery during meal times.

As far as I was concerned, the next few days were golden. Jane was in no immediate danger, Dr. Daley told me, and I found being with the boys was a fresh and totally unexpected delight.

The first evening when we went across the road for supper, the boys were already in bed but howling because they missed their mother.

'A job for you two Fathers,' Mrs. Pring said sharply. 'Upstairs with you and calm the little ones while I get you something to eat.'

Till then, my most vivid memory of the two children was of them swapping books and occasional blows in the front row during Mass. Danny hadn't endeared himself to me by always shouting out as soon as I entered the pulpit, 'Daddy, are we going home now?'

The boys, looking alike with their blue eyes, round faces and brown hair cut in a fringe, were in adjoining rooms. Mrs. Pring introduced us first to Francis, a precocious child, whom Fr. Duddleswell was detailed to look after, and then to Danny, my charge.

Danny, with a white moustache where his evening cup of warm milk had flecked his upper lip, was sitting up in bed. He was sucking his thumb which made him look like a dreamy squirrel nibbling a nut. I warmed to him at once.

After a few moments, he said in a gruff voice comical in one so small, 'Daddy, I want a cuddle,' and I put my arms around him and started on a story. I had hardly spoken three sentences when his quiet, deep breathing told me he was asleep.

I laid him down gently, blessed him and was about to leave when I caught snatches of the conversation in the next room. I sat beside Danny and eaves-dropped.

'Why are you cold, bed?' Francis was saying. 'Get warm soon, won't you, 'cos the sheet is cold on Francis's legs.'

'Francis,' I heard Fr. Duddleswell whisper, 'you must not bite your nails.'

'Why?'

'Because they will scratch your insides, that's for why.'

'It's all right, Father Doddles, I always chew them well before I swallow them.'

'Is that so? Well, go to sleep, little feller. And that is an order from your parish priest.'

'Could you go to sleep if I told you to, Father Doddles?'

'I suppose not.'

'It's not as easy to go to sleep as some mummies think.' There was a creaking of the bed before Francis added, 'Going to sleep is very hard when it's not easy.'

'Try counting sheep,' Fr. Duddleswell suggested.

'One, two, three, six, four, eight, nine, ten.'

'Go on, Francis.'

'There's too many for my numbers, Father Doddles.'

'Close your eyes, then.'

'Why?'

'So that you can see your dreams better.'

'Why?'

'Dearie me, anybody would think you are a Protestant. You must close your eyes to save on electricity.'

'Danny needs a light on when he goes to bed 'cos the dark hurts his eyes.'

'Does it now?'

'Danny says that when he goes to sleep he can't remember what he's been dreaming about.'

'Uh huh.' Fr. Duddleswell was plainly lost for words on hearing such a deep thought.

'Do you dream, Father Doddles?'

'Sometimes.'

'Nice dreams?'

Fr. Duddleswell was not keen to divulge the contents of his sleeping mind even to a three-year-old. 'Sometimes,' he repeated.

'Sometimes,' Francis said, 'mine aren't worth watching. And sometimes I drop off the top of big buildings.'

'What happens?'

'I'm lucky so far. I always fall awake before I hit the ground or my nightmares gets me.'

'That *is* lucky.'

'And sometimes I do funny things.'

'Like?'

'Like doing as I'm told.'

'Go to sleep.'

'I can't cos you haven't said my prayers.'

'Nor have I.' And Fr. Duddleswell rattled off the Our Father, Hail Mary and Glory Be. Afterwards, he said, 'So *there*, Francis.'

'But, Father Doddles, when are you going to say some proper prayers?'

'You didn't like the ones I said?'

'Not very really.'

Fr. Duddleswell made up a few impromptu prayers for Mummy and Daddy and Danny and Francis as well as a very moving one for Father Doddles.

'You're not very good at prayers, are you, Father Doddles?'

'Am I not?' He sounded grieved at a child questioning his professional competence. 'You say your own, then.'

'Please, God,' Francis whispered loudly, 'can I have a flat head?'

'Whatever for?'

'So's I can stand on it, of course. Shush, Father Doddles. I'm saying my prayers.'

'I am sure I beg your pardon.'

'Please God, I wish I could whistle without a whis-

221

tle. Please God, I wished I was a millionaire so's I could buy an ice cream.'

'Wait,' Fr. Duddleswell said. 'Here's threepence. For an ice cream.'

'Please God, don't bother about making me a millionaire till tomorrow night. Amen.'

'I am sure the Almighty God will hear you, Francis.'

'Course He will. He's got ears and eyes all over His body.'

'He has?'

'Like a dragonfly. Only you can't see Him 'cos He's got a infinite quite big towel over His head.'

'I did not know that, truly.'

'Oh, yes. He's got the biggest head there is.'

'Bigger than mine?'

'Much?'

Fr. Duddleswell whistled. 'Is that possible?' I heard his feet scrape the floor as he stood up. 'Now I am off to eat me rations for the night. Sleep well. I will turn off the light.'

He crossed to the door and I heard the click as he switched the light off.

'Father Doddles?'

'Yes, Francis.'

'I usually find sleeping don't take long once you've started.'

'God bless you.'

'In the name of the Father and of the Son and of the Holly Ghost. Amen. God bless *you*, Father Doddles.'

Jane Martin's condition continued to improve. Her ankles went down and her blood pressure was almost normal. As a precaution, the doctor decided to keep her in hospital.

I visited her every day to assure her the children were well-behaved.

'It's very kind of you, Father,' Jane said, trying to be brave.

'I'm really enjoying myself,' I told her.

And it was true. Danny was teaching me things I had not grasped before. For instance, that the only way to get to love a small child is by making the effort of picking him up and holding him tight. In other words, by physical contact. Because of my isolation and training in the seminary this had been alien to me.

More importantly, Danny taught me something new about God. It's not too much to say that Danny fundamentally altered my religion. Up to that time, whenever I thought of God in Jesus' terms as 'Our Father', I had automatically seen myself as a helpless child, resting in his Father's arms.

But now, as I cradled Danny to sleep each night in my arms, I felt I understood God better by identifying with Him in His infinite power and concern. I was so fond of Danny, I would defend him to the death, whatever wrong he did, whatever he became. So *that's* what God is like, I said to myself with the thrill of a new discovery. And *that* must be what my priestly title 'Father' means.

Mrs. Pring had so much housework to get through that Fr. Duddleswell and I took to bathing the children and getting them ready for bed. Danny wore a nappy at night. Mrs. Pring made me put it on him because she didn't trust Fr. Duddleswell with a safety pin.

The little boy fascinated me with his expressive gestures and the miracle of developing thought and language. When, for example, he said 'Bye' his right arm was extended in an exquisite curve and only his dimpled hand waved goodbye from wrist to fingers in a movement as perfect as a butterfly's.

He said to me one night:

'You was good to me.'

'No, Danny, you *were*.'

'Yes, I were.'

'No, Danny, I *was*.'

'Was you, Daddy?' At which point I gave up and

223

told him the story of the three bears until he dropped off to sleep as soundly as if I had preached him a sermon.

'Father Doddles,' I heard from the next room.

A trifle warily. 'Ye-es?'

'How can you see with those bits of glass over your eyes?'

'Try them for yourself.'

After a pause. 'I can't see a thing.'

'I am able to see through them because I am a priest, you follow? And priests can do all sorts of wonderful things.'

'Like wearing a little white collar.'

'What d'you mean?'

'How do you get your head in that little white collar? Is that a miracle?'

'I was born with it on,' Fr. Duddleswell replied modestly, doubtless crossing his fingers.

'Do you wear it in the bath?'

'Not very often.'

'Where do you keep your wife?'

'I do not have one.'

'Why?'

'I don't want one.'

'Why, Father Doddles?'

'I am too ugly, you see.'

'Yes, you are too ugly, you see.'

'Besides, I've lost my hair.'

'Where?'

'It just disappeared.'

'Is that a miracle too?'

'It disappeared like magic, to be sure.'

'Did the wind blew it away?'

'Look you here, keep still, little feller. I want to get you dressed for bed.'

'I'm busy at the moment.'

'But I want to put your pyjamas on.'

'They're my pyjamas.'

'I want to put them on *you*.'

'I'm busy at the moment.'

'You must go to bed, Francis. D'you hear me speak to you? You are tired.'

'I'm *not* tired.'

'Well, I am.'

'Then *you* go to bed, Father Doddles.'

'I bet you Danny is asleep.'

'Danny is the best baby in the world now that Jesus is dead.'

I remembered that Francis was responsible for killing off Jesus early that year.

There was the sound of a scuffle before Francis said:

'I have just caught a very, very, very good idea.'

'Yes?'

'Can I have a piece of chocolate?'

'Later.'

'I don't like later. I've not cleaned my teeth yet.' A few more seconds of rustling. 'Is it later now, Father Doddles?'

'No 'tis not.'

'Chocolate, where are you?'

'Here it is, you scamp.'

'Where were you painted, Father Doddles?'

'Painted?'

'Yes. Where were you painted black like that?'

'These are me clothes, not paint.'

'My Mummy says you are not as black as you are painted.'

'Before you gobble up that chocolatle, little man, let us say our prayers. Our Father Who art in heaven . . .'

We found ourselves walking across the road earlier each evening to do our chores. Fr. Duddleswell liked Francis a lot. He said of him, 'He will make a fine priest one of these days, that little feller.'

He did not feel quite so friendly towards Francis the first evening we tried to coax the boys to eat their supper.

Mrs. Pring had just ordered Danny to take his

foot out of his mouth while he was at table when Francis filled his spoon with soggy, pink blancmange and catapulted it in Fr. Duddleswell's direction. It plopped and made a huge splodge in the middle of his cassock.

Mrs. Pring grabbed a damp dish cloth to sponge Fr. Duddleswell down but before she did so, she genuflected to him and muttered quickly, 'O Sacred Heart of Jesus, I implore/The grace to love Thee daily more and more.'

Ostensibly to help Mrs. Pring but chiefly because we so enjoyed it, Fr. Duddleswell and I joined forces in bathing the boys. We ourselves got a soaking, naturally. Once we even had to return home before our evening meal for a change of clothes.

As luck would have it, there were the two Miss Flanagans at the front door. They looked at us, then at the cloudless sky, then at us again and asked, 'Would it be too much to ask you, Fr. Duddleswell, to hear our confession?'

After the bath each night, it was cowboys and indians. Francis parading in nothing but a policeman's helmet, carried a six-shooter, while Danny in only a pair of Indian moccasins, brandished a tommy-gun.

Then the unexpectedly arduous job of dressing them for bed. Once, when Francis had put his toe in Fr. Duddleswell's eye for the second time, I heard my parish priest complain, 'God Almighty, 'tis worse than putting trousers on a centipede.'

On one occasion, after the bathing session, we were changing the boys on Francis's bed. Danny was in his pyjamas and I was holding his hand when he began to cry. He tried to tell me something but because he couldn't sound the 's' and the 'th' at the beginning of certain words, I didn't grasp his meaning.

'Why's he crying?' I asked Francis.

'Because you won't give it back.'

I pleaded not guilty. 'I haven't taken anything from him.'

'Yes you have. Give him back his thumb.'

'I suddenly realized what Danny meant by, 'I want to 'uck my 'umb' I released his hand and he proceeded contentedly to do just that. He took his thumb out a few moments later to tell us:

'My Uncle Billy died but 'e's very 'appy now.'

According to Mrs. Pring, Uncle Billy was really their great-grandfather who had died in January aged eighty.

'I'm sorry,' Fr. Duddleswell and I said together.

'He died like 'is,' Danny said as he closed his eyes. 'And then he 'miled,'—his rosy face lit up as he showed all his teeth—'like 'is.'

Francis hooted with laughter at Danny's funny expression and immediately started to cry. It was one of those sudden and unexpected transformations from laughter to tears that I was reading about in Dostoievsky at the time. *His* characters always seemed to be subject to the sharpest switch of the emotions. I had thought this incredible until I actually witnessed it in the boys and saw that it took place in me, too, continually. What defence mechanism operated inside myself, I wondered, to have made me unaware over the years of something so obvious?

Francis was crying because Uncle Billy, to whom he had been deeply attached, didn't visit them any more. One set of the children's grandparents had been killed by a bomb during the war, the other set had emigrated to South Africa. White-haired, white-bearded Uncle Billy was their favourite older person.

'Did I ever tell you the story about Billy the Snowman?' Fr. Duddleswell began.

The children sat upright in anticipation of a story.

'Well, now, one day not so long ago—'

'Once upon a time,' Francis corrected him.

'Indeed. That is what I intended to say. Once upon a time, it started to snow. And it snowed and it snowed and—'

'It snowed,' the boys contributed.

'And when it stopped, two little fellers called Francis and . . .'

'Danny.'

'Indeed. Francis and Danny made a snowman. They put some snow into their buckets and patted it down till it was hard as wood and built . . .'

'A snowman.'

'Francis said to Danny, "But it hasn't got a name yet." '

'Uncle Billy,' the boys cried together.

'If you wish. They called it Uncle Billy because he had white hair and a white face and beard, you follow?'

'Did he have eyes, Father Doddles?' Francis wanted to know.

'This nice little feller, Francis, put two pieces of coal for his eyes and the other equally nice little feller Danny put a piece of coal for his nose.'

'No, Father Doddles.'

'Why ever not, Francis?'

'Because snowmans always have a carrot for a nose.'

'So they do. Well, now, Danny gave Uncle Billy a carrot for a nose. And they gave him a twig from the tree for a mouth.' Fr. Duddleswell paused. 'Is that right?'

The boys nodded.

'Francis put his daddy's hat on the snowman and his own scarf round Billy's neck.'

'Why?'

'To keep him warm, of course. But Uncle Billy was still cold, so the two little fellers placed pebbles—'

'What's pebbles?' Francis asked.

'Small stones down the front of him to make him an overcoat.'

'And a white pipe in his mouth?' Francis said.

'Of course. And every day, the boys went into the garden to talk with Uncle Billy and play around him in the snow. But came the warmer weather when the snow began to melt.'

'Ah,' the boys said, disappointed.

'The sun turned very warm, y'see. And on the roofs and the pavements where the snow had been there was left only a wet patch here and there. Then it dried up altogether.'

'What about Uncle Billy?' Francis said.

'Uncle Billy was lucky. He lasted longer than the rest of the snow because he was made firm as wood to start with. But even he began to—'

'Melt.'

Fr. Duddleswell knitted his lips and nodded. 'Many days after all the other snow was gone, Uncle Billy still stood in the garden. But even he could not last for ever. He melted and dripped and his pipe fell out of his mouth and his hat fell over his eyes and he sagged. Like this.' And Fr. Duddleswell dropped his shoulders.

'It's not fair,' Francis said.

'And why ever not?' Fr. Duddleswell asked. 'Uncle Billy did not mind. He said to the little fellers, "Francis and Danny, I have been with you a long, long time." His voice was so soft by now they could hardly hear him. " 'Tis time for me to go." "Why, Uncle Billy?" the boys said. "Because, me boys, all of my friends are up there." '

'Where, Father Doddles?'

'Why, up in the sky, of course. All the snow goes up there when it melts.'

'Inwisible?' Francis asked.

'Almost. Uncle Billy's friends had all become white clouds in the sky. And Uncle Billy said, "Me boys, I am off to join me friends. Without them, I am lonely, y'see. I am going with them on a lovely journey to see the world. But every time I pass over your house, I will nod to you." '

'So he will come back, Father Doddles?'

'Oh, yes. All the time.'

There was a pause for the boys to reflect before

Fr. Duddleswell asked, 'Did you like that story, Francis?'

'Ye-es.'

'You do not sound too definite about it.'

'You're sure,' Francis said, 'he had a carrot for a nose?'

One evening, the lads so missed their mother, there was nothing we could do to calm them.

'They are singing the black psalm,' Fr. Duddleswell said, defeated.

Mrs. Pring, hearing the little ones cry, left her ironing and sat them side by side on the bed.

'Now, my darlings,' she said, 'what is round, has no bottom to it and yet it holds two joints of meat?'

'I give up,' Francis said.

Mrs. Pring held up her finger with the wedding ring on.

'What do you find in a sock that is sometimes very big and yet it doesn't weigh as much as a feather and you can't even see it?'

Fr. Duddleswell went up on the toes of his right foot to show a large white circle in the heel of his sock. 'That reminds me,' he said.

'Not you, Solomon,' Mrs. Pring said irritably. 'Now, my darlings, what is the name of a little house with lots and lots of windows that you can't see through, a house so small it won't even hold a baby mouse?'

By the time Francis had guessed it was a thimble, the cheeks of both boys were dry and they were ready for sleep.

'Children are very special people, Father D,' Mrs. Pring said gloatingly. 'You can't impress *them* just by turning your collar back to front. Their respect you've got to earn, see.' She turned about and walked off in maternal triumph. 'Supper in five minutes.'

The test of our affection came on Friday afternoon when Mrs. Pring said she was so tied up, Fr.

Duddleswell or I would have to take the boys for a walk.

'I have me parish to look after,' Fr. Duddleswell objected.

Mrs. Pring answered him with a quote from one of his own sermons. 'St. Charles Borromeo used to say, "One soul is diocese enough for a bishop." Well, Father D, you've got two dioceses to look after while I get on with ironing your shirts.'

She put the pushchair in the hallway and left us to work out which of us was taking the boys on their outing.

' 'Tis more than an Irishman's reputation is worth to be seen pushing anything on four wheels,' Fr. Duddleswell complained, 'and here is meself a priest of God.' He pondered for a moment. 'Tell you what, Father Neil, let us toss for it. I will do the honours in case you swallow the coin, like.'

He winked at me and pitched the penny in the air.

'Heads,' I called.

He waited until he had a good sight of the coin resting on the back of his hand before calling, 'Heads.'

To cheat, this man didn't need a two-headed penny.

I wasn't having this. '*I* called heads, Father.'

'Tell me truly, me uncooked curate, did I ask you to call?'

'It's a sin to cheat,' I protested.

'God help us, I did nothing of the sort, Father Neil. Did I even win? I did not. It was a dead heat, like.'

'What if I had called tails?'

'Why are you standing here discussing hypotheticals, Father Neil, when there is a job of work to be done? We both of us called correctly, you cannot deny it. So, to avoid the apple of discord, we will compromise and take the boys for their outing together. There will be no scandal given that way.' His eyes twinkled. 'Folks will think this is an altar boys outing.'

Apart from a few quizzical stares, the only embarrassing incidents occurred in the grocer's where we were shopping for Mrs. Pring.

I had just stopped Francis from taking off his shoes and socks when he tried to put a penny in a dog's mouth, believing it to be a wooden model used as a collecting box for the Blind. After that, Danny, inevitably, said, 'I want to do . . .'

'Yes,' I said loudly.

Mr. Billings, the grocer, offered us the use of his facilities.

I glanced at Fr. Duddleswell and he whispered, 'Not on any consideration.'

Realizing the pointlessness of tossing for it, I did the necessary.

Outside, Fr. Duddleswell thanked me profusely. 'One day, Father Neil, I will build a basilica in your honour.'

The boys insisted on sitting on a wall for two minutes like old men watching the traffic go by. Then I hit on the splendid idea of taking them to an antique shop in the window of which stood a huge brown bear, stuffed and moth-eaten. Far from being entertained, they screamed in terror at the sight of it.

'It's only a bear, boys,' I assured them.

'It's not,' Francis said. 'Bears always have a hat and a tie on.'

We couldn't argue with that, so we walked them to a sweet shop to console them with an ice cream. It was a great success for about fifteen seconds, which was how long it took for the magnitude of our mistake to dawn on us. A white Niagara went cascading down their chins, necks and arms, spattering jackets, trousers, socks and shoes. By the time the boys had finished, Fr. Duddleswell and I were ourselves a sticky mess.

As we walked home a good deal wiser for the promenade, Fr. Duddleswell was muttering, 'Who would have thought it needed six adults to look after two little children.'

Jill Bennett met me at the door. 'Someone phoned about Mrs. Martin, Father.'

It was eight o'clock on Saturday evening and Fr. Duddleswell was out on a parish visit.

'Yes, Jill?'

'They say she's very poorly, Father.'

'Was it the hospital that rang?'

'Dunno, Father. I thought you knew. They want you to ring back.'

I telephoned the hospital. The sister in charge of the maternity ward thanked me for calling and told me that Mrs. Martin had been taken to the labour ward an hour before.

I was so stunned, it didn't occur to me to leave a message for Fr. Duddleswell. I was racking my brains, trying to remember what had to be done in the case of premature babies or babies likely to be still-born.

My job was to instruct the doctor or midwife, especially if they were non-Catholics, on how to baptize the baby in the womb, if that was necessary, and which part of the body to aim for.

There was a standard emergency procedure. They should baptize the head if possible, saying, 'If you are alive, I baptize you in the name of the Father and of the Son and of the Holy Ghost.'

As I pedalled to the Kenworthy General, I prayed fervently that the happiness of the previous week would not turn sour on us. At least, I told myself, I'll be able to tell Don Martin I've done my best.

I walked into the hospital unchallenged and took a seat outside the labour ward. A Nurse Jenkins saw me there. She had recently been assigned to casualty where we had met.

She pointed to the labour ward. 'Going in there, Father?' I nodded. 'Difficult birth, is it?'

'Yes, Nurse.'

233

'Well, you'd better get togged up for it.'

She led me to a room not much bigger than a cubicle where she helped me into a large green overall which she tied at the back. She handed me a white linen cap and, finally, a white mask.

'Thanks, Nurse.' My breath bubbled the mask as I spoke.

'Someone's bound to come and collect you in a minute or two, Father.'

I waited half an hour. It seemed like two days. All the time, I was becoming hotter and more agitated. Eventually, I knocked loudly on the door of the labour ward.

A nurse, dressed as I was, appeared. 'Father?'

'Yes.'

'Name, please.'

'Martin,' I said. 'Mrs. Martin.'

She stepped outside and took my arm. 'She's in a bit of pain. Still some way to go, I'm afraid. All you can do at the moment is pray. I'll be back in ten minutes.'

It was nearly an hour before I saw the nurse again. 'I'll take you to her now,' she whispered. 'You will be of most help to us if you hold her hand, comfort her, you know. There's gas and air handy. When the pain is worst, just cover her nose and mouth with the mask and tell her to breathe slowly and rhythmically.'

Jane, in a long white gown was strangely old, almost unrecognizable. A chalk face with dank brown hair plastered over her forehead. A drip was in her arm.

At the door, I whispered to the nurse, 'The baby?'

'Leave the worrying to us, *please*.'

I sat down beside the bed and took Jane's hand. 'Jane,' I said. But she did not respond. She seemed alone and far away.

I pressed a cool sponge to her face and hands. She looked up gratefully. I made to put the sponge to her lips but the sister in charge, an older woman, motioned me to stop.

Jane began to groan as a contraction came upon her. I put the mask over her face and told her to breathe deeply. The nurse looked at me as if to say, 'That's right.'

As in the burial at sea, I lost all track of time. The contractions were coming at briefer intervals and with growing intensity. Occasionally, the nurse put a sort of brass horn on Jane's belly and listened intently for the baby's heart beat.

Once the nurse said to me, 'Foetal stethoscope. Care to listen?'

I pressed my ear to it but could hear nothing. That didn't exactly cheer me up. She wouldn't have asked me to listen to the baby's heart if it had stopped. Would she?

I felt hot and slightly nauseous. The nitrous oxide and the antiseptic were getting to me.

More and more, it seemed to me that I was in the presence of death. And Jane with two small boys and so young.

I wanted to ask the sister or the nurse if they had read Mrs. Martin's file and knew about the two previous difficult births. But both of them were too busy and preoccupied.

From the delivery room next door came a high-pitched, blood-curdling scream as a mother gave birth. 'God the Father,' I said to myself. My mind went back to Ross, the gypsy boy. 'Let the child live, Father. I demand it. Please.'

An elderly doctor in a white coat poked his head round the door for a quick word with the sister. I heard him say, 'I've read the case-history of this one, Sister. I'll be around if the Houseman wants me. Get him to give me a call.'

Good, I thought. They do know it's an emergency.

Five minutes passed before I realized the doctor was none other than Sir Godfrey Ward. A picture of his investiture at the Palace was in the Chaplain's room. Jane's case must be serious if one of the country's leading gynaecologists was in attendance.

Thirty minutes later, the Houseman arrived, looked at Jane and said to the nurse, 'Get Sir Godfrey, please.'

Soon the nurses wheeled Jane into the delivery room and I followed wondering how I could possibly interrupt the doctors' and nurses' concentration for a moment to tell them about intra-uterine baptism with a syringe in an emergency. If the baby was born dead and was unbaptized, he would go to Limbo not Heaven.

Sir Godfrey appeared and for fifteen minutes I virtually closed my eyes as Jane groaned and sometimes screamed.

She stopped screaming for about ten seconds and then the screaming began again. This time, the sound was thinner and higher-pitched as if she had almost run out of breath. I opened my eyes and there, upside down in the nurse's hand, was a baby boy.

'Is he all right?' I almost shouted, alarmed at seeing the baby's blue face.

In spite of her mask, it was clear that the nurse was smiling. 'Of course, a perfectly normal birth.'

Like Francis, I experienced the see-saw of emotions. From terrible fear to exhilaration. That's enough for one night, I thought.

The nurse slapped the baby's back and cleaned his throat out with a tube.

I thanked God for His mercy. I took Jane's hand and whispered in her ear, 'Well done. The third Musketeer.'

I was asked to leave for a few minutes. When I returned, Jane was sitting up in bed, bathed but still in a daze. The baby, wrinkly-faced and wrapped in a blanket, was in a perspex cot.

The nurse said, 'Seven pounds two ounces.'

'Wonderful,' I said.

The sister picked the baby up and placed him in

my arms, 'Congratulations, Mr. Martin, on a beautiful baby boy.'

My joy switched back madly to dismay. My mask bellowed at the mouth but no words came. I nearly dropped the child.

I looked across at Jane and she was looking at me, amazed.

I whispered to the sister. 'He's very nice. But he's not mine.'

The sister said hoarsely, 'You're not the father?'

'Not in the way you mean.'

'What the blazes . . .' the sister began. 'Mrs. Martin, isn't this your husband?'

Jane didn't recognize me. 'My husband's in Cairo. Isn't he—'

'No, he is not,' the sister called over her shoulder. 'I'm just off to get Security.'

I raced after her. 'I can explain, Sister.' After a quarter of an hour, I succeeded and we had a cup of tea together.

My watch showed two-thirty. Realizing the presbytery door would be bolted, I had reconciled myself to spending what was left of the night in the garden shed.

In spite of my recent ordeal, the last week had been worth it. It was nice being a daddy as well as a father. Don Martin was luckier than he knew.

I had pushed my bike through the side gate when I noticed a light on in Fr. Duddleswell's study. I went round to the front door and found it wasn't bolted, after all.

'What a here-and-thereian, y'are, Father Neil. The Playboy of the Western World. In the name of God, lad, I thought the bats or the fairies had eaten you up. You leave no word and wander off till the stone of night is well nigh rolled away. Where have you been?'

Before I could explain, he said, 'I phoned the police and two patrol cars are out looking for you now.

237

I called casualty at the hospital and, thanks be to God, you were not there.'

'No, I wasn't.'

'Mrs. Martin, Jane's sister-in-law, has herself gone down with 'flu. Her husband rang and Jill Bennett says she gave you the message.'

'She did,' I admitted.

'He rang again to say his wife was very poorly and to ask if we could still cope across the road. You did not return the first call so I presumed you had gone to see Diana.'

'No, Father, I didn't.'

Anyway, before you tell me what you have been up to at this late hour, I think you should know that I rang maternity. Jane has just had her third.'

'A boy.'

'Indeed.'

'And it's okay.'

'Seems so, Father Neil. But d'you not think you ought to pop along and see the pair of 'em to make sure, like?'

Twelve

FIDDLER UNDER THE ROOF

One morning in mid-Lent, all the signs were that a cat was expiring in agony in Fr. Duddleswell's study. When I went to investigate, I found my parish priest playing the fiddle.

As I entered, he removed the offending instrument from his chin. 'Did y'like the tune, Father Neil?'

I hadn't realized there was meant to be a tune to it. 'It sounded vaguely familiar, Father.'

'I will take you home again, Kathleen.'

I snapped my fingers very convincingly. 'Of course.'

'I am practising, Father Neil, for the greatest festival of the Church's year.'

Is there an Easter concert?'

He coughed. 'I was referring, I'd have you know, to St. Patrick's Day.' He played a few more bars. 'Well?'

'Very.'

He sniffed and repeated his question. 'Well?'

Not knowing what reaction was expected of me, I started humming the line, *To where your heart will find no pain.*

'And why are you humming *that*,' he demanded, 'when I just played you the opening of *When Irish eyes are smiling*?'

I had no plausible excuse ready to hand so I said, 'What did you think I was humming, then, Father?'

He scratched his head without answering. 'This year, Father Neil, we are holding a monster meeting of the race. Bishop O'Reilly is himself threatening to preside at the evening service. Mind you, he is not such a bad feller really, when he forgets he is a bishop.'

'How often is that, Father?'

He cleared his throat. 'About once in a decade.'

'Religion,' I said, smiling, 'has spoiled many a nice man.'

'True, true. The Bishop's father, so I believe, was a carpenter in Kilkenny but his son had notions from the time he was a child of moving higher and becoming a Bishop.' He put his fiddle to his chin. 'After all, as the Bishop said once in a sermon, "Whoever heard of a carpenter who made his name in the world?"'

239

He continued softly playing unrecognizable melodies that somehow stirred his soul. With eyes closed, he said, 'Yourself has an important part in the proceedings, Father Neil, naturally.'

'I'm not expected to preach the sermon on St. Patrick?'

'Indeed not. I am asking Canon Mahoney to do just that.'

'Thank God,' I laughed, very relieved.

'No,' he said, his chin vibrating against the base of the fiddle. 'Since I discovered your talent for it in the New Year, I am wanting you to tell a funny story at the evening concert.'

'I am no good as a comedian,' I protested.

'Am I world class at the fiddle?'

'Haifitz could learn a thing or two,' I said, without specifying.

He scowled at me. 'You are right, Father Neil, you are none too good at the comicals.' He put on his mischievous smile. 'A chance for you to shine, lad, like a star on a frosty night.'

'*Galway Bay*!' I made a guess at the current noise in an effort to change the subject.

He shook head and violin together. '*By Killarney's Lakes And Fells*.' He played on before suggesting, 'You recognize it now.'

'Of course,' I said, warily, in case he had switched tunes without warning. 'A great favourite.'

Mercifully, he fell to musing, to his own accompaniment, on the olden times.

'Ah, dismal was the day'—scratch, scratch—'me father left the happy land of the Troubles'—scratch, scratch—'and took the emigration to England.'

Dismal for some of us, I thought, wanting to plug my ears.

'This is a pagan country, there is no denying it.'

'It's the people they let in,' I said.

'No, seriously, Father Neil, on a bus in this country, so I am told, not even the women will give up their seat to a priest.'

'I'm astonished.' I hoped he would notice the ambiguity of tone.

'There is only one advantage in being English, as far as I know.'

'Which is?'

'Unlike the Scots, the Italians and, above all, the Irish, English people cannot commit mortal sin.'

'Delighted to hear it, Father, but tell me why.'

'An Englishman's motives are always too mixed.'

More soul-stirring music before: 'Father Neil, what is an Irishman? Tell me that, now.'

I kept silent, sensing disobedience was demanded of me.

'A white English-speaking negro, that is what.' The violin gave off a plangent sound. 'We do not belong to the native race of the place. Oh for that land God made across the water where all the fields are fresh and green.'

I remembered the old saying, 'Ireland is a very good country to live out of.'

'You have only to contrast an Irish face with an English face, Father Neil. Mine and yours, to take a for instance.'

'Yours is much prettier,' I said, loud enough for him not to hear.

'Someone once said, Father Neil, when God makes an Irish face, His kindly hand brushes straight up, y'follow?'

'And the English face, Father?'

He dipped his violin. 'Downwards, lad, downwards. So the whole effect is one of, um, deceit'—scratch, scratch—'and being closed like a clam.'

'Was the "someone" who said that an Englishman, by any chance?'

For reply, he almost poked his bow in my eye.

I did my best to sound irritable. 'Father, I really think you are the one to tell that funny story.'

'Stop your whimpering, Father Neil, and I will buy you some ointment for your nappy rash.'

At that moment, Dr. Daley was ushered in by

Mrs. Pring. At the door, he lifted his right hand in a poetic gesture. ' "If music be the food of love," as Yeats has said.'

Fr. Duddleswell placed the instrument down on the desk and sighed, 'Donal.'

'Charles,' Dr. Daley said with an equal passion. 'I would recognize that playing anywhere, even with my eyes closed.'

'You would?'

'Surely. I don't want to flatter you, Charles, but I do not know anybody who plays the fiddle exactly like yourself.'

'I am out of practice and that is the truth,' Fr. Duddleswell replied coyly.

'Tut-tut. The imagination is boggled at what it would hear, Charles, if only you took the fiddle out of its case more than once a year. Why even the stone lions in Trafalgar Square would not be able to keep their feet still.'

'Too kind,' Fr. Duddleswell purred, 'you are too kind. But thanks to you for the good word, anyway.'

Dr. Daley's build-up was now complete. 'You wouldn't have by any chance a drop of . . .'

'During the forty days, Donal?'

'You are not wanting to take me off my life-support system simply because it is Lent? Dear, dear, *dear*. Besides, Charles,' he undid the top button of his shirt, 'I have a hair-shirt on underneath that scratches worse than a fiddler's bow.'

'What is wrong with water, Donal?'

'Apart from everything, Charles? Well, now, to be scientific about it, I'm sixty per cent water already and I don't want myself diluted further. Anyway, didn't St. Pat himself say, It's a Christian thing to relieve the first necessity?'

'Donal, for the last time, can you not give up the whiskey at least during Lent? Yes or no?'

'I am surprised at your unpatriotic fervour.'

'How so?'

'You know as well as I, Charles, that Irish has no

242

words for yes and no.' The doctor shook his benign head. 'Not words that spring readily to an Irishman's lips, that's for sure.'

Fr. Duddleswell said, 'Your eyes are that glassy, you could take them out and put them in again without damage.' But, doubtless still feeling how well his old friend had just scratched his back over his playing, he relented.

'God bless you, Charles, till the day the big bell rings slow for you.'

As Fr. Duddleswell poured, Dr. Daley was saying, 'Indeed, you play like an angel from Heaven, Charles.' Whenever there was a hint that the dispensing hand might slacken or halt, he repeated, 'Like an angel,' until it rallied.

When the glass was full Dr. Daley held it up to the light. 'What a great stranger you are,' he said. 'Now Charles, to business. As you are aware, the St. Pat's Day committee has elected me its chairman again this year.'

'Donal, before you go on, since I have just throttled me conscience and done you a disservice, would you care to do something for me?'

Dr. Daley took a satisfying sip. 'Anything, Charles. *Anything.*'

' 'Tis me knees, Donal. There is something the matter with 'em.'

'That is the penalty, Charles, for trying to walk to Heaven on them during Lent. Good job I have brought my tool kit with me. Sit your holy fundament down there.'

While Dr. Daley fumbled one-handed in his black bag for a hammer, Fr. Duddleswell sat down meekly on his desk. He lifted his cassock while the doctor tapped his knees, one by one. On the second, the foot kicked so violently that Dr. Daley's glass went flying across the room.

'Dear, dear, dear, dear, dear, dear, *dear*,' Dr. Daley said gloomily. 'That foot will have to come

243

off, Charles. I cannot have it shamelessly destroying glass after glass of the liquor.'

'Fill up again, Donal. And tell me your diagnosis. Housemaid's knee?'

'I have a furious thirst on me this morning that is drinking me dry,' the Doctor said, as he replenished his glass. 'It's water on the knee, all right.'

'Not so!'

'I have been trying to impress on you over these many years, my consecrated friend, what filthy stuff the water is and now, will you believe me? it is flowing like the Irish Sea twixt your skin and your knee caps. Tut-tut.'

'And the treatment, Donal?'

'Stick to the whiskey, Charles, and for the time being pray humbly on your bum. It's not fair on your charming little knees to place such a terrible burden on them.'

When we were seated comfortably, Fr. Duddleswell explained why he had asked the Doctor round. 'Y'see, Donal, this year St. Patrick's Day falls on the eve of Palm Sunday.'

'It does,' Dr. Daley said, contemplating the contents of his glass, as if for him all drinking days were much alike.

'Indeed, which is why I am thinking this year, out of respect for our Blessed Lord's Passion, the concert—'

'Yes?'

'Ought to be dry.'

Dr. Daley instinctively reached out for a refill to withstand the shock. 'A thirst more or less sudden has seized me by the throat.' He looked at Fr. Duddleswell incredulously. 'Dear Charles, your ideas must have gone to your head. Shall I examine next your noble dome for you?'

'Donal, I am *not* off me chump.'

'Charles, are you expecting the Irish faithful to wet their throats with spittle?' A heavy swig. 'Are

244

you wanting our concert hall to be melancholy as the graveyard of Clonmacnoise?'

'The day before *Palm Sunday*, Donal?'

'Next, you will be asking the kiddies to give up the sweets on St. Pat's day.'

'I am no saint meself,' Fr. Duddleswell began.

'Not even your severest critic would accuse you of being *that*, Charles.'

'But, I am having no tearing drunks hereabouts as Holy Week begins.'

'I will look after the bar myself, like I am its guardian angel.'

'And the fox will look after the hens.'

'Why, Charles, it is all right, I am telling you. I have a hundred helpers who can handle a shillelagh, any one of whom on his own could clear the fair.'

'Have it your way, Donal. I am only the parish priest in this place.' The irony being lost on Dr. Daley, he added, 'But 'tis against me better judgment, truly. As I always say, "The family that drinks together, sinks together." '

'What else, Charles?' the Doctor enquired, with the ease of a man who has won the major battle.

'Dancing, Donal. Let everything be done decent, like.'

To advertise my presence, I said, 'Not cheek to cheek?'

Fr. Duddleswell returned my look stolidly. 'Not *anything* to *anything*,' he growled. 'I will not have the colleens in this parish being fingered feverishly like rosary beads.'

'Understood,' Dr. Daley said smoothly, as if at his advanced age this was a problem that was none of his.

'A fresh lick of green paint, Donal, for the Saint's statue.'

'Surely.'

'I am having Mrs. Joseph Arbunathy personally bring some shamrock over the day before the feast so 'tis fresh for the Bishop to bless. Does that about cover it, Donal?'

'It does.' And the Doctor sipped happily.

'You are sure, Donal,' Fr. Duddleswell said pointedly.

'I almost forgot,' Dr. Daley said. 'The committee has asked me to invite yourself to—'

'Uh huh?'

'Kindly play the fiddle for us at the concert.'

'On one condition,' Fr. Duddleswell said, stretching his luck.

Two worried weeks passed. Fr. Duddleswell was trying on a lovely old lace alb specially laundered for the Bishop to wear on the great day.

''Tis beautiful,' Fr. Duddleswell said, admiring himself up and down. 'What do *you* think, Father Neil. No flattery, mind, I am not one to be flattered by flattery.'

'Beautiful, Father.'

A conceited smile spread over his face. 'You took the word out of me mouth.'

'Yes, I did,' I admitted, edging towards the door.

'Now, Father Neil, what about that funny story you volunteered to tell?' I pleaded ignorance of his meaning. 'You remember how I blackmailed Dr. Daley and threatened I would not play the fiddle this year except you were allowed to tell a funny story.'

The door was already open. Another second and I would have made my escape. Unfortunately, Mrs. Pring chanced to be barring the way, Fr. Duddleswell called her in.

'Now Mrs. Pring, as y'know full well, I am not such a one as courts flattery.' He indicated the precious alb. 'Tell me truly, what d'you think?'

She gave him a cold stare. 'Arsenic in old lace,' she said, and closed the door on me.

'I knew *she* could be relied on to let me down,' he

fumed. 'Oh, that woman is a load on me stomach. One day she will go to the bad place.'

'See you later, Father.'

'Stay, son of me praise,' he ordered. 'Cheer me up with your funny story.'

It wasn't the time or the place. 'I can't possibly,' I said, before I began:

'There was once a meeting of all the nations of the world.'

'Where was this meeting taking place, Father Neil?'

'I don't know, Father.'

'He does not know,' he muttered darkly to himself. 'This is a *funny* story, Father Neil. Make it Bognor or Blackpool.'

'Blackpool, Father.'

He laughed. 'That is very comical. Who would ever have suggested that all the nations of the world should meet in Blackpool?'

'*You* did.'

'Oh, get on with you, Father Neil.' He proceeded to pull the alb over his head.

'And while they were there, they decided to ask God which of all the nations in the world is dearest—'

'Hell's bells,' he cried.

'You've heard it before, Father?'

'I have just put my fist through the lace on the bottom of this alb.'

I headed for the door. 'I'll tell you it another time, Father.'

He signalled his intention to suffer on. 'You were saying, Father Neil.'

'They wrote a message to God: "Which nation in the world, God, is nearest to Your heart?"'

Fr. Duddleswell was still examining the tear in the lace. 'And how, pray, did they convey this message to the Almighty God?'

I hadn't given that a thought. 'Perhaps they put it in a rocket, Father.'

'Easier if they burn the scroll the query is written on.'

'Thank you, Father. So they burnt the scroll the query was written on. And there appeared a dove.'

'Not a pigeon,' he exlaimed mischievously. 'Only the other day, one of Billy Buzzle's gave *me* a very interesting message from heaven.'

'In the dove's beak was a piece of paper that fluttered down out of the blue. The President of the nations there assembled picked it up and—'

'Of what nationality was this President?'

'Er. Does it matter?'

'It does, to be sure.'

I couldn't see why but I said, 'Since the meeting is in Blackpool, the President had better be—'

'Switch the meetin' to Dublin, Father Neil.'

'Of course, anything to make it funnier. So the President of the Republic picks up the divine message and reads: "All nations—"'

He cut across me. '"Dear Mr. de Valera, All nations—".'

'"All nations are equally dear to my heart",' I took up.

''Tis too improbable,' he declared. 'God loving Russia and China the same as Italy and Spain and old Ireland?' He bit off a loose thread from the alb. 'You are sure you cannot play the piano?'

I was getting fed up with his interruptions. 'Wait,' I insisted. '"All nations are equally dear to My heart. Yours, Almighty O'God."'

He lifted his glasses on to his forehead to inspect the torn lace more closely. 'I am waiting, Father Neil.'

'Goodbye,' I said.

'Is that, too, part of the funny story?' He saw that it wasn't only the lace alb that was the worse for wear. 'No, dead serious, lad, that is very amusing indeed. Is that "Almighty O'God" meant to indicate that God—?'

'Comes from Aberdeen,' I said, slamming the door on my back.

'Big Paws, you leave Father Neil's food alone, you hear me? Or else.'

Mrs. Pring gave Fr. Duddleswell this stern warning as he attempted to snatch one of my slices of toast at breakfast.

'I'm not having the Law of the Claw in this house,' Mrs. Pring went on, 'not when Father Neil's as thin as a wax taper already.'

'God help us,' Fr. Duddleswell cried. 'I will get me tin hat and hide down the dug-out.'

He had taken up the Lent fast in earnest, mainly to control his weight, I think.

His resolve was first noticed on Ash Wednesday. He appeared at breakfast with a black smudge on his forehead and declined to eat as much as a boiled egg. Not a priest to do things by halves, he looked as if he had just climbed down the chimney.

He was faithful to the fast in the main, measuring out meticulously the food the Church allowed on an inaccurate pair of kitchen scales he'd borrowed from Mrs. Pring. But he had these horrible lapses when he ravenously raided the food put in front of me.

Another of his Lenten whims was to have the church door locked as soon as Mass commenced. He posted a trusted parishioner near the exit with the key, ready to open up if a child fell sick or a woman fainted. But God preserve the key-bearer if he otherwise unlocked the door before the celebrant had left the altar.

'I want the Almighty God to have the honour due Him,' was his exlpanation. The truth was he wanted everybody inside the building for both collections.

On Friday, March 16th, he rang Dr. Daley to remind him that St. Patrick's statue had not yet received its annual lick of paint.

'Nothing must go amiss this time, Donal,' I heard

249

him say. 'I was misfortuned enough the last occasion the Bishop paid us a visit when a silly dog tried to eat him.'

Dr. Daley sent someone round immediately to make the Saint look spick and span enough to be borne on high in the procession.

That evening, Mrs. Arbunathy called at the presbytery with a sackful of shamrock. Fr. Duddleswell thanked her warmly and retired to his study to examine it. In the long journey across the water, the shamrock had begun to wilt. He placed it, therefore, in a wooden box and left it in the garden to soak up the night dew.

'Father D, you won't get me wearing any of that stuff,' Mrs. Pring declared.

'I am sure I beg your pardon.'

'I'm not going to be a hypocrite and pretend I'm fond of the Irish when I'm not.'

Fr. Duddleswell was snorting like a horse with a heavy cold. 'If you ever harboured the ambition of being me housekeeper in Heaven, Mrs. Pring, you can forget it entirely.'

'Talking to you, Father D, is like talking to a wall without ears.'

Remembering it was Lent, he controlled himself with an effort. 'Woman, would you kindly open that door this side and close it the other?'

Next morning when the great day dawned, the discussion about whether Mrs. Pring would or would not wear shamrock seemed academic. It had vanished in the night.

Thirteen

THE DAY OF THE SHAMROCK

Fr. Duddleswell rushed madly into my study. 'Father Neil, you would not be playing cruel tricks on your lovable old P.P.?'

'What, Father?'

'Jasus, I can feel the Big Black Fox breathing sourly on me cheek.' He really did look as if death had come for him at that moment. 'Start digging the hole down for me, lad. I am a gone man, so I am.'

Suddenly he *knew* what had become of his shamrock. He crossed to the window, opened it and, finding a new lease of life, roared:

'You bloody iniquitous goat.'

Down to the garden and another roar in the direction of Billy Buzzle's bedroom.

Billy's sleep-lined face appeared. You had to admire his presence of mind.

'Happy feast day, Father O'Duddleswell,' he yawned.

Fr. Duddleswell explained with belligerence why his prospect of happiness had dimmed overnight.

'Father O'Duddleswell,_ *why* are you getting steamed up over a few miserable ounces of green stuff?'

'Green stuff,' Fr. Duddleswell cried. 'You bad potato, you Oliver Cromwell, you Black and Tan.'

'Your fault,' Billy said. 'You drove my goat frantic with your fiddling, I shouldn't wonder.'

Fr. Duddleswell was furious. 'I am warning you, at all the Sunday Masses, I am telling me parishioners that you and your Tory goat annihilated all our shamrock on St. Patrick's Day.'

It was getting to Billy that something of consequence had taken place for which he was being held responsible. 'You wouldn't do that to me, Father O'Duddleswell? Please, no.'

'Indeed, I will, you rapparree. Me people would forgive you anything, Mr. Buzzle, even the stench of pig. But not ruining our festival by causing a famine of shamrock in the parish. That is the sin against the Holy Ghost, y'hear?' He banged the fence. 'No Irishman will ever take a bet with you again. Else I will refuse him absolution.'

'Father O'Duddleswell, wait.' Since his protagonist gave no sign of waiting: *Wait,* I tell you. I promise you, you won't see that goat no more after today. My Pontius don't like him. The stinking goat keeps butting him in the flank, anyway. I'll send him into the wilderness. Agreed?'

The goat which had slipped its lead in the night came prancing towards Fr. Duddleswell. A superb animal to look at.

I had called through the open window, 'Find him a good home, Billy,' before I realized what I was saying.

'As for you,' Fr. Duddleswell said stridently, as he stormed into my room, 'I want you to get a replacement for the shamrock.'

'Fly over and back to—?'

'Father Neil,' he groaned. 'Go to the park, lad, and pick whatever clover you can. Enough of the shamrock has come through the post for me to put a coating of it on the top. Pray the Bishop will not notice anything untoward.'

I was already slipping out of my cassock. 'How long have I got, Father?'

'Take as long as you like, Father Neil, provided you are back here within the hour.'

* * *

Grabbing Mrs. Arbunathy's sack, I cycled to the park. It was raining. I was wearing my raincoat as well as a muffler to hide my collar.

Clover was in short supply. I searched for it in the wet grass on my hands and knees. If not clover, anything that would pass as shamrock.

Next to the part was a series of allotments surrounded by a tall, wire fence. Because of the foul weather, no one was working the allotments. I decided to climb over the fence and look for a shamrock-substitute in more promising surroundings.

I was about to make my ascent when a police patrol car passed by. I bent down to tie up my shoelace. When I stood up, the car had gone. *Laus Deo semper*.

The fence presented no problems to one my height and at last my luck had changed. I came across yards and yards of chickweed. A gentle tug and it came away in big streamers. Within five minutes, the sack was full.

' 'Morning, sir.'

The two policemen in the patrol car had returned. 'Good morning, Officers.' Caged in, I was forced to address them through the wire.

'Short visit, sir.' The taller of them, with a brush moustache, acted as their spokesman.

'It's raining,' I said, outwardly calm but inwardly in turmoil.

It was an improbable tale I had to tell. Who would credit that I was looking for something like shamrock on a wet Saturday morning in someone else's garden allotment? Before coming to St. Jude's, I had never been in trouble with the police.

'Forget your key, did you, sir?'

'I don't have a key. Not to that gate.'

'You do have other keys, do you, sir?' I made no reply. 'What were you doing in there, sir, taking a stroll?'

'You wouldn't believe me if I told you.'

'Let me be the judge of that.'

I tried him and, afterwards, he acknowledged I was right in the first place.

'All right, sir, climb back over here.'

In my nervous state, my foot stuck in the topmost hole in the wire and I nearly broke my ribs as I fell forward on the policemen's heads.

'Open up that sack,' the taller policeman said, adjusting his cap.

I obeyed. He saw there were only weeds. His companion muttered, 'He must've realized we were on to him.'

'Tip *all* the goodies out, please, sir,' the senior policeman said.

It was nothing but chickweed.

His companion noticed for the first time that I was wearing a clerical collar. He again muttered behind a gloved hand, 'I reckon we've got a nutcase here, Jim.'

Jim said, 'Shall we book him?'

'What for? Nicking weeds?'

'Look here,' Constable Jim said, coming over stern, 'we can't have this sort of barbaric be'aviour. Not on our patch. In future, if you want weeds, you grow 'em, understand?'

They marched off—self-consciously, I thought—to their car. Greedily, I stuffed the weeds back into the sack and cycled home.

I fended off Fr. Duddleswell's congratulations. He noticed because he said:

'Are you celebrating Mass, Father Neil, that you turn your back on me like this?'

In common with Mrs. Pring, I was determined not to sport greenery of any kind that day. I even made up my mind to alter the funny story I was being made to tell. It would end: 'Yours, Almighty God. P.S. The Saint dearest to my heart sends his love, the Englishman, Patrick.'

254

If the audience didn't find that amusing, too bad. I didn't become a priest for laughs.

'Father Duddleswell, Father Boyd, a hundred thousand blessings on the both of you.'

The Bishop, his thin shoulders covered by a scarlet cloak, his red-ribbed cassock spattered with green, was in sparkling mood.

Remembering, no doubt, that next day was Palm Sunday, he pointed to his limousine and said, 'I would prefer to travel by donkey myself, like our Blessed Saviour, y'see? But would the Holy Father hear of it? He would not.'

We knelt on the pavement to kiss his ring before bowing him into the house where Mrs. Pring, in a shamrock-patterned apron, was introduced. My bosom heaved and suddenly felt bare. Mrs. Pring, my only ally, had betrayed me.

Waiting in Fr. Duddleswell's study was Canon Mahoney, the Bishop's own theologian, as orthodox as St. Augustine. The Canon, bald and friendly, possessed a torso like a big D. By choosing him as guest preacher, Fr. Duddleswell indicated he wasn't intending to take any risks.

The Bishop wasn't long in noticing the glaring absence of shamrock on my person. 'Father, you are surely not one of those,' he asked me, 'that have no respect for the land of saints and scholars?'

'On the contrary, me Lord,' Fr. Duddleswell put in gallantly, ' 'twas Father Neil who supplied us with the shamrock you are about to bless.' He plucked half the display off his own cassock and pinned it on mine. 'It goes with the colour of your gills, lad.' he whispered.

Soon he was the one turning green. The Bishop said:

'Father Duddleswell, I would have you know I have a nice surprise in store for you.'

I think for one moment Fr. Duddleswell was expecting the Bishop to say he was promoting him to Canon.

'Yes, me Lord,' he gulped.

'After your good housekeeper has served us an evening meal as arranged, Monsignor Pat here and myself will be attending your concert.'

'But, me Lord,' Fr. Duddleswell protested, thinking of the alcohol on sale, 'that cannot be.'

'And why ever not?' the Bishop enquired suspiciously.

''Tis too great an honour to bestow on any parish,' Fr. Duddleswell whimpered.

The Bishop beamed as if to say it was for self-sacrifices of this sort that he was consecrated in the first place.

While the Bishop was vesting in the sacristy, Fr. Duddleswell took me aside.

'At some point in the ceremony, Father Neil, I want you to root out Dr. Daley. Warn him that the bloody Bishop is coming to the concert, so it must be *dry*, like.'

I promised and waited for my opportunity.

The Bishop, in gold cope and mitre, bestowed his blessing on the congregation as the ministers and servers processed slowly round the packed church. St. Patrick's statue, borne on its platform by four strong men, headed the procession and the Bishop brought up the rear. The choir and congregation were in excellent voice with, *O Patrick, hail, who once the wand'ring race.*

Examining my thoughts, I was surprised at the calmness with which I was facing what I sensed, for no reason I could pin down, to be impending disaster.

It began as soon as the men set down the statue on a table on the sanctuary. The Bishop arrived and, with an onrush of unrehearsed emotion, stepped forward to kiss it. Fortunately, he first clasped the statue with both hands and thus discovered that the paint was wet. Certainly he lost a glove which spent the rest of the ceremony glued to the statue, but at least his lips didn't have to be wrenched free from the Saint's tacky feet.

During the early part of the ceremony, I could hear the church door being rattled noisily. I wondered why Fr. Duddleswell, on this day of days, still insisted on the door being barred against latecomers.

The sermon was good, at any rate. Canon Mahoney took as his text St. Patrick's words: 'I was a stone lying in deep mud until the Mighty One in His mercy took hold of me and put me on top of the wall.'

He spoke of Patrick's 'Vision of the Night' when the young Saint read a letter addressed to him which began, 'The cry of the Irish' and he thought he heard the cry of those who lived near the Western sea beseeching him, 'Come again and walk among us.'

A prayerful man was Patrick. He managed each day to get through thousands of ejaculatory prayers and all one hundred and fifty psalms, many of them at night while he was up to his neck in icy water.

The genius of the Saint, the Canon said, was to take a piece of wood sorrel that grew in abundance in that wild, wet land and by it to elucidate the ineffable mystery of Catholicism. The preacher's words were memorable for their simplicity.

'Now, my dear brethren, you all know the sacred Trinity is the heart of our holy faith, even though we cannot make head nor tail of it. It is a mystery of faith, which is to say it is more of a riddle than is a riddle itself. Three persons in one God. Is not the very point of Almighty God revealing this mystery to us, now, to make us realize how shamefully ignorant we are? Besides, my dearly beloved brethren, what need would there be of the submissiveness of faith if you or I understood the words, "Three in one and one in three" which I am now preaching to you about.'

After the sermon, the Bishop blessed the three-leaved symbol of faith artfully spread out by Fr.

Duddleswell in a silver bowl. From time to time, the Bishop poked his ungloved finger among the greenery as if he could not believe his eyes.

Fr. Duddleswell saw personally to the distribution of the 'shamrock', then the Bishop led the congregation in reciting the rosary.

This was the best opportunity I would have of slipping away from the sanctuary in search of Dr. Daley. He was in the back row, snoozing. I woke him up and briefed him on both the problem and Fr. Duddleswell's drastic solution.

'Lord save us', the Doctor said hoarsely, 'the Great Statesman of St. Jude's is cracking his whip like a whale's tail tonight. Is Charles wanting us all to suffer from the dry rot?'

'That's the message, Doctor.'

'Thank you kindly, Father Neil. I have an hour to sort this out while you clergy are at dinner. Leave everything to me.'

The church door was still being rattled furiously so I went to investigate. The custodian of the key that evening was Tim Fogarty. To my surprise, Tim was himself pushing and tugging at the door.

'What's up, Tim?' I asked.

'Trouble, Father.' He was whispering so that the crowd in the vicinity wouldn't hear him. 'I locked up, as ordered, when the procession started. Then some idiot came late, found the door locked and tried to open it from the outside with his own key.'

'Now it's jammed?'

'Can't shift it, Father.'

'Hope nobody faints,' I said. 'I suppose, though, you can always take them into the sacristy.'

'Sure, Father. I'll try and get this open before the ceremony is over.'

A second, more horrific thought struck me. 'I only hope there isn't a fire, Tim.'

'What's that,' somebody enquired next to Tim, 'did somebody mention a fire?'

Tim shook his head vigorously to stop a panic and

I hurried back to the sanctuary where I was due to expose the Blessed Sacrament for Benediction as soon as the rosary came to an end.

Everything went well until I was putting the Blessed Sacrament back into the tabernacle. The last two hymns to be sung were, *Father of all those far-scattered sheep of Christ* and the gem of them all, *Hail glorious Saint Patrick, dear saint of our isle.*

Either I was seeing things or the congregation was leaving the church *via* the sacristy. My eyes swept over the moving throng and I had no difficulty in lip-reading what the ushers were saying. One word: 'FIRE. As I removed the monstrance from its stand high above the altar, it was clear to me that the only flames on view were coming from the candles.

People near Tim Fogarty must have picked up our snatch of conversation. My 'fire' had swollen into a full-scale rumour that the whole building was ablaze.

The ensuing panic was arguably the most orderly ever seen. Still bellowing out *Hail Glorious Saint Patrick* and genuflecting at the top of the centre aisle, the congregation was making its way through the sacristy, into the presbytery and out into the street.

What with the din of the organ and the full-throated singing of the choir in the loft and the ministers on the sanctuary, none of them realized that the church was being evacuated.

I returned, guilt-ridden, to my place at the side of the altar. What could I do but wait for the rest of the ministers, still with their backs to the pews, to grasp what had happened?

After the last tear-filled reduplication of *For God and Saint Patrick, For God and Saint Patrick, For God and Saint Patrick and our native home*, Fr. Duddleswell, to the Bishop's left, said, 'And now, me Lord, your final blessing.'

The Bishop inclined his head for Monsignor Pat to put the mitre on him; he took his crozier from an altar server and turned round to face a completely empty church.

Several hundred people had left without trace. It was, as Fr. Duddleswell commented later, the greatest disappearing act since the earth opened and swallowed the enemies of Moses.

'Father Duddleswell,' the Bishop said shrilly.

Fr. Duddleswell had sunk to his knees, facing the altar with his eyes closed, to await the blessing. He too turned and looked about him as if he were peering into a mirror and couldn't find his own face.

There was nothing for it. We genuflected and returned without ceremony to the sacristy where Tim Fogarty started to apologize for the strange occurrence.

I wasn't letting Tim take the blame for me. I butted in with, 'It's all my fault, Father.'

'What d'you mean, Father Neil?'

I admitted I had initiated a rumour about a fire.

'A further thing,' the Bishop said, poking me in the back with his crozier, 'who are you, Father, to alter the lines of the great hymn to "Ever bless and defend the sweet land of our birth, Where the *chickweed* still blooms as when thou wert on earth"?'

'I'm sorry, my Lord.'

To atone in part, I went into the house for some turpentine. I released the Bishop's glove from the Saint's statue and gave it back to him.

'Thank you, Father,' he said, sniffing it, 'but for the rest of this day I will be leaving my iron fist naked to the elements.'

When things had calmed down a little, Fr. Duddleswell put his tiny teeth to my ear and grinded out, 'You know the worst thing of all this, you Sean O'Clod?'

'No,' I said miserably.

'There was no final bloody collection.'

Dinner was not an outstanding success, though the charity of St. Patrick gradually made itself felt.

'A famous crowd tonight, me Lord,' was Fr. Duddleswell's incautious opener.

'At the start, Father, there was that. But'—he was remembering the antics of Billy Buzzle's black labrador on his previous visit—'stranger things have happened to me in your church.'

Fr. Duddleswell held up a bottle of best Sauternes. 'Me Lord, I do not suppose . . .'

'Very, very kind of you, Father, but not in Lent. And tomorrow . . .'

'Palm Sunday,' I said.

'But,' the Bishop went on graciously, 'far be it from me to prevent the rest of you from enjoying yourselves.'

Fr. Duddleswell, Canon Mahoney and I bowed our heads. The Bishop's secretary, Monsignor Patrick O'Connell bowed his, too, as he bent down to open up a leather bag at his feet. From it he drew a well-known brand of tonic wine, uncorked it and filled the Bishop's glass.

'You have brought your own wine, my Lord.'

I shouldn't have said it. I had resolved not to put another foot wrong. But somehow such a resolution always made me clumsier than ever.

'It is not wine really,' the Bishop said darkly. 'It is a health food. The doctor makes me drink it for my liver and lots of other ailing bits and pieces of me.'

I noted its high alcoholic content printed on the bottle but said nothing.

Even so, we were on the upward slope.

'Know what the Prods say?' the Bishop asked. 'Give the Catholics a Pope and a potato and they'll be happy.' He dug into his succulent roast duck. 'There is a great deal of truth to that, Fathers.'

We all nodded solemnly as we too stoked up.

The Bishop turned approvingly to Mrs. Pring. 'A wonderful meal, Madam.'

Mrs. Pring smiled and curtseyed before Fr. Duddleswell said, 'Three cats we have had, me Lord, and they all left home on account of her cooking.'

Mrs. Pring was grateful for the guffaws that greeted the remark. It saved her blushes.

'Me father, God rest him, had a saying, me Lord,' Fr. Duddleswell went on. 'Three sights may be seen on St. Pat's Day in Spring; ploughing, sowing and harrowing.'

'When I was a lad on the farm,' Canon Mahoney contributed, 'we always called the 17th "the day of twenty-seven works". Those were the days, they were indeed.'

A comfortable mood of nostalgia settled on the company. The Bishop, with sweet melancholy, said:

'I cannot promise myself too many more St. Pat's days like the present. Soon I am for that land lovelier than Ireland and further off even than America.'

'Never', 'Do not say that, my Lord', ' 'Tis a sin almost to say so', came from the other diners.

'True for you,' the Bishop insisted. 'Yet I am on the black side of sixty, is that not so?' He was viewing life through the small end of the telescope. 'Ah, I do remember twenty years past when I was made a bishop. The Apostolic Delegate called me to him and said, "Monsignor O'Reilly, the Holy Father asks if you will consent to be consecrated bishop".'

A deep sigh as if he still could not believe his luck two decades afterwards.

'And I replied to the Delegate, thrice beating my breast, "Excellency, *Domine, non sum dignus*, I am not worthy, not worthy, not worthy." '

There was a pregnant pause before I blurted out, 'But you did say yes, my Lord.'

The Bishop looked at me sourly. 'I did. It was a traditional command of the Holy Father couched in courteous question form.'

'I'm very glad you said yes, my Lord,' I said, braving it out.

The Bishop ran his tongue over his teeth as if to test their sharpness. 'For the life of me, I do not see why, Father Boyd.'

That was when I made a quick decision against the English version of my funny story. A few moments later, I decided I wouldn't tell the Irish version either. I might mess up my lines and drop another clanger so that the Bishop sent me to another diocese. Instead, I would do a recitation.

'One thing I never could understand about St. Patrick,' Fr. Duddleswell put in, rescuing me again. 'When he preached and rich ladies threw their jewels at his feet, why did he throw them back?'

No member of the clergy round the table was able to suggest an answer to a puzzle of that magnitude.

Our group walked round to Tipton Hall. From it emerged the sound of pipes, fiddles, accordions and general merrymaking.

Inside, the place was packed with Irish and fellow-travellers. I saw enough shamrock on the poles alone to fill a barn.

As we entered, a hush descended, the dancing stopped and couples unclasped hands.

'Please do not let us interrupt you,' Fr. Duddleswell called out, and gradually the gaiety returned.

Dr. Daley stepped forward and hurried us past the bar to a semi-circle of seats at the back where a plush red chair had been made ready for the Bishop.

I had time to see a notice on the wall behind the bar giving the price of 'Adults' Shandy'. There were small bottles beneath another sign that said 'Adults' Lemonade and Gingerbeer'.

'Doctor,' the Bishop innocently said, 'your shandy has a grand head to it.'

With a masterly mental reservation, Dr. Daley replied, 'We felt sure your Lordship wouldn't want to see alcoholic beverages on sale the day before Holy Week begins.'

Later, I managed to slip away and have a word with the Doctor at the bar. The shandy, of course, was Guinness, lemonade was gin and tonic, gingerbeer was whiskey and soda.

'Where did you get all the little bottles, Doctor?'

'Needs must when the devil drives, Father Neil.' He hid his mouth behind his hand. 'By courtesy of the National Health Service.'

'Not bottles for . . . ?'

'You cannot legislate for necessity, my boy.' He smiled. 'They are new ones. But when I put them to their rightful use, I will get some interesting readings, to be sure.'

I winked at him. 'I'm glad you got your own way, Doctor.'

'Was I not born and bred in Ireland, Father Neil, where all you need to know is written on the door?'

'What's that?'

'Why, *push* and *pull*, that's what.'

Fr. Duddleswell sneaked over for a word. 'Donal,' he declared, 'you have gone over me head.'

Standing half an inch above him, the Doctor said good-humouredly, 'Not so difficult, Charles.'

'Donal, I will not have you back-seat driving me parish, d'you hear?'

The Doctor banged his breast, drum-like. 'I intended no offence, Charles.'

'Do you not realize a lie goes on one leg only? If the Bishop finds out, I will be demoted to curate.'

Dr. Daley winked at me. 'What could be worse than that, Charles? Will I get yourself a glass of whiskey against the awful possibility?'

Fr. Duddleswell gritted his teeth and walked away in disgust.

Dr. Daley called after him, 'Neat, Charles, or with a dash of arsenic?'

'Dear, dear, *dear*,' I said.

Dr. Daley put his thick arm round my shoulder. 'Father Neil, I hear it was yourself that cleared the church this evening.'

'Without even a shillelagh, Doctor.'

Dr. Daley breathed alcohol fumes all over me. 'Well, you have my profound thanks, anyway.' He pointed with his free hand to some of the women dancing a jig to a pipe accompaniment. 'Did you ever hear the saying, Father Neil, that Irish women have a dispensation from the Pope to wear their legs upside down?'

I followed his finger. 'Lots of them in this room seem to be wearing their thighs around their ankles,' I said.

He squeezed me harder. "It must be the shamrock next your heart, Father Neil, that is making you so irresponsibly eloquent.'

'Do *you* dance, Doctor?'

He relaxed his grip. 'God, I couldn't dance a jig now if you bought me a distillery.'

'Not even with that incentive?'

'Indeed not. My legs are stone deaf, they won't do a thing I tell 'em. Mind you, I was once one who could dance till today was the day after tomorrow. In my bloom and with a drop in, I could move my legs faster than now I can move my fingers.'

He moved his fingers there and then as if he was rapidly playing scales on the piano.

'I'm not telling you a lie, Father Neil. At one time, these legs of mine could do anything but talk. Why, I could kick 'em so high even the birds had to get out of my road.'

'Could you do the splits?'

'Could I do the splits? Don't remind me of it. So swell was I at doing that, the bystanders were afeared I'd slice myself in two from my crutch to the crown of my head. And, now, Father Neil, see what cruel tricks life plays on you.' He pulled his paunch in to look down his baggy trousers. 'My stilts complain at present if they only for a few yards have to carry me.'

'Carry you *and* a few glasses of whiskey.'

'D'you think *that's* why they decline the weight of my body?' He faced me, his red eyes popping. 'Anyway, how did *you* know I like the occasional glass?'

The Master of Ceremonies called a halt to the proceedings to announce the star turn of the evening.

Everyone applauded in anticipation of Fr. Duddleswell's annual performance. Mrs. Pring, who had just come in, nudged my elbow. 'Didn't I always tell you that man is only stage-Irish?' she said.

He stood out in front, fastidiously tuning his fiddle.

'Believe me, Father Neil,' Dr. Daley said ambiguously, 'when our Charles starts to run his bow across the strings, even the Bishop will lose the power to sit still.'

Cries of 'Shush', 'Be quiet there', as Fr. Duddleswell began in earnest.

After a few seconds of unrecognizable wailing, Billy Buzzle, who had come to pick up bets and make new contacts, started up, *In Dublin's Fair City*, and everyone joined in with, *Where girls are so pretty*.

The singing tailed off as Fr. Duddleswell lowered his bow, heaved a monumental sigh of wrath and exclaimed, 'That is the next tune, if you will have the patience. I am commencing me recital with, *I will take you home again, Kathleen*.'

When he had finished what I presumed was a medley and the stamping and applause had died down, he made the next introduction himself.

'And now the next to stand out on the floor is me curate.' Applause. 'Me curate who is a sayer of witty things, has a funny story to tell. Believe me, and you may have to take me word for it, 'tis exceedingly funny, coming from an Englishman. So make sure you do not hold his race against him and give him a generous round of laughs.'

At which everyone laughed spontaneously and clapped while I, red-faced, took up my position in the centre of the floor.

' 'Tis not a funny story at all, at all,' I said, mimicking without meaning to and nervously stroking the shamrock on my cassock.

To my surprise, laughter hit me in the face.

'Since tomorrow is Palm Sunday, I think it's more fitting for me to recite a sacred poem.'

266

The laughter, this time, was more hesitant as if the audience was not sure whether to believe Fr. Duddleswell or me.

The poem I had chosen was one I had come across, while I was a seminarist, in an *Anthology Of Irish Poems.* It had a simple Christian theme which reminded me of Pascal's famous words, 'Jesus will be in agony until the end of the world.'

'The poem is called, *I see his blood upon the rose.*'

For a full twenty seconds, the audience whispered among themselves before they settled down, no longer in any doubt that this was serious stuff. I took a deep breath before—

> I see his blood upon the rose
> And in the stars the glory of his eyes,
> His body gleams amid eternal snows,
> His tears fall from his eyes.

The people, seated and standing, were still as stones. Never had I been listened to with such rapt attention. It encouraged me to speak out more dramatically.

> I see his face in every flower:
> The thunder and the singing of the birds
> Are but his voice—and carven by his power
> Rocks are his written words.

No question, they were eating out of my hand.

> All pathways by his feet are worn
> His strong heart stirs the ever-beating sea,
> His crown of thorns is twined with every thorn,
> His cross is every tree.

I bowed but to my surprise, after what I took to be a pretty good rendering, no one applauded. Nothing at all stirred except where a few women were dabbing their eyes with their handkerchieves.

I walked over to where the Bishop's group was seated. Still no movement. The whole concert hall was as quiet as the church after the congregation had left.

The Bishop himself blinked to clear his eyes. Shaking his head mournfully, he took my arm and pressed it with obvious affection. 'Beautiful' A deep intake of air. 'Perfectly beautiful.'

His reaction set the pattern for the rest of the evening. People kept coming up to me and gazed gratefully into my eyes without words or touched their forelocks, saying, 'T'ank you kindly, Father. A t'ousand t'anks to yer.'

I was wondering if I had missed my vocation. Should I have taken up the stage as a career?

It was enough for me that the Bishop had metaphorically put his kid gloves back on. He patted the chair beside him and sat me down.

'Father Neil,'—so it was Christian name terms now—'when I was a little lad in Kilkenny, this was before you were born, what was there for us to eat at home? Only praties and stirabout.'

'Ah,' I said sympathetically.

'Happy days, Father Neil. My dear mother, may she be at God's right hand, was at Mass each day and at all the Masses every Sunday. But did we complain if the Sunday lunch was cold?'

'No, my Lord.'

'Indeed we did, Father Neil, but we knew, all fourteen of us, that she was in the right.'

'Of course, my Lord.'

'Saints usually are, isn't that so, Pat?'

Monsignor Pat, who hadn't been following the conversation, said, 'You do, my Lord.'

The Bishop looked at me and bit the inside of his mouth. 'Do you know the real problem of Ireland, Father Neil?'

I set aside the obvious answer, 'The Irish,' and shook my head to indicate the problem was unresolvable except by a Bishop.

'Somebody said, Father Neil, all the troubles of Ireland spring from one simple fact: a very silly race ruling a very intelligent one for too long. Would you agree with that?'

I drew my head back as if that needed a lot of thinking about.

'Another thing, Father Neil, why do the ballad and the dirge characterize our luckless, green and lovely land?'

'It's a shame,' I said, not daring to propose a possibly unacceptable solution.

'It is because, in a famous phrase, everything in Ireland, Father Neil, is too late, that's why.'

He released his grip on my arm. 'Now, be a good lad, go across there'—he pointed to the bar—'and fetch me a drink of Adults' gingerbeer.'

'Do you think you should, my Lord?'

'Do you think I shouldn't, Father Neil?'

I shook my head and went to the bar to tell Dr. Daley the bad news. When he handed over the small bottle and a glass I turned round to see the Bishop and Fr. Duddleswell gazing challengingly upon me. The first seemed to be saying, 'That's right,' and the second, 'You bloody dare.'

Fr. Duddleswell was King but the Bishop was Emperor. I returned and poured out the drink for the Bishop. He took it and raised his glass with, 'To the little gentleman in velvet.' Having sampled it, he said, 'God prosper you, Father Neil. The best gingerbeer I ever did taste.'

Fr. Duddleswell looked relieved. He and I presumed that Dr. Daley had cleverly had a harmless drink in reserve for just such an emergency.

When nobody was looking, I smelled the bottle. It was whiskey, all right.

The Bishop drank five gingerbeers on the trot. When he left on Fr. Duddleswell's arm at nine o'clock, after once more demanding to hear, *Hail Glorious Saint Patrick*, he looked decidedly the better for wear.

* * *

'Thanks for the apron, Father D.'

It was the hour of our evening drink. We had left the concert soon after the Bishop, Fr. Duddleswell having given strict instructions to Tim Fogarty that everybody was to be out on the street before Palm Sunday.

'You're not so bad, considering,' Mrs. Pring said, smiling.

'Considering what, Mrs. Pring?'

'Considering you're so awful,' she said.

'Bring yourself over here,' he said, 'till I thicken your ear for you.'

Mrs. Pring wished us good night and went to bed.

'That woman has tongue enough for six sets of teeth.' Fr. Duddleswell was in his most benign mood. 'D'you know what the Bishop said to me on parting?'

'No, Father.'

' "That assistant of yours," says he, "is the most promising curate in the diocese".'

'Was he drunk?'

'Naturally,' he grinned. 'Anyway, the open palm to you, lad. Well done.'

'Sheer luck, Father. That poem I chose just caught the spirit of Passiontide.'

He looked at me curiously. 'Nothing of the sort, Father Neil.'

'No?'

'Indeed not. D'you not know who wrote that poem?'

'Joseph somebody or other.'

'God hasten it to us. 'Twas Joseph Plunkett.'

The name meant nothing to me.

Another sceptical look in my direction. 'You are not pulling me leg, like?'

'No.'

'Wait till I tell you. Joseph Plunkett was in the Easter Rising.'

270

'Never!'

'His intended was Grace Gifford, a lovely young girl with great artistic talent. And a Protestant at that. They were the good old days, you follow? when 'twasn't Catholics against Protestants but Irish folk against the foreigner.'

I sniffed at his interpretation of the good old days.

'Well, now, Father Neil, Joseph Plunkett was in prison. And on the night before he was executed, Grace Gifford was allowed in and they were married by candlelight in the prison chapel. After, the chaplain left 'em alone for ten minutes only. That was when Joseph gave his brief little wife the poem, written in his own hand, that you recited so beautifully tonight.'

'So it's a rebel poem,' I gasped.

'In an English manner of speaking only. Joseph Plunkett *was* a rebel certainly. The sort that every Irishman condemns. Until a British firing squad proves 'em wrong, if you're still with me.'

I could do nothing but shake my head incredulously again and again.

If God is an Irishman, I thought, it explains an awful lot.

'And you *really* knew nothing of this, Father Neil?'

'Nothing.'

'Oh, Father Neil, sometimes I ask meself if you, with your Buster Keaton face, are the cleverest curate I ever had or the dumbest.'

I finally accepted that my New Year's resolution to wise up had been a failure.

'The dumbest', I said. 'I'm like a sheep.'

'And who but the silly sheep will inherit the earth?' He took my arm in a fatherly grip. 'I am fast coming to the conclusion we are a fine pair, lad, you and I.'

I liked the sound of that. 'Are we, Father?'

'Indeed and indeed. Here am I, the shaggy old ram in charge of the flock. And here is yourself, Father Neil, a dear little baby lamb who is only woolly on the inside.'

THE END

Saint Patrick's Day 1978